CIAO, STIRLING

THE INSIDE STORY OF A MOTOR RACING LEGEND

VALERIE PIRIE

Biteback Publishing

First published in Great Britain in 2019 by
Biteback Publishing Ltd
Westminster Tower
3 Albert Embankment
London SE1 7SP
Copyright © Valerie Pirie 2019

ISBN 978-1-78590-463-9

10 9 8 7 6 5 4 3 2 1

A CIP catalogue record for this book is available from the British Library.

Set in Minion Pro

Printed and bound in Great Britain by
CPI Group (UK) Ltd, Croydon CR0 4YY

MIX
Paper from
responsible sources
FSC® C020471

For Boo and Pop Pop

CONTENTS

PART ONE

NOT PAID TO ASSUME

DECISION TIME

The bronzed, broad-shouldered, slightly balding, rather shy young man stood up. I was completely taken aback. I had expected him to be far taller than he was. Politely, he stretched out his arm to shake my hand and said, 'Goodbye. Thank you for coming along.' This was not to be the final goodbye, however. It was to be the beginning of an exceedingly long and enduring relationship.

The man standing in front of me on this rather chilly spring evening was Stirling Moss, the racing driver, whose name had already entered the annals of the English language as the reply to the question asked of many an overenthusiastic speed merchant: 'Who do you think you are, Stirling Moss?'*

I was ushered out of the offices on that dark moonless night by Stirling's manager, Ken Gregory. Before he escorted me off the premises into an almost black void, he asked me where they would be able to contact me later that night.

'My home telephone number,' I began, but Ken interrupted me.

'Is that where you will be tonight?'

'No,' I replied. 'I am going out to dinner with some friends.'

'Do you have their number?' asked Ken.

---

* I was once out driving in a little NSU with racing driver Hugh Dibley, a good friend of mine and Stirling's (who would later drive for SMART), when I arrived at some traffic lights in the outside lane next to a lorry. Hugh had the window open (we were going flying) and the lorry driver yelled, 'Who does she think she is – Stirling Moss?' To which Hugh replied, 'No, just his secretary!'

This was my first lesson in answering the question that is being asked, not what one thinks is being asked.

'Yes...' I replied, hesitantly.

'Would you please give it to me then?'

I gave him the number and promptly forgot about the interview as I struggled home amongst the dregs of the rush hour and made my way to my friends' house in Surrey.

The call from Ken Gregory, offering me the job for which I had been interviewed that evening, came during the middle of dinner and I was caught completely off guard because I was asked to make a decision on the spot about whether or not I wanted to join the outfit.

I had never expected to be in the running, let alone be offered the position of Stirling's secretary, so I had not really thought seriously about the prospect. This job interview was the first that the secretarial agency I had joined had sent me on, and they had pretty much forced my hand to go along because they had already made the appointment first before telling me.

I had already made up my mind that I did not want to remain a secretary all my life because I had been in a job for three months and was bored to tears all day long. It was a grace-and-favour job, which had been given to me by a friend of the family. After leaving college, I had rebelled against working as a secretary and, in desperation, the family had asked a neighbour to help out by trying to persuade me that working for his company would be fun.

Isn't it always the way when you don't want to be good at something, it turns out that you are? This happened to me at the rather 'posh' secretarial college I was forced to attend: I had succeeded in coming second out of the whole year, much to the annoyance of the principal as well as myself, the problem for her being that I was a

4

bit 'mouthy' and would always try to have my say. Sweet sixteen I was not.

I quickly assimilated my thoughts and decided that anything would be preferable than the mind-numbing work that I was doing at that point. Instantaneously, I decided that it would probably be the best offer to come along for the time being and thought that it might be a good idea to give the job a whirl for a year or so and then move on to greener pastures. This was quite an acceptable thing to do at the end of the '50s, so I accepted the offer there and then.

Later that night I laughed to myself thinking about a girl in my class at school called Sylvia McGhie, who had harboured a crush on Stirling Moss for a long while, and remembered how we all got heartily sick and tired of her ticking on about him. None of us schoolkids were the slightest bit interested in the man, or motor racing, for that matter – and it came to the point when none of us wanted to hear his name again. Ever. And so we told her in no uncertain manner to shut up about him.

Little did I know then that he was to play such a large part in my life, and vice versa.

● ● ●

After his major accident in April 1962, when he had to retire from professional motor racing, I could never watch Stirling drive in his distinctive white peaked helmet without a feeling of nostalgia. On the couple of occasions that I saw him sitting in an open single-seater, tooling round with his head tilted to one side and in his familiar light blue, good-weather overalls, with his arms outstretched and his hands on the small, three-spoked steering wheel at a quarter to three, it would affect my whole being. I felt the same about him as an individual. I could never imagine that a time might come when he wouldn't be there.

I knew that he would always be around somewhere in the world to give me advice and support.

Friendship is not about feeling obliged to see someone on a regular basis and, over the years, our friendship grew stronger and stronger. There was always an unspoken understanding that we were there for each other, whenever or if ever needed. Stirling was my mentor and supporter but, most important of all, he was my closest friend, who understood and believed in me (as I did in him) and he would never let me down. I just hope that I meant the same to him.

Neither of us hardly ever uttered a cross word to each other during our more than sixty years of friendship, which began in 1958, although that is not to say that we always agreed on everything as, especially in the office, we certainly did not. I gave in my notice on numerous occasions, and I recently remembered when his note of apology fell out of a book I was reading that he once gave me an ultimatum. But, I suppose that is just a normal employer/employee reaction in the heat of the moment – and there were quite a few such moments. We both had very strong but very different personalities and temperaments, and my true character took quite a while to come through and mature. Stirling always prided himself on the fact that I was young enough to still be moulded – by him.

When I first joined Stirling Moss Ltd, I was a complete innocent and was immediately plunged headlong into a totally different environment from the one I knew and in which I felt comfortable. I also knew very little about life in the Big Smoke, but I was to learn – and very quickly at that. Stirling was a young man in his prime and he was in a hurry. However, life is strange and neither of us knew, at that time, how many incidences in both our lives would throw us together so much and to such an extent that it would lead to such deep bonds being created between the two of us, not only of friendship but of loyalty and, I suppose, a unique belief and understanding of each other. We knew each other's strengths and we knew each other's weaknesses and would always bat on the same side. We did not always see eye to eye, but each could persuade the other on most occasions – the exception being the subtleties involved in the game of cricket! There wasn't enough action in cricket for Stirling, so we would agree to disagree if ever the subject arose! He even became a convert to golf in his later years, which was another of his earlier aversions.

●   ●   ●

After I joined the company, I very quickly learnt that I had to stand on my own two feet to survive and, in particular, with Stirling. In fact, that became the basis of our whole friendship, our 'partnership', if you like, because I would always hold my own with him and always give him an honest opinion, to the best of my ability, although I generally had to give in to him if he did not agree with me because he *was* the boss! Very few people in his entire life ever stood up to him and I was one of probably only three (apart from his parents and his sister, Pat) along with David Haynes and Norman Solomon.

Stirling was almost at the height of his fame when I began to work for him as his personal secretary but, after his star had waned somewhat and I officially stopped working for him full-time, I had finished up as general dogsbody/Girl Friday and company director as well. When I first started working for him, his name was hardly ever out of the newspapers. In terms of column inches, he ranked third in importance after Her Majesty the Queen and Sir Bernard Docker's outrageous wife, Lady Docker – until she finally blotted her copybook with Prince Rainier and was subsequently banned from Monaco. He then moved up to the number two slot. Consequently, the press was always to play a tremendously large and important part in Stirling's life and those involved with him.

Stirling was the first to understand that if he did not appear regularly in the British press his popularity would wane and this would affect his worth and his livelihood. As a result, he put almost as much hard work and dedication into maintaining his own publicity as he did in remaining at the top of his sport.

A QUAINT HIDEAWAY

I was living at home when I first started working for Stirling Moss Ltd; home, at that time, was in Surrey. I commuted daily to work, initially by train and then by underground to the old Trafalgar Square tube station (which was still fully operational back then) and it was extremely convenient for William IV Street, which is just off Trafalgar Square and where the office was then situated.

I don't ever remember being asked at my interview whether I could drive or not but it would obviously have been a requirement of the job specification. I suppose, when I joined Stirling, the only thing that I had in common with him was that I had always wanted to drive a car and that, as a child, my ambition had been to drive a general around (in the war). Shades of *Foyle's War*, I suppose, and when I first started with Stirling I was just as prissy as the girl driver in the ITV series. I had taken my driving test just as soon as I possibly could, when I reached the legal age of seventeen, having learnt to drive on a private estate the year before with a private instructor, who was a policeman.

The office itself was most unusual, to say the least, because it was the very opposite of plush. It was tiny, utilitarian, functional and tucked away out of sight. Consequently, it was invisible to anyone who did not actually know where it was and, even if they had the address, it would still prove a challenge to find.

How different the office seemed when I turned up for work on my first day of employment. I had only been to it before at night-time but, in daylight, the full quirkiness became apparent.

The front door was in the middle of an open-air walkway, about three metres wide, which ran along the rear, at first-floor level, of a high-storey terraced block of Nash buildings. The white, gloss-painted wooden door housed a simple Yale lock. There wasn't a letterbox and the no-nonsense, small electric bell rang out shrilly in the early morning air as I waited for the door to be opened.

When it did, I was quite surprised to see Stirling's manager, Ken Gregory, standing there. He welcomed me in rather formally and with great dignity. I had imagined that Stirling would have been in the office on my first day, but he was not.

Almost immediately after my arrival, 'Mr' Gregory informed me that I was always to defer to and address Stirling as 'Mr' Moss. Although this was 1958, I found it rather strange and it sat rather uncomfortably with me during my first twelve months or so with the company. As a result, I went out of my way to call Stirling nothing to his face unless I really had to, although of course one would always refer to him as 'Mr' Moss when alluding to him indirectly or on the telephone, for example. After all, I was not addressed as 'Miss' Pirie in the office.

From what I was to gather in dribs and drabs later, in addition to Ken managing Stirling, he also managed another British racing driver, Peter Collins, and an Italian driver and was secretary to one of the four major motor racing clubs at that time in the UK, which eventually became known as the British Racing & Sports Car Club (BRSCC). He had gained much of his admin experience at the number one club, the RAC (Royal Automobile Club), which held overall responsibility for motor sport in the UK, where he had worked in the competitions' department after being demobbed from the RAF. Whilst at the RAC, Ken had also tried his hand at motor racing whenever he could come by the odd car, which would always be owned by someone else, and he had rather naturally run across Stirling through being involved with the sport although, as it turned out, their friendship had, in fact, flowered and developed because of Stirling's predilection for the opposite sex!

Ken was a northerner and when he came to work in London, after the war, he rented his own bachelor pad which (rather conveniently for Stirling) 'happened' to have two bedrooms. By sheer chance, Stirling found out about Ken's living situation whilst chatting to him at a formal motor racing dinner very early on in both their careers and, quick as a flash, he decided it would be a great idea if he had a bolt-hole in London whenever he wanted – for his convenience, of course, not necessarily Ken's! At the time, Stirling was still living with his parents, who were leasing a twenty-acre smallholding in Bray, Maidenhead, which had always been 'home' to Stirling, although he was born in Surbiton. Stirling reasoned in a whisker of a second that

Ken's flat would be all too perfect for him to use because he could take his conquests back there and 'entertain' them. Stirling's keen eye for 'a bit of skirt', even as an adolescent (let alone in his mid-teens), had tended to get him into rather a lot of hot water, and he was finding it almost impossible to contain his male testosterone under his mother and father's beady eyes down on the farm. Remember, this would have been at the end of the '40s.

Ken showed me what little of the front office there was, where I would spend most of my working days. It was partitioned off from Stirling's side of what had once been one large room by a flimsy piece of hardboard, which contained a hatch and a door, the former for communicating from the secretary's desk with whoever was sitting at Stirling's desk on the other side of the partition and vice versa. The small door had been built into the partition so that the two 'rooms' could be closed off at any time, whenever anyone wanted to speak in private, but I subsequently found out that it didn't work very well because more or less everything could be heard, whether the hatch and the door in the partition leading from my office to Stirling's side were open or shut. I was, therefore, to become privy to all the secrets of the entire office, a detail that I rather naturally spared Ken and Stirling.

There was not a great deal to see in what was to become my office. Behind a plain, four-legged, wooden desk was a dark, four-drawer, khaki-green filing cabinet and a small, solid-looking safe with a six-inch brass handle and combination lock, which sat next to the filing cabinet on the floor. Under the high windows, which ran along the front of the office at the back of the building, sat a couple of chairs for the use of visitors who were generally unwanted (even if they had made an appointment with the 'Great Man' himself).

Once I had been given this cursory tour of the office, I was invited to take my seat behind the desk, on which was sitting a rather bat-tered Remington typewriter, which had clearly seen better days. It was an unprepossessing dark metallic fawn colour and, noticing that the ribbon was red and black, I wondered why they would want to use the red. It turned out they didn't, and Stirling was delighted the first time I bought all-black ribbons for the typewriter because it doubled the usage and halved the cost. He viewed this as being a real bargain. It was my first brownie point.

I do not remember ever using the typewriter when I was sent along for the interview with Stirling but, many years later, he informed me that the sole reason that he had chosen me to be his secretary was because I knew the correct punctuation for addresses on letters and envelopes. Well done, that secretarial college! They, too, had been meticulous about the correct forms of address and Stirling was also incredibly fussy about this – in fact, I would say he had a fetish about it – and would never accept any form of 'modernisation' when it began to creep in. Before being knighted he would be addressed in correspondence as: Stirling Moss, Esq., O.B.E., F.I.E., 21, William IV Street, London, W.C.2. Frankly, I am not quite so sure that it was for this reason that he chose me at all because he often used to laugh and tell people that he only took me on because, at my young and tender age (seventeen), he knew he could mould me to his ways, which is pretty much what did happen although, at that time, he didn't quite know how young I actually was.

Ken explained how the two-line switchboard by the hatchway worked. This also directly linked Stirling's office (Covent Garden 0581/2) with his own office at the BRSCC, which was situated nearby on the other side of The Strand, a few minutes' walk away. It had been a happy coincidence that the two offices were so close to one another when Ken took on the job of official secretary at the club. Not that Stirling ever popped round to see Ken; he would always telephone him and if Ken was out or not available he would become exceedingly vexed and frustrated.

Ken began jostling a few papers, preparing to dictate a number of letters to me, and the ordeal began.

This was make-or-break time for me because I had somewhat exaggerated the secretarial experience I told the agency that I had, and it was far too late by now to own up. I had done precisely three months' work experience. I hadn't used my shorthand very much and, although I was very quick at everything I did, I generally found my shorthand difficult to read back. It was for this reason that I always wrote down the correct hieroglyphic because, in the past, I had often relied on asking someone else who knew shorthand to read it back for me. However, I was now on my own and there was no one to ask. I was later to find that Stirling would always be OK about this if I got stuck, but Ken was a different animal altogether. It certainly did wonders for my memory.

After he had finished dictating, Ken informed me that he was going out. He gave me a key to the office and I was left to hold the fort.

The letters didn't take long to get through and, with nothing better to do, I took further stock of my surroundings.

UTILITARIAN AND UNPRETENTIOUS

Behind the front door, immediately to the right of the entrance and concealed from view by the inward-opening front door ran a long, light corridor, which had shelving running along its entire length on the left-hand side, opposite some windows. The shelving was hidden by some extremely modern (for the time) kitsch bluish/greyish/cream hessian, horizontally striped curtaining, behind which were a whole load of box files and other general paraphernalia required for running the office and for organising Stirling.

Stirling's part of the office was probably just a bit smaller than my own. An old, orange sofa sat underneath the window at the front of the building facing the street and there was an ordinary, upright, single wooden chair with a green, padded leather seat, which had been placed at ninety degrees next to his desk, with its back against the partition. His run-of-the-mill office desk was exceptionally neat and tidy. On it was a diary, a flip calendar containing writing utensils and a couple of phones. And that was about it. What did this indicate apart from the fact that it belonged to a neat and tidy, practical person? I was later to find out that this was only the half of it.

The wallpaper behind the desk was intriguing and it reminded me of my interview when I could hardly take my eyes off it, which was probably the reason why Stirling had chosen it in the first place and, as I later found out, had hung it himself – to take the attention off himself when he was talking to a visitor. Like mine had been, most people's eyes would keep straying to look at the back wall. Strangely, he was exceptionally shy.

The wallpaper had a pale, almost apple-green and white background on which several different sizes of large silver and gold gear or watch cogs were interlinked and intertwined. It was only on the one wall (as was the fashion of the day) behind the desk, the rest of the walls having been painted white. I was to find out that the old orange sofa was hardly ever used.

There were two options for visitors to take to get up to the offices of

Stirling Moss Ltd. The most usual course of action during office hours would be to enter through a small door, half hidden in the middle of the block, just back from the pavement, situated between three or four shops and a restaurant-cum-burger bar on the corner of the street (long before the advent of McDonald's). This latter enterprise was owned by Stirling, his father, Alfred Moss, and Ken Gregory.

On pushing the front door open, visitors would be faced with an old, narrow, rickety, well-worn and bare wooden staircase, which led up to Alfred's dental practice's reception area on the first floor, and behind reception sat a veritable dragonara. Nurse Newley was a formidable, middle-aged woman. A fairly attractive nurse/receptionist, she was always dressed in an immaculate white uniform with a midnight blue elastic belt running around her waist, which was fastened with an intricate, filigree silver buckle. She generally wore a nurse's cap, white stockings and white shoes. This nurse, who we all thought, rightly or wrongly, was Alfred Moss's mistress, would act as a first-class deterrent to anyone thinking of trying to 'drop in' on Stirling, which he never ever welcomed or appreciated. She would filter any unwanted guests and prevent them from going out through the back door behind her domain, onto the flat, asphalt, roofing/walkway. However, as I was to find out, she held no fear for any of the irascible, cranky-yet-fun-loving racing drivers who dared to invade her territory from time to time.

The second option visitors had would be to walk along the entire length of the block at street level to the now non-existent traffic lights at the crossroads with St Martin's Lane where, if one looked very carefully, there was a stone staircase made from sandstone to match the building, which had extra-wide and very long steps. These steps led up from the pavement to the first-floor rear walkway, which was accessed through an open sandstone archway above the top of the steps; the whole entrance blending in naturally with the rest of the block and being virtually invisible.

The steps had been constructed in days of yore for race horses to walk up to their stabling (hence the distance between the steps), with Stirling's office previously having been part of some of the stabling. The jockeys used to live above the stabling on the second floor of the building and this room, immediately above Stirling's and my own office, formed part of Stirling's father's London hideaway, and we always used to laugh about it and call it his 'love nest'. If this assumption was true, then Stirling was definitely a chip off the old block!

Access to the office was on the left, about halfway along the broad asphalt walkway, at first-floor level. Down below, on the other side of this walkway was an enormous, corrugated-iron inverted V roof, which partially covered a particularly spacious, open-air site, which was being used as a garage for car repairs. It was bang next door to the Georgian church of St Martin-in-the-Fields, virtually facing the National Gallery and the National Portrait Gallery, which is just off Trafalgar Square at the beginning of the Charing Cross Road. During the week, the garage could be quite noisy and smelly. Thankfully there was the second door further along the walkway on the left, which led back into the dentist's reception area where one could seek refuge if caught in the fumes.

Later that first day, Ken came back to sign the letters I had typed up, which I had left lying in the wire filing tray for him on the shared desk in the inner office, and, after reading them through thoroughly and signing them, he asked me to post them on my way home. He also explained that 'Mr' Moss had been away racing up north at Aintree over the weekend and was doing some testing on the way back, but would be in the office later on in the week.

THE WHIRLWIND

As it turned out, it was Wednesday morning when Stirling hurtled into the office. I was sitting typing when the door suddenly burst open and the whirlwind appeared.

We generally didn't keep the door locked during the day if anyone was inside the office, and I don't know who was more surprised, Stirling or me, but I think it was probably him, because he had totally forgotten for that instant that there would be anyone else in the office, so occupied was he always with his own thoughts. After regaining his composure, he said a cheery hello and disappeared into his own side of the office. I then heard him plonk his shoulder bag on the floor with a big thud, sit down at his desk and begin going through his mail, totally ignoring me. But, I was soon to find out that the comparatively slow pace of life during my first couple of days in the office was to change dramatically into a veritable tornado when he was around.

Once he had finished reading the mail and had scribbled a few notes, he started talking to me through the hatch. He was sorry that he hadn't been there to greet me on my first day and wanted to know, was I getting on OK and was there anything I needed? I must also tell him if I encountered any problems – all this was said in virtually one breath – and then the phones started ringing, non-stop. It was as though all hell had been let loose and the whole world was linked up to our tiny office and he had set the tripwire in motion so that everyone knew that he was around and, of course, they all needed to talk to him personally and urgently. It was pandemonium.

With so many people wanting to talk to Stirling all the time, it would be some months before I would learn how to distinguish the type of calls that he would accept and those he would not. That first year, I must have really driven him wild, in more ways than one. I had always been brought up to tell the truth, whatever the consequences, (the exception being the rather large white lie about my age that I had told the secretarial agency) and I found that I was unable to say that Stirling was out when he was in. However, I think he learnt a lot from this fault of mine as well, because he found himself talking to people he didn't necessarily want to talk to and he soon became quite adroit at fending them off fairly quickly and moaning to me afterwards, 'Valerie, you really must…'

The impression I got of 'Mr' Moss that first day was that he was very pernickety, knew precisely what he wanted to achieve, would do everything at top speed to obtain it and if it didn't happen yesterday his frustration would begin to boil over. Patience was never to be one of his fortes, although he became exceedingly tolerant of my somewhat chaotic filing system later on. Conversely, at times he would become incredibly quiet, thinking and sometimes sniffing and checking his nails – occasionally even whipping out a nail file to deal with any rough edges – at the same time as jotting down notes to himself. He left nothing to memory, continually scribbling on little scraps of paper and ticking off or crossing out the items on the list, once each item had been dealt with to his entire satisfaction. He was exceptionally polite and approachable and was extremely courteous to me and – initially – very considerate. That didn't last long! On the other hand, like him, I was extremely shy and initially felt completely out of my depth.

I suppose it was fortunate that I was quite a bright, yet rather wilful person and, during my years with Stirling, what with being left on my own for so much of the time and with ever increasing responsibilities, this trait would increasingly come to the fore. Making decisions never fazed me, whether they were right or wrong, and, of course, a hundred and one problems and business propositions would present themselves whilst Stirling and often Ken were away. Of course, I would naturally always take any decision with the best of intentions, which Stirling always appreciated. Only once was I conned, and by the person who had previously employed me, who had, by then, gone on and set up his own rather trendy advertising agency. Fortunately, despite my words being deliberately misrepresented, Stirling believed my account of the conversations that had taken place whilst he was away, and this so-called family friend had to back off, but inevitably it caused friction at home.

Once he had organised himself and had settled back into office life that first Wednesday, Stirling gave me a bit of dictation at breakneck speed and, as soon as he had finished, he rushed out of the office, shouting at me when he was halfway through the door that he wasn't sure exactly when he would be returning but to leave the letters and stamped envelopes in the basket on his desk and he would sign and post them himself.

Long after he had left the building, the phones continued to ring endlessly, so, in between trying to type up his letters, I dealt with all the calls as best I could, whilst fending off queries as to exactly who I was on many occasions. These queries, I found out later, were either from members of the media or people in his circle who hadn't a clue that Stirling had been thinking of taking on a new secretary. As if it mattered.

He blew back through the door again much later in the day and I handed him the list of callers on a sheet of paper. I had left the letters as instructed on his desk and he started to go through them with a fine-tooth comb, checking to see that they were correct – and correctly punctuated! However, when he realised that I wasn't doing anything, he busied himself, explaining the filing system and showing me his way of writing and sending out the fan mail.

The autographed photographs were all signed personally and were provided free of charge by BP, to whom he was contracted for his oil and petrol, and it was one of my responsibilities to ensure that the supply of signed photographs didn't run out, particularly when he was to be away for any length of time because he would religiously sign every photograph, in ink. Despite his distaste for contemporisation, he would later take to using a biro on the whole.

LEARNING THE ROPES – AND OFFICE POLICY

He then explained that it was the policy of the office to answer every communication received, however crazy it might be – and some letters were really bizarre and not very nice at all, I can tell you. I very quickly learnt that the majority of the public were kind, sane and respectful, but that there were definitely a few weirdos out there. Some would be what were then termed as 'religious cranks', others would be extraordinarily venomous and others were sexual perverts. We also used to receive mountains of letters from young men and schoolboys, asking for advice on how they could become racing drivers, and I soon developed a series of charming yet pretty standard replies to answer the question, although all through the history of motor racing, one basically had to have an awful lot of money and an awful lot of talent to drive cars competitively. Primarily, it was the money that came first, because, without a car (and later perhaps a kart), no matter how talented a person might be, he had to be able to demonstrate his potential on a circuit.

Every day, I was to collect the morning mail on my way in from the dentist's receptionist and open it if no one else had done so and sort out which mail he should deal with and which should be left for Ken. He would always personally sign the letters, which accompanied an autographed photograph (so the recipient would receive two signa-tures) if he was in the country, but I was to deal with them and other standard types of enquiries when he was out of the country. Ultimate-ly, I would write the majority of Stirling's letters for him, even when he was in the country. I would just put them on his desk for signature and he would sign them, more often than not, without reading them, and the only letters he would answer personally were those which, for one reason or another, I did not consider I could, or should, deal with. All letters that were marked 'Personal' were to remain strictly unopened until such time as he could deal with them himself. This went without exception, unless I was expressly told to do otherwise.

At the end of my first week, Stirling went off to another race meet-ing and I was to be left on my own again, apart from Ken blowing in from time to time to keep an eye on me and to keep Stirling's business affairs in order. Whenever Stirling arrived back in the country after a race, he would only be able to spend two or three days maximum in the office mid-week before he would nip off again. Consequently, because it was such a limited time, every man and his beast seemed to know when he was around, and I soon realised that I had a lot more learning to do – and very rapidly.

Talk about being thrown in at the deep end!

AN EPIPHANY

The timing of my appointment, just after Easter, had been made mainly because of Stirling's racing calendar. When I arrived on the scene, he was due to be around a little more than usual so he would be spending rather more time in the office than he would normally and, gradually, as the stiffness of the relationship between employer and secretary began to soften a fraction, I actually began to enjoy working on a one-to-one basis and with such a diverse array of things to do. My appointment had been timed so that he would have a good run-in period to get to know me a little better and vice versa (his one and only previous secretary, Judy Noot, having left a little earlier in the year).

Looking back at this initial period, I think that Stirling began to be slightly concerned when he realised that I was a complete and utter ignoramus regarding motor racing and felt that I needed educating. So, just before he was going to compete in the annual *Daily Express* meeting at Silverstone at the beginning of May, barely a month after I had started working for him, he asked me if I would like to go along to watch the racing because he was going to be driving in two or three events there.

As I left work on the Thursday evening, Stirling gave me instructions on how to get to the house where he and his wife, Katie, would be staying. It was in Buckingham and I was to arrive no later than 8:30 a.m. on the Saturday morning. Little did he dream that I would have to get up with the birds that morning to take the milk train via Waterloo across London, in order to arrive in Buckingham at the stated time and that, when he first asked me, I had imagined that we would all be driving up together.

That was my second lesson in learning that I was not paid to assume, a phrase Stirling uttered on very many different occasions – as did I with him.

This would also be the first of very many hundreds of hours that I would find myself working for Stirling on an unpaid basis, although, to be fair, not much work was involved on this particular occasion, just my time.

It was about 7:30 a.m. when I somewhat nervously made my way to the address that Stirling had given me: Castle House, Buckingham. That was all.

It was a damp and misty morning when I arrived at Buckingham Station and, as I nervously followed the instructions I had been given, I checked with a couple of early morning risers I came across along the way to ascertain that I was going in the right direction. The house seemed to be miles away from the station. I was not used to walking but I trudged on, feeling slightly scared because of the all-enveloping film of early morning mist around me and being in unknown territory. At last, I arrived outside some high, wrought-iron railings and was surprised to see that Castle House, as the name suggests I suppose, was an imposing mansion. I later found out from John Bristow-Bull, its ebullient owner, who looked very similar to the English caricature of John Bull, that the site actually dates back to the Norman era but the house itself was built in the fifteenth century and it not only contained a priest's hole, which was built during the Reformation, but also a ghost.

The tall gate let out a long whine as I pressed the latch down and pushed it open. The central flagstones leading up to the imposing and majestic front door were somewhat uneven, and John himself responded to my timid rapping with the large, heavy knocker.

Wearing a blue and white striped pinny and brandishing a rather large, well-used, blackened frying pan in his left hand, he welcomed me with open arms. His effusive greeting to a total stranger somewhat overawed me as I was bidden to follow him down the hall to his enormous stone-flagged kitchen, where he was preparing breakfast himself for all of his guests, who were coming down the stairs in dribs and drabs.

No one ever knew very much about John but whenever anyone asked about his background he always claimed to be a relative of the Prince of Wales (Edward VIII), although he always laughed and added that he had actually been born on the steps of a house where his mother was staying as a guest in Germany, immediately before the First World War. Years later he told me that, one night in his youth, he was gambling with the 'in' crowd in a house right at the western end of Piccadilly when it was raided by the police and when one young man was asked for his name he gave it as being Edward Albert Christian George Andrew Patrick David Windsor. When asked for his address and the reply came back as 'Number One, London' the policeman was not at all amused and said, 'Now, now, sir, we've 'ad our little joke, now what h'is your real h'address...' The address the young man had given for the property was the name by which the Duke of Wellington's ancestral house, Apsley House, has always been known and the house was being used by the Royal Family in that epoch, on this particular evening for a little bit of a flutter in both senses of the word!

And, the rest, as they say, is history.

• • •

Stirling had not long been married and this was the first time that I was to meet his Canadian heiress wife, Katie, who, I thought, was absolutely stunning: very vivacious and exceedingly charming. She had a close-cropped pixie-style haircut, wore hardly any make-up and seemed to me to be the antithesis of Stirling because she was very gay and amusing.

FAIR'S FAIR

Stirling had been staying at Castle House ever since he had had a monumental fall-out with the Very Reverend the Rector of Wicken. He used to stay at the large, rambling rectory in the Northamptonshire countryside, just a stone's throw from Silverstone, on the recommendation of a friend and it suited him very well. It was reasonably priced and was pretty secluded, but its top attraction was that, when he first heard about it, not many other people knew of its existence as a B&B. However, as normally happens when people find 'a good thing', word begins to spread and this was to be no exception. The fact that Wickhen Rectory offered very good value and that it was very handy for Silverstone made it a little too popular for Stirling's liking. However, the final straw that broke the camel's back was when Stirling met his match with its owner.

Now, apparently, the good Rector liked to go to bed early and used to leave his guests to help themselves to whatever they wanted in the bar and they would leave a note for him so that he would know in the morning what they had taken. Initially this was fine and worked very well indeed. But, as the popularity of the establishment grew, he decided that it would be far easier for all concerned if, instead of charging them for what they had had, he would just add a mandatory daily charge of ten bob (fifty pence) onto each bill per guest when they left. But, he had counted without giving any thought to Stirling, who was a teetotaller for all his racing life – and, at that time, rather proud of it.

Rather naturally, the first time the mandatory charge appeared on Stirling's bill, he felt that the levy was grossly unfair so he had a word with the good Reverend about it, but the Rector would not see reason. He absolutely refused to make Stirling the exception to his rule and, ultimately, there was a stand-off. The Reverend would not back down. Stirling was absolutely livid because he felt that he had been cheated and he eventually and very grudgingly paid the surcharge, swearing never to set foot in the establishment again – and he did not. He never was a good loser but this went beyond the pale because he felt that the Rector was being completely unreasonable and unfair. And this is how he came to be staying at the much nicer and very exclusive Castle House, which was his and his chosen friends' personal fiefdom for Silverstone, even though it wasn't as close to the circuit as was the Rectory.

Over breakfast round a good-sized wooden kitchen table covered by a chequered tablecloth, there was a lot of talk and laughter and a fair amount of speculation amongst those who had stayed the night as to whether or not the ghost had appeared. No one sitting round the table had been disturbed by the usual screams when it did appear and the couple who were using the room where it generally made its presence known had not yet surfaced. Stirling had seen the ghost just once and that had been enough for him. He had refused thereafter to sleep in the room again so John had switched him to the bedroom where Katherine of Aragon had slept when she visited Castle House during the reign of her husband, Henry VIII – though hopefully not on the same mattress.

Stirling wasn't taking the slightest bit of notice of any of the chatter that was going on around him and was gobbling down his full breakfast of bacon, eggs, sausages and tomatoes, accompanied by tea, toast and marmalade, as though it was probably going to be his last meal. He had hardly noticed my arrival apart from a brief nod and a bright rhetorical question, 'Had a good journey?' Still munching his last mouthful, he stood up brusquely and darted out of the kitchen to collect his bags, simultaneously shouting to me and Katie, who had just introduced herself, to hurry up and get into the car.

We had hardly scrambled into the sleek, low vehicle outside, when we shot off to the circuit via a shortcut Stirling knew through the back lanes of Stowe public school. Squashed into the rear of the sports car as I was, my memory of the journey is of pretty sandy-coloured, exceedingly straight, tree-lined roads and being driven at very high speed. We arrived at Silverstone some twenty minutes or so later.

Once Stirling had shown each of our passes to the overzealous officials at the entrance on the outer side of the circuit, we drove across the tarmac itself and into the paddock area behind the pits, which was situated in the infield of the circuit.

As soon as the car came to a stop, Stirling jumped out and dashed off, leaving Katie and me to our own devices. Looking around, the first thing that I noticed was that those of the general public who had gained access to the paddock seemed to be mingling quite freely with everyone else. I was like a lost soul. Katie suddenly realised that I was just standing by the car not knowing what to do and immediately took me under her wing. She was kindness itself and we started to wander around the large open space that was littered with cars and people. It was obvious

27

she was very popular with all the other drivers and she introduced me to everyone she stopped to talk to. She was very easy-going and very different to Stirling. Tall (much taller than Stirling), dark and slim, she had a twinkle in her eye and was always laughing and joking, whereas Stirling generally seemed to take life a little too seriously.

The terraced concrete pits, such as they were, were more or less open to the elements. Grey breeze blocks had been used in their construction and the rough partition walls, made of the same material, separated each pit from the other. Along the front ran a solid concrete counter, about four feet high. The pit roofing was originally made of corrugated iron, but by this stage in its life it was a bit leaky to say the least. The mechanics would either wait and watch the race, squatting on the pit counter or just in front of it, whilst the others would hang around at the back of the pit, trying to dodge out of the way of the drips from the roof whenever it rained.

They had to leave sufficient space on the counter for the time-keepers to stand and do their job properly, and what a difficult and important job that was. The more professional timekeepers used split-second watches so they could time every single car in the race if they wanted to, and the amateurs generally used three stop watches attached to a board.

There were practically no facilities for anyone at Silverstone at the end of the '50s, whether the public, drivers or officials, and the circuit was a flat, windswept old aerodrome. One main stand had at least been built for spectators, which was on the last corner before the start/finish line, across from the pits.

I subsequently found out that the two wooden adjoining loos in the paddock were positively archaic. They couldn't even be called privies. Each contained a metal bucket and, of course, there wasn't any running water. The old wooden doors, each incongruous, with a small, flimsy yet spruce and newly-painted black, sliding lock, had definitely seen better days, and had obviously been well weathered by the ferocious and blustery gales that drifted across the wilds of Silverstone in those dim and distant days. The whole place seemed inhospitable – and no one had warned me to bring any proper warm clothing.

The noise of the cars in the paddock was ear-splitting – there certainly weren't any ear protectors in those days – and the all-invading smell, which I found out much later to be that of Castrol R, was *the* smell of Formula One motor racing. Those were the days and that was motor racing.

Stirling was driving in three races during the day and Katie organised for someone to drive us out to two or three of the furthest corners on the infield so we could watch the cars as they came roaring round. I thought that it was absolutely thrilling to be able to stand so close to the cars as they came into view and sped past, trying to hold the correct line, and I was terribly disappointed when Stirling was forced to retire in the big race.

Katie and I had been given our instructions to be back by the car as soon as Stirling had finished his last race and, rather fortunately, Katie asked me how I was going to get home. I looked at her in astonishment as, once again, I had rather imagined that I would be given a lift back to London, but apparently that was not on the cards either. Luckily, there were quite a few non-motor racing celebrities attending the meeting that day that Katie knew and she very kindly asked Edmund Purdom, a well-known actor of whom I had never heard, to give me a lift back to London and, rather grudgingly, he agreed. He had a white, open-top MG sports car with red leather seats and I had the distinct feeling that I wasn't going to do much for his image.

As for Stirling, it would never have crossed his mind to think about how I was going to get home from that cold, bleak and isolated circuit, situated right in the middle of nowhere, deep in the heart of the Buckinghamshire countryside. His mind would be mulling over the day and focusing on what needed doing to the car and where he was going next, as well as thinking what he would need to organise and take with him. At this juncture in his life, having almost reached the peak of his career and popularity, he had a one-track mind, focused solely on his motor racing activities.

DEATH

Death is not the greatest loss in life.
The greatest loss is what dies inside us while we live.
NORMAN COUSINS

May arrived and Stirling was scheduled to be away for at least three or four weeks, although he told me he might nip back between Monaco (the second of the Grandes Épreuves that year, but the first in Europe) and Zandvoort (Holland) so life went on without 'Mr' Moss. However, I still had plenty to learn and keep me occupied. The days passed very quickly and I increasingly began to find that I enjoyed working alone and making my own decisions.

During those first few weeks, a couple of drivers were killed and the press was in constant contact with the office, wanting a quote from Stirling on this, that or the other, and he would only think it polite to answer or return their calls whenever he could.

If he was away, I would try to contact him and ask him to give me a quote, which I could relay back to the journalist in question and any others who might subsequently telephone, but it wasn't always that easy to get through to him because there wasn't the technology around then that there is today. In fact, sometimes it could take a couple of weeks to contact some countries, with all calls going through the international operator.

Archie Scott Brown was the first driver to die on my watch. He died from the burns he sustained in a sports car race in Belgium when he went off the road and hit the memorial to another renowned pre-Second World War British racing driver, Dick Seaman, who had also died of similar burns at exactly the same spot, nineteen years earlier.

Archie was two years older than Stirling and today his look-alike would probably be the ex-world champion Nigel Mansell. He had the same high, broad forehead, bushy eyebrows, a little moustache and chubby rosy cheeks. His mother had contracted German measles during the pregnancy and, as a result, he had been born without any shin bones, clubbed and reversed feet and only one good hand. However, he turned out to be a talented driver, even though he was always at the mercy of the international driving clubs, most of which barred him from competing in Formula One events.

His death made a deep impression on me, probably because 'Mr' Moss was not in the office on the Monday after the accident and it seemed as if the whole world and its master began calling in to ask for a quote from Stirling on Archie. Being on my own, I was totally flummoxed because this was the very first time for me when there wasn't any let-up from callers whatsoever. The clamour was quite incredible, each journalist vying with the other to be the first with an 'exclusive' follow-up on the story.

At long last, Stirling rang in mid-morning and I was able to give him the names of all those who wanted to speak to him. He told me that he would ring a couple of the names on the list directly and asked me to ring round the others with the quote that he then gave me.

This was the first occasion that I had to dial up and speak to the press directly for any length of time and it was the first crisis of any sort with which I had had to cope single-handedly. After ringing the reporters back to give them Stirling's quote I suppose I felt much more confident and competent as a result.

To me, the word 'death' at the time was nothing more than a word used in conjunction with a name and meant that the person wasn't going to be around any longer; in this case, poor Archie. I did not associate this death or, for that matter, any of the other deaths in the years to come, with Stirling.

When Stirling did eventually appear back in the office, he had topped up his tan in Italy and the south of France and, apart from dealing with the mail, he spent an enormous amount of his time researching his future travel arrangements. Names such as the Hotel Bristol in Monte Carlo, the Huis ter Duin in Zandvoort and the Lochmühle in Germany are still engrained on my mind and run off the tongue as smoothly as though it was only yesterday.

BEING PAID TO TRAVEL THE WORLD HAD ITS PROBLEMS

Quite often, Stirling could be seen in his office, huddled over a thick paper-backed directory containing details of all the airline flights in the world working out which airline he would prefer to take and which would be the cheapest flight to his chosen destination. Remember, there wasn't the internet and he didn't like using a travel agent because he did not trust them to do the job as well as he could do it. He would also ask me to ring around to get quotes and confirm connections and the two of us would be at it for quite a long time before he would eventually make up his mind which airline(s) he would choose on what day, and then it would often be handed over to me to make the final flight bookings with the airlines directly. Stirling always preferred to be left in charge of his own arrangements as much as possible. Being the perfectionist that he was, he never believed that anyone could do a better job than he could do himself and he was never prepared to trust anyone sufficiently to try them out, apart from myself, who he could see and hear in the background. He would keep half an ear on what I was doing to make sure it was correct. He was very pernickety.

Stirling would often be offered the cash equivalent of a first-class ticket as part of his start money to wherever he was going to appear. He always liked this because he would then book 'steerage', as we used to call economy seats, so he could pocket the difference. He could travel perfectly adequately in steerage and it would give him a lot more money (which he could put into the company). Actually, everything he earned was put into Stirling Moss Ltd and he was paid a salary, as of course was I (which he always kept reminding me about), all of which had to come out of the start money he was paid for racing, plus the fees for personal appearances, promotions and so on. Consequently, he would always come down on me very hard whenever he thought I was being extravagant and spending too much petty cash. He could never quite make me see his point of view about this because I reasoned that, if I spent the money, he wouldn't have to pay tax on it. His standard reply was always, 'Yes, but I have to earn it first!' I just didn't get it.

Stirling Moss Ltd had been formed in 1955, three years before I arrived on the scene, not, as many people thought at the time, as a tax dodge but because, with Stirling being out of the country for so much of the year and his own personal signature being required on all the contracts and endorsements that were made on his behalf, it had become totally impractical to run his affairs efficiently. The formation of the limited company permitted two of the three directors to sign on his behalf. The other two directors on the board of Stirling Moss Ltd at the time were his father, Alfred Moss, and his manager, Ken Gregory. I was to replace Ken as a director when there was a parting of the ways with Ken after Stirling's enforced retirement from motor racing, and, much later, his third wife, Susie, replaced Stirling's father after he died.

THE IMPOSSIBLE WAS POSSIBLE

The first Grande Épreuve (the term used to describe any of the Grands Prix races which counted towards the world championship; not all Grands Prix being Grandes Épreuves) of the 1958 season had been won by Stirling in Argentina. In a Grande Épreuve, specified points were given to the top, final placings and an additional point would be awarded to the driver putting up the fastest lap, regardless of which position he finished in. This point would be added to his tally in the world championship table. Other non-nominated races were also called Grands Prix and were held at various places around the world, such as in New Zealand or in Sweden, but wins and places there did not count towards the world championship.

The race in Argentina really had caught the imagination of the public at large, particularly the British, who always seem to appreciate an underdog or someone who comes up trumps against the odds – and Stirling certainly proved it on that special Sunday in mid-January 1958.

He was driving Rob Walker's privately entered little Cooper Climax and he had had a real fight on his hands because he was up against the might of all the factory teams, whose cars were generally acknowledged to be faster than Rob's somewhat outdated Cooper.

Even I had read about this astonishing feat in the national press before I joined the company, but Stirling never ever considered that it was one of his better drives. Don't ask me why; I could never understand it, but he was the driver on that particular day and, strange to relate, he was always pretty modest about his driving. His proudest win? Probably the 1955 Mille Miglia, but his best and most satisfying race was undoubtedly the 1961 Monaco Grand Prix. He always said that he thoroughly enjoyed every minute of this race when he had to keep the Ferraris at bay by outsmarting and outdriving them. At the time, he was probably at the very peak of his abilities. He returned from that particular race deeply elated and highly satisfied.

THE GOOD OLD DAYS

There was never a dull moment at William IV Street. If I wasn't taking dictation or typing letters, I was busy doing a hundred and one other things. In the '50s and early '60s, there wasn't a fixed amount of start money for appearing in Formula One races – or any other race for that matter. (I was once asked by Ken Gregory to go along to lunch with him and John Eason Gibson, Secretary of the BRDC, because he thought he would do rather better in his negotiations on Stirling's behalf because John and I were both Scots. And he did!) Terms had to be negotiated on an individual basis for every race and/or race meeting, generally over the phone. As Stirling pulled in the crowds like no one else he was generally allotted more start money than any of the other drivers. There weren't any restrictions as to the number of races in which a driver could compete on the same day (although the regulation permitting drivers to swop cars and continue competing in the same race stopped at the beginning of 1958), so it was not unusual, particularly in the UK, for Stirling to appear in two or three races at the same race meeting on the same day.

The rules of Formula One racing in the early '50s were pretty complicated even then, but they didn't keep changing quite as much as they do today.

It was, however, a relatively easy matter of acquiring a racing licence. A person who held an ordinary driving licence could simply apply for one, in the case of British drivers, from the British governing body, the Royal Automobile Club. Later, however, one had to complete a type of apprenticeship by competing in half a dozen club events, which were the most junior of junior races (or rallies for which one required a separate international licence).

In the main, any would-be racing driver would enter his/her own bog-standard saloon car, which they would just tool around in, trying to keep out of everyone else's way, just to get a 'signature' for good behaviour after the race from the secretary of the meeting, but it was obligatory to go the full distance and finish the race. Others (such as myself later on) would beg or borrow a bog-standard or slightly souped-up version from someone else and have a go, bearing in mind that they had to behave reasonably well in order to gain the required signatures. Six good race reports (even just tooling around at the end) and you became a racing driver – of sorts! The same process went to obtain a rally licence.

After obtaining their official racing licences, people could participate in all types of competitions, including international events, and in any type of racing, from saloon cars and sports cars to top-flight racing, which was Formula One, followed by Formula Two and Formula Three, although I don't believe that anyone went straight into a Formula One car. Other specialist formulas were added, such as Formula Libre, as the sport evolved and became increasingly popular, as of course was saloon car racing because it was more affordable and fun. Incidentally, at the end of the '50s, there was only one female driver in Formula One, Maria Teresa de Filippis, an Italian, who was not very fast, though there had, of course, been other female drivers in the past, including Aileen Moss, Stirling's mother, but not in a Formula One car.

In addition, at the end of the '40s and the beginning of the '50s, anyone with a racing licence could qualify a car for a race, without the actual nominated driver being present to qualify the car himself, just as Stirling's colleague and friend Ken Gregory had done for him on a few occasions in his early years. Whenever Stirling was competing in another race elsewhere on the same day as practice at a different venue or, as it is known today, qualifying, the time Ken put up (on Stirling's behalf) would determine Stirling's place on the grid at the start of the race, normally the following day.

As mentioned previously, right up until 1958 drivers in Formula One races could also take over the drive of another person's car during a race. The replacement driver would take up the accredited position of the previous driver and the final position of the car would be determined by the position in which the car finished after passing the chequered flag, i.e. over the finish line. This final result would not normally be attributed to the original driver who started off in the car or to the pair of drivers, but to the person who finished the race in the car. In other words, it was permissible for Stirling to take over another driver's car, which was, for the sake of example, lying in ninth position and wherever he worked himself up to (or down) would be recorded as his final position. For example, this happened in the 1957 British Grand Prix at Aintree, when Stirling took over the Vanwall of his injured teammate Tony Brooks and worked his way up through the field to win the race – all perfectly permissible back then.

The 1958 season would certainly have been a completely different story had the rules not been altered and Stirling had been allowed to take over the number two Vanwall, but they were, so that was that. However, Stirling was still allowed to compete in all types of different cars on the same day, from saloon car racing and sports car events to Formula racing.

The Vanwall team, to whom Stirling was contracted for the 1958 season, had not been able to send any of their cars to Argentina; hence Stirling had little choice but to drive the Cooper Climax if he wanted to drive in the first qualifying event of 1958 in the calendar of events scheduled by the FIA (Fédération Internationale de l'Automobile, the sport's overall ruling body) for the Formula One world championship. Apparently, Vanwall were really worried about how the new fuel regulations, which banned normal driving (alcohol) fuel in favour of avgas, would affect their engines and they were not completely satisfied that they had solved the problem in time for the race in Argentina. However, Stirling's second drive in a Grande Épreuve that year, the first since I had joined the company, would be driving the new Vanwall in the sunny climes of Monte Carlo.

PITCHING UP UNANNOUNCED

Although the office was hidden from outsiders, I never knew who might pitch up and come through the door at any given time.

The first occasion that Katie visited the office after my arrival there (and well after Silverstone), was when she blew in like a breath of fresh air and announced, 'It's pissing down with rain.' I had never heard rain described like this so later that evening I asked someone (much to their amusement) what it meant, and was duly told.

Stirling made it fairly plain to her that she wasn't exactly welcome in the office. He didn't get up from his desk and shouted at her through the partition, 'What are you doing here?'

Completely unperturbed by this bluntness, Katie moved further towards his door and, poking her nose into his office, replied, 'I was in the area and thought that I would drop by.'

'We are very busy in here,' he snapped.

She smiled sweetly and, with one foot in Stirling's office and one in mine, she began to talk to me.

'Valerie's very busy too,' he grumbled. 'Please don't disturb her.'

Serenely and confidently, she calmly moved inside the inner sanctum and plonked a kiss on his head.

'We really ARE very busy here,' he reiterated.

Still unruffled, she went on talking to him but as she only received a couple of grunts, she soon made up her mind to be on her way as quickly as she had arrived. She winked at me, waved her hand and was off.

Stirling never ever appreciated his routine being interrupted by anyone and he would not tolerate people just 'dropping by' unexpectedly – and that included his own wife.

A MIXED BAG OF PERSONALITIES

One cloudless, sunny morning, I had left the office door wide open and was busily working away when two tall, good-looking men ambled through the doorway. One was lean and handsome, with thin fairish hair and a craggy face. His eyes twinkled permanently and he had the slightly pursed, pouting lips that many Frenchmen possess. The other was a total contrast to the first. His hair was dark and his matching elegant goatee beard and moustache had been clipped very precisely. He was not quite as tall as the other man but was by no means short, yet he was equally handsome in a totally different way and he moved in a slower, more deliberate manner. They were both exceedingly well dressed in clothes that were casual yet chic, with a slightly foreign-looking cut, which the British have never quite been able to attain – or is it that the British just don't comport themselves as well?

The clean-shaven man spoke first with a decidedly French accent.

''Allo,' he said. 'We knew zat Stirleeng would not be 'ere so we decided to come and see what 'eez secretary 'eez like.'

I blushed.

The other man added in a sing-song voice, 'Oh, he keeps the best things hidden away for himself.'

It turned out that the fairer-haired man was the charming Franco-American driver Harry Schell and the other was the laconic Swedish driver, Joakim (Jo) Bonnier, who unfortunately burnt to death in the classic 24-hour sports car race at Le Mans in 1972 after a slower driver had pulled out in front of him. Stirling always considered slow drivers to be a menace, particularly at Le Mans, because he said that the drivers in slower cars just tooled around in their own little world and would only become aware of the presence of a faster car bearing down on them when it was almost up their exhaust or, he would more probably have said, 'it was up their chuff'. He felt that Formula One was much safer than sports car racing because one always knew who one was up against in Formula One, whereas in sports car racing, there were often too many drivers of lesser abilities and capabilities driving cars of widely varying sizes and speeds on the same circuit at the same time. (One could argue that that was all part of the competition and, indeed it was and still is, although one rarely sees F1 drivers driving anything other than F1 cars these days – the main exception at the time of writing being Fernando Alonso.)

Harry Schell was a great charmer and womaniser, being half French and half American (although the French part was rather more dominant). He lived in Paris with his regular girlfriend, although, as I later found out and had to deal with on his death, he had a girl in every port (as did the majority of drivers, whether or not they were married.)

Harry and Jo were like chalk and cheese, apart from their love of the opposite sex and motor racing, but they rubbed along together well on the international motor racing circuit as they roamed the world as gentlemen racing drivers. The two of them were almost inseparable travelling companions.

Unbeknown to Stirling, Harry and Jo became great mates of mine and, in fact, in London I became Harry's informal banker. I had a very soft spot for him because he just oozed charm. He would generally arrive in the UK, literally penniless but with his pockets stuffed with French francs or American dollars, and he would borrow a tenner (a week's wages for me) until he was able to change his money into pounds.* Harry would always repay me without being prompted

---

* Quite often, the organisers used to pay the start money in cash and the drivers would obviously keep a lot of it to pay for their expenses; credit cards appeared on the scene at a much later date.

and often he would bring me little presents, such as French cuisine in pretty pottery containers. He also used to send me postcards from wherever he was in the world as would Stirling, who once brought back a colourful certificate verifying that I had crossed the equator when I had probably been hard at work or tucked up in bed in the UK!

The pair didn't normally book a hotel until they arrived in London because they found they could usually negotiate a better price if they rolled up on the day. They preferred to stay at either the (old) Berkeley in Berkeley Street, or the Westbury in Conduit Street, which links New Bond Street with Regent Street and, because they were friends and didn't get on each other's nerves, they would share a twin-bedded room together because it helped them to cut down their expenses. In his early years, Stirling used to share hotel rooms with Ken or other male friends who used to travel with him, which did raise a few eyebrows at the time, but similarly, it was purely a matter of trying to keep down his costs.

I never knew when the pair would pitch up but had Stirling known about the arrangement, he certainly would have banned them from the office, accusing them of wasting his secretary's time, not to mention using his telephone, 'which costs money, which I have to earn'.

Amongst the other 'regulars' who used to call when I first started working at William IV Street were the charming diminutive French driver Maurice Trintignant (uncle to the film star Jean-Louis Trintignant); the American drivers Masten Gregory from Kansas City, Missouri, who was small and lean, and because he was so short-sighted always wore large, horn-rimmed glasses (and who I once had to lock in the office after he became over-amorous with me!); and the curly-haired Carroll Shelby from Texas, who would tower over most in his shiny, black embroidered cowboy boots. He would even wear these boots when he was racing, together with a most extraordinary outfit, which consisted of thin, blue and white striped trousers together with a matching bib, which was held in place by two large silver-coloured suspenders that were attached to straps that came over from the back waistband and locked onto the bib. He normally wore a white T-shirt underneath. Sometimes, these drivers would turn up when Stirling was there and at other times he was not. Should he be in his office, his welcome would be decidedly indifferent, to say the least!

SHIFTING SANDS

It was always an unbelievably busy office when Stirling was in the country, with a constant stream of visitors coming and going. He considered these interruptions to be infernal irritations but conceded that most were an evil necessity. All those who had made appointments were, on the whole (if they were not the press), representatives from his sponsors, all of whom contributed quite a sizeable amount to the kitty each year, or people who had a business proposition to discuss with him.

However reluctant he may have felt about these meetings he would always make himself available, but rarely would he move out of his office because he considered that the travelling would be 'a total waste of his time'. He even used to persuade outside broadcast TV crews to come to interview him, when the office would be transformed into a micro studio, with huge arc lamps and wires trailing around all over the place. The disruption these crews caused meant that it was virtually impossible to get anything done whilst they were there (not to mention the fact that this was anti-productive workwise!) and, once a recording had started, woe betide if any of the telephones rang.

'Turn those bloody things off,' Stirling would yell, exasperated that the whole thing couldn't be done in one take, yet it was normally the direct private line in his office that would ring, which of course would be my fault. It always was!

This private line was particularly handy when he was abroad or whenever he was out and wanted to get hold of me urgently and found that both the other lines were busy. Yes, I had to grow another tentacle, all in the line of duty!

The first time someone appeared at the door to interview Stirling after I joined the company was John Timpson from the BBC, who later became an anchor on the *Today* radio programme with Brian Redhead and chair of *Any Questions*, and he offered to show me how to work the lumpy machinery that he had to lug about with him. Fortunately, Stirling was occupied on another matter when John first turned up so he didn't react as he would have normally about someone diverting my attention from my work. I was most impressed with the device, although it would have looked positively archaic in this day and age. It did even then.

First of all, the tape was encased in an extraordinarily large and heavy khaki tin box with a lid, about two feet wide and eighteen inches high. The two holders for the tape were on the top, each about five inches wide, and John was expected to carry this chunky equipment around with him wherever he was sent. Fortunately for him, the UK was not at war with anyone at the time.

Stirling was (unfortunately, as far as I was concerned) so impressed with the machine that, as soon as he could, he acquired a couple of tape machines and, if he was abroad, he would ask someone, no matter who, to deliver the tape(s) personally back to me in the office so I could transcribe them. I loathed working with tapes – and still do – and would grumble to him like mad about having to transcribe them, but I had to admit from his point of view that it was a useful system, which did speed up things quite considerably – for him. Everything always had to be done totally for his gratification and benefit at top speed and with accuracy. As it was ever thus, although it wasn't immediately noticeable, at least to me.

The racing calendar really only started at Easter in Britain, with the traditional Goodwood meeting, and would run out of steam come the end of September. Meanwhile, other races came and went and all the while, Vanwall continued to try to sort out the problems with their cars right up until May, endeavouring to get them running and handling more efficiently. However, they did decide to send the new car on its first outing for Stirling to drive in the second Grande Épreuve of the year, the Monaco Grand Prix. No one was particularly surprised when, almost predictably, he was forced to retire due to mechanical failures, least of all him.

The following weekend at Zandvoort, known for its sandy dunes that affected the course and the cars quite considerably when the wind blew sand onto the circuit, it would turn out to be a slightly different story, much to Stirling's delight. The Vanwall mechanics had obviously slogged their guts out on the car all week between Monte Carlo and the Dutch Grand Prix and I was absolutely thrilled for Stirling when I heard a snippet on the radio early on the Sunday evening news, informing listeners that he had won the race there – and by a lead of no less than forty-eight seconds. In fact, he lapped all the other cars apart from the two BRMs (British Racing Motors), which came in second and third, one of which was driven by my friend Schell, and the other by Jean Behra. Motor racing was a reasonably popular sport back then, but it did not warrant much coverage and this clip was aired on the BBC most likely because it involved Stirling. Had someone else won the race, it probably wouldn't have been mentioned at all.

By now, Stirling was racing virtually every weekend on the Continent and he left Ken Gregory and myself to hold the fort. He had a further mixed bag of successes and failures. He retired during the 1958 Belgium Grand Prix at Spa-Francorchamps, again with engine trouble, but, at the French Grand Prix at Reims in early July, he came second to Mike Hawthorn, who was in a works Ferrari (Hawthorn's only win of the season). Once again, however, this race was marred by the death of one of Hawthorn's teammates, the Italian Luigi Musso.

Stirling returned home for the next Grande Épreuve, which was the British Grand Prix. This year, it was to be held at Silverstone, rather than at Aintree, where it had been held the previous year (it used to alternate) when he had won. Once again, he retired with engine failure, the race being won by the other British Ferrari driver, the debonair Peter Collins.

Then came the fateful German Grand Prix at the Nürburgring.

Stirling was forced to retire after three laps with magneto problems and would have been packing up to leave the circuit when, seven laps later, tragedy struck. Peter Collins, who had not long been married to the American actress Louise King, went off the road and was thrown out of his car as it hit a tree and somersaulted.

Peter was rushed to hospital in Bonn suffering from severe head injuries and died later that day.

Not only did this come as a bombshell to all the drivers, but it also came as a great shock to the British public because of the perceived rivalry between Stirling, Mike Hawthorn and Peter Collins, although it was quite well acknowledged that Stirling was the fastest driver of the three, given the same car and conditions.

Mike had been far closer to Peter Collins than Stirling ever was, mainly because they were both extroverts, whilst Stirling was an introvert. Stirling and Mike both rallied round to do all they could for Peter's widow Louise, who they both respected and, if the truth be known, had both rather fancied before Peter carried her off after a whirlwind romance of less than a week.

Apparently, Stirling had suggested to Pete that he should contact Louise if ever he found himself at a loose end in Coconut Grove in the States, and he had, with the inevitable result. The marriage was initially met with such disbelief in the racing circle it was likened to Stirling entering into a monastery or Mike Hawthorn giving up booze! (Louise's first husband, John Michael King, appeared in the original production of *My Fair Lady* and I always associated the song, 'On the Street Where You Live' with her.)

Unsurprisingly, on the Monday after the accident, there was a barrage of phone calls at the office and, once again, I had to hold the fort, although some of the newspapers were able to contact Stirling directly in Germany because he had had to cancel his immediate plans to come home to help in the aftermath of Peter's death.

Stirling was pretty subdued when he did get back to the UK, but he immediately immersed himself in office affairs, which soon took his mind off the weekend's traumas.

There wasn't much time for Stirling to share many thoughts or feelings with me that first year – even if he had wanted to – because we were like passing ships in the night. However, a certain amount of empathy had begun to grow between us and, by mid-season, circumstances created a new bond, which came to a head towards the end of August.

By now, I had found Stirling to be a fairly intense, rather shy young man, and that is perhaps why he was outwardly never really full of his own importance. To me, he was just a regular type of guy who had a lot on his plate, a lot of drive (pardon the pun), an abundance of ambition – where second best was never on the cards – but, increasingly, it also seemed to me that he was rather pennywise as well as being pound-hungry. It had become abundantly clear to me that if anyone wanted his time – or any part of it – then they had to pay for it, whether it be for a garage opening, an interview with the BBC or just driving competitively. He would not budge an inch unless he was going to get some type of pecuniary reward for it. He would not necessarily be averse to a little quid pro quo from time to time, but only because there was something in it for him. So far as he was concerned, time was always of the essence and, although he derived his income from people paying him for his time, he was not at all bothered if they chose not to use him. And he didn't come cheaply, either, especially when he really didn't want to do something.

BIG-TIME CHARLIE POTATOES!

Not long after my appointment, Stirling was ensconced in his office, deep in conversation with someone, when he suddenly shouted at me through the open hatch and asked me to go to pick up some things for him from his flat in his car, which meant negotiating the perennially busy Hyde Park Corner (and I had never driven in London before). He pushed the keys through the hatch and told me that Katie would let me in. I went downstairs to street level, only to find a gleaming, pale green, DB3 Aston Martin staring at me. Up until that time, I had never driven anything more powerful than a Hillman Minx.

I gulped, put the key in the door and settled into the driving seat, but do you think I could find where to put the ignition key? Feeling like a complete idiot, I climbed back up the stairs to the office and timidly asked where the ignition was. Back downstairs I went and, after finding it and putting in the key, I then couldn't find the brake. Somewhat apprehensively, I climbed back up the stairs again. Even more timidly, I asked where the brake was and Stirling told me exactly where it was without even raising an eyebrow. Quite frankly, I was utterly amazed and rather pleasantly surprised.

At this juncture, had I been the owner of the vehicle, I think I might personally have been ever so slightly worried about lending such an expensive car to such an obvious novice but, seemingly, this just didn't come into the equation with him. His expectations have always been of the very highest and he certainly does not suffer fools gladly.

When I pulled up at the kerb at the address that Stirling had given to me – Challoner Mansions – I thought I must have made a mistake. I was outside a small, drab and gloomy mansion block of flats in a rather seedy backwater of West Kensington, a stone's throw from Queen's Club tennis courts. I had imagined that he would have lived in a much smarter area and, as I climbed the dark, dank stone staircase to the second or third floor, it crossed my mind that I wouldn't like to have to lug up my shopping such a long way.

However, there was an even bigger surprise to come. Once inside the cramped hallway, Katie beckoned me into the living room, which was completely covered with a miniature electric railway track, trains, stations and scenery.

I was just about to ask Katie why it was there when she threw up her arms and hands outwards, simultaneously shrugging her shoulders and, lifting her eyes skywards, she sighed and said, 'Stirling,' and left it at that.

Whilst driving back to the office, I thought to myself, 'What a strange place for Stirling to live, let alone an heiress.'

After the incident with the Aston, I was often asked to go on errands. Trying to fit in little jobs was difficult when Stirling was around because he always wanted me to be in the office so I mostly tried to slip out when he was away, but this was also wrong if I was out when he telephoned. One could never win with him! But, that would come to change somewhat over the years.

BEHIND THE SCENES

Whenever he got back from racing, he would bring in the overalls that he had been wearing and I would take them off to the dry cleaners in one of the small alleyways off St Martin's Lane to be cleaned (I always wondered why Katie didn't do this) and, once I had collected them, they then had to be taken to be fireproofed before the next race, which involved coating them with a mixture of borax, boric acid and water. I also used to trot off to Herbert Johnson on New Bond Street on a regular basis, where Stirling bought his helmets and had them renovated and/or resprayed. In fact, he started quite a trend with some of the other drivers, who also admired the helmet's attractive lines and copied him by buying and wearing this make, but Herbert Johnson was probably one of the very few places in the world which didn't give him a discount of any kind at all for recommending their goods to others! He was actually quite vain as far as his appearance was concerned and liked to be seen as being quite 'with it' and fashionable.

On a couple of occasions, I was sent to a building at the top of St Martin's Lane to collect brown, foolscap envelopes in which, I later learnt, were 'top shelf'-type magazines, and on a couple of occasions I had the distinction of being the only woman standing in line with a whole load of bowler-hatted men in Soho, waiting to buy tickets for the Raymond Revuebar. I gather this show was like the Folies Bergère, although I am told the ladies went totally unclad on stage.* Presumably, the spectacle at Raymond's was permitted because such performances were run under the licence of a private members' club, which overcame the rules of the land.

• • •

Alfred Moss, Stirling's rather portly, grey-haired father, used to waft in and out of the office at regular intervals, always brandishing a cigar in his hand and leaving that unmistakable smell of stale cigar smoke – which pervaded even the paperwork – and giving Stirling the benefit of his advice, more often than not, unasked. They argued frequently and would often end up raising their voices and shouting at each other. On one particular occasion, they didn't even bother to close the flimsy intercommunicating door. The debate became increasingly heated and the atmosphere electric. They were shouting so loudly that I really thought that everyone in the rest of the building would be able to hear them. I felt nervous and embarrassed because

---

* The musical *Hair* was the first time people were officially allowed to appear nude (and, specifically, move) in public and that was in the mid '6os.

I was completely out of my depth, never having come across anything like this before. Suddenly, I began to laugh hysterically – and I couldn't stop. They both stopped shouting at each other and looked at mousey little me in utter astonishment. The little secretary was actually daring to laugh at the two grown men arguing. And then, they began to laugh. And they couldn't stop, either. Nothing ever was said but I swear from that day forward, Stirling began to develop a slight sense of humour.

A CATASTROPHIC SLIP-UP

But back to 1958: by the time the Portuguese Grand Prix came around in Oporto, Stirling (with Vanwall) and Mike Hawthorn (Ferrari) were running neck and neck in the world championship points table, and it was here that Stirling showed his true colours in the most unusual of ways – sheer and unadulterated chivalry and honesty.

Stirling won the race, but afterwards he heard that Mike had been disqualified for pushing his car in the wrong direction back onto the circuit after running out of road and he went and had a word with him. After his chat with Mike, and because Stirling had actually witnessed the incident, he made a point of going to see the organisers to tell them his side of the story which was contrary to the official report they had received. Subsequently, Mike was reinstated and, back in the running. He was also awarded the one valuable extra point for putting up the fastest lap of the race, which would count towards the world championship that year. In all honesty, Stirling thought he had that crucial one point in *his* bag; he was later to find out that his pit had held out incorrect information for him during the race.

52

Boards used to be hung out as the drivers passed the pits, giving them information about their position in the race and their lap times. Nowadays, all this – and more – is given to them over the radio by their respective teams, including giving the drivers direct instructions (to go faster, slower, etc.) In Stirling's day, however, all this was pretty much left up to the driver to decide.

Because the on-track rivalry at that juncture was so fierce between him and Mike for the world crown, he was absolutely devastated when he realised that he hadn't put up the fastest lap. He knew his own capabilities and he knew that he could easily have gone a lot faster out on the circuit that day. And, what a lifelong mistake this was to prove to be. That one point was to be crucial to Stirling because it was that one point that would hang in the balance until after the result of the last and final Grande Épreuve of the year was known. This was to be held in Morocco, two very long months later in the middle of October.

Contrary to what people thought at the time, Mike and Stirling were good friends when they weren't competing against each other, although Hawthorn was totally different in character to Stirling. In fact, Mike had been one of Stirling's ushers at his wedding the previous October, as had Peter Collins. Mike was a totally different animal to Stirling and their personalities were complete opposites. Absolutely chalk and cheese. Mike preferred to live life to the full and he certainly enjoyed his booze, whereas Stirling would rather live a far quieter life outside motor racing. Stirling was always totally professional and he felt it his duty to give the public good value for money. Whenever he won a race and went out to drive the mandatory winner's lap, he was renowned for unfailingly acknowledging the crowd's support by raising his arm in a gesture of thanks as he went past. The spectators loved it and loved him for it. It always seemed to me that Mike was probably more in it for the fun of racing and the lively social life that went with it, plus, of course, it gave him a very reasonable way to live.

Once back in the office after the race in Portugal, Stirling looked visibly distraught, as usual checking his nails, which he always did whenever he was anxious and had a problem or was thinking hard, and, for him, he was quite snappy.

At last, I heard a big sigh and a 'Valerie will you come and help me with this, please? I want to check my championship points.' And, there and then, we methodically began going through the results of each of his races for the year and his fastest laps. We must have done it at least three times but we always came up with the same old answer and the result was not what he wanted, but it did give me what turned out to be a brilliantly simple yet extremely useful idea.

I would log all his race results with times after each event and keep them for reference. This had never been done before and it was subsequently to involve me in a tremendous amount of research (another job to do in my 'spare' time when he was away!) because I had to unearth all his previous results, going back ten years. These records have been such a valuable tool over the years that I don't know why he had never thought about logging them before I arrived on the scene.

It was even stranger because he meticulously kept a daily diary wherever he was in the world and it would be the very last thing he would attend to at night, regardless of where he was or who he was with. The only academic subject at school that he was really ever good at was mathematics. He would always jot down the practice times, car details and so on (not necessarily his own), plus the rest of his thoughts or daily activities in his diary but, bizarrely, he would never record any precise details of race day itself. Many years later, when I was working through his diaries on a task for him, it rather amused me to see that he always became a little confused when crossing over the International Date Line! However, as a racing driver, being good at maths was certainly helpful for him in working out gear and axle ratios and so on.

Without the internet, it took me some time to dig up details of all of his past races, but it also helped me to increase my knowledge about his racing years and his life leading up to the time when I joined him.

NOT FOR THOSE WHO KNOW!

The following is a little of what I found out about his racing career before I joined him.

It all began on 2 March 1947. Stirling was seventeen, if my maths is correct, and his first competitive car was a BMW 328, which he had persuaded his father to buy from a fellow dentist. After driving around his parents' property at Bray in a little Austin 7 and the like from a very young age, Stirling had 'caught the bug' and, having sized up the BMW, he pestered his father to allow him to compete in it, which he eventually did in a Harrow Car Club trial on that date in March. He won the event and, as a result, he was presented with his very first motoring trophy, the Cullen Cup.

And that was the beginning of how Stirling Craufurd Moss became the first ever professional motor racing driver. He began to show his colours at a few more events that year and people began to take notice of him, not just for his skill and youth, but also for his name.

At the beginning of the 1948 season, Stirling did receive a smack in the face because he sent in an entry to compete in the Shelsley Walsh Hill Climb, which the organisers chose to turn down. If every organiser had felt the same way about him, his career would have been over in an instant, but fortunately they did not. His second entry for the Prescott Open Hill Climb was accepted and he finished fourth. After that, there was to be no stopping him. He notched up six consecutive wins in his next six events, quickly coming to the notice of the other drivers (most of whom were quite old) and enthusiastic spectators.

The following year (1949), Stirling was determined, come what may, to compete in a 500cc single-seater, much to his parents' dismay, but eventually they gave way and lent him some money to complete the purchase of a Formula Three Cooper, fitted with a 500cc JAP engine. He entered and competed in four hill climbs and various speed trials, pulling off nine wins that year. He also set new class records and put up the fastest time of the day in three of these outings.*

His international racing debut came in 1949, when he raced in Switzerland, France and Holland as well as some English events with some success, this time in a modified F3 Cooper chassis that he had bought, using a non-too-reliable borrowed 1000cc JAP engine. The old 500cc engine, with which he had competed the previous year, was used for some of the other events that year as well.

The turning point in Stirling's career came in 1950 when he was asked to drive for the works HWM (Hersham and Walton Motors) team to compete in Formula One and Two races. He had now become a 'proper' professional racing driver, in as much as he did not have to

---

* Because of the different power of the engines, cars were classified according to their power, and fastest time of the day speaks for itself – it means setting up the fastest time of anyone regardless of class on that particular day, but not necessarily a lap record. A lap record is the fastest time that anyone puts up at a particular circuit and irrespective of circuit conditions in a particular class of car.

pay for all his own motor racing and he would receive a percentage of start, prize and bonus monies. He was always adamant that he would never pool his winnings, but he did insist that his mechanics should receive a certain set percentage of them and this, I believe, was specifically stipulated in all of his contracts.

He raced with HWM all over Europe and, if he wasn't racing for them, he competed in his own modified Cooper F3, using the old JAP engine until it was decided to replace it with a Norton engine. He fervently hoped that he would at least be able to cover all the running costs with the prize and start monies that he and his father managed to negotiate for him.

He also managed to get himself a drive later that year in the infamous nine-hour Tourist Trophy sports car race at Dundrod in Northern Ireland, where he had never raced before. At the eleventh hour, he had persuaded a chap called Tommy Wisdom (driver and subsequently *Daily Herald* motoring correspondent) to lend him his brand-new Jaguar, which had come virtually straight off the assembly line. Against all odds and all comers, Stirling won the event, having driven all through the night in howling gales and torrential rain. This would prove to be the turning point in his career.

The next day, the newspapers were full of his exploits and the somewhat unusual name of Stirling Moss was on everyone's lips. Who was this curly-haired young lad who had sprung from almost nowhere and had beaten all the very best in such atrocious conditions? It was a name which would keep cropping up in the future on the front pages around the world, and for a very long time to come. Because of this win in the borrowed Jaguar, at the end of the season Sir William Lyons, who headed up the Jaguar Car Company in Coventry, signed up Stirling as a Jaguar works driver in sports car races. His first race for them in a works car was the Italian Mille Miglia the following year (1951) in the 3.5 litre Jaguar. He also drove a C-Type Jaguar for the factory at Le Mans.

By 1951, the Martin-Norton, which became known universally as the Kieft (CK51), had been built for Stirling to race in Formula Three events and was a car that he loved and which he held in particular regard, despite its looks, which were not perhaps aesthetically pleasing. All the while, he continued to attract attention to himself, whether it was by setting a fastest lap or a lap record. But 1951 was not his finest year and 1952 was to be even worse. Stupidly, as it turned out – and he was always the first to admit it, even though going there was for all the right reasons – Stirling decided to leave HWM after his first race for them in Bremgarten because he was tempted to go and drive for Leslie Johnson in his Bristol-engine G-type ERA (English Racing Automobile). He believed that he could help to develop the car so that it would be ready and fully competitive as a F1 car for the revised rules under which F1 would be run in the future.

The ERA was not a success and it was fortunate that Stirling had kept the Kieft Norton to fall back on during 1952, because he managed to keep his name in the winners' frame by winning Formula Three races in it.

By now, he had become involved in the design and building of yet another new car with London garagiste Ray Martin but, disappointingly, this car was to prove pretty unsuccessful. This was coronation year, 1953, when everyone hoped that the new, young Queen would be able to help lift the UK out of its doldrums and cheerlessness as it was trying to recover in the aftermath of the war years. It was during that year that one of Stirling's rivals, Mike Hawthorn, who was also coming to prominence in the public eye, signed on as a works driver with Ferrari. By the year end, Stirling was a worried man.

Knowing that Mercedes was putting together a Formula One team for 1954, Alfred Moss and Ken Gregory (by then Stirling's manager) made an appointment to meet the infamous German team manager, Alfred Neubauer, in Germany to see if they could persuade him to give Stirling a place in the Mercedes team. But, although Neubauer had certainly heard about Stirling's prowess, he told the duo that he felt that, as far as he was concerned, Stirling was really an unknown quantity and that it would be far better if he could properly prove his worth. He also added that his name would never even be considered as a potential Mercedes works driver until he had done this.

During the conversation, Neubauer suggested to Alfred and Ken that it might be expeditious for them to acquire a 250F Maserati because he felt that it was quite a competitive car. Subsequently, a new car was ordered from the Maserati factory in Italy. This was defiantly modified for Stirling's driving position at the works in Modena, which included moving the brake pedal in the cockpit from the right-hand side to the middle (i.e. the accelerator was moved to the more traditional position to the right of the brake!). Unfortunately, in the well-known Italian tradition of procrastination, the Maserati was only delivered well into the 1954 season. However, Neubauer was to be proved correct. The car was fairly fast in Stirling's hands, but what really sealed Stirling's immediate future was demonstrating his prowess in it to 'the great man' in Switzerland. At the demanding Bremgarten circuit against the might of the whole of the Mercedes team, which also included that year's world champion Juan Manuel Fangio from Argentina, and the official Maserati team, Stirling, in his own Maserati, qualified third on the grid and led the race for sixty-eight laps. This, together with his performance at the Italian Grand Prix was sufficient to impress Neubauer, and he subsequently went to join his idol Fangio as his number two in the Mercedes team the following year, 1955.

After this outing in Switzerland, Stirling was immediately asked by Maserati to become a semi-official works driver. A deal was cut whereby Maserati would enter and maintain the car that he had bought from them free of charge but, officially, the car would still be privately owned by Stirling Moss Ltd. This meant that, for the rest of the season, the car would be fully run and maintained by the factory at no cost to him. So the upshot was that he would not have to buy any more parts or accessories or pay any more bills for his Maserati whatsoever for the rest of the '54 season. This also meant that, in future, the stress, strain and anxiety of keeping his car on the island in one piece would virtually be eliminated. Struggling to do everything on a shoestring had certainly added to Stirling's worries and stress right up until this point in his career, with the exception of his time with HWM. Consequently, he now determined to test his own abilities alongside the other Maserati works cars. He decided to drive his Maserati well *under* the given maximum limits set by Maserati to all their drivers, just to prove to everyone, including himself, that he could equal their performances with less power under the same conditions, or even better them.

A short while after this arrangement had been made with Maserati, Stirling did revert to being a private entrant once more because of the death of one of the Maserati works drivers in a race. The official Maserati team decided to withdraw all the team cars for a while as a mark of respect to the dead driver. Stirling never could see eye to eye with any of the top brass, or whoever decided to do this. He certainly would not have expected this to happen if he were to die racing, neither would he have wanted it. In his mind, once a fatal occurrence had taken place, it did not make any sense to him whatsoever to withdraw the rest of the team cars. He felt that there was absolutely nothing anyone could do about an accident after the event. To back up his argument, he always quoted the fact that none of the organisers of an event ever considered stopping a race in its entirety on such occasions unless the damage on the circuit was too dangerous for the other drivers to continue racing. Only in the rarest of occasions would a race be paused long enough for the wreckage to be cleared and then the race would be restarted. Stirling was a pragmatic person and withdrawing the rest of the team cars really did not make any sense to him at all. Of course, after the fact, as a matter of respect to the dead driver, whoever it may have been, whenever possible Stirling would make a point of attending the funeral and/or memorial. But, to him, whenever such incidences occurred, it was always a case of 'the show must go on'. He therefore told Maserati that he would continue to race as a private entrant until such time as the Maserati team became fully operational again. Subsequently, all his entries were *pro tem* switched to the name of Stirling Moss Ltd.

For the past few years, Stirling had also been competing in a few prestigious rallies and, in 1954, he won the Coupe des Alpes rally in a works Sunbeam Alpine and was presented with a Coupe d'Or for his third consecutive win, a feat only to be repeated once ever again (by Jean Vinatier in 1971; the first being Ian Appleyard in 1952). Stirling was the second winner – of only three ever – of a Coupe d'Or.

It had by now become apparent that Stirling was a 'natural' in any car that he chose to drive and, although rallying is a different technique altogether from racing, it didn't seem to stop him from getting on with the job he was being paid to do.

By the beginning of 1955, the contract had been signed with Mercedes-Benz and Stirling found himself at Hockenheim testing the fuel-injected straight eight-cylinder engine W196 Mercedes, which he found to be much heavier to handle than his own Maserati 250F that he continued to drive in events that year when Mercedes were not sporting a car for him.

The efficiency of Mercedes was legendary and whatever Stirling wanted, Stirling had – be it a special seating position, a mirror or a steering wheel. He was in his element.

Two things should be mentioned at this juncture. Juan Manuel Fangio was without any question of doubt whatsoever, a worthy, multiple world champion in a F1 car, but he was not as versatile as Stirling and was not capable of driving quite as competitively and with such pinpoint accuracy in any other genres of the sport. This went for most of the other drivers (to date) as well, the reasons being quite inexplicable.

One of the mysteries of Stirling's year with Mercedes was whether or not their number one driver Fangio held back to allow Stirling to win on his home turf in the British Grand Prix at Aintree that year. The only person who ever really knew the answer to that question was Fangio himself and he took this secret with him to his grave, although Stirling did ask him on several occasions. But the records show that Stirling did win the British Grand Prix in the Mercedes and, in fact, notched up a new lap record as well. It was his first major win in a Grande Épreuve and set him up, yet again, as a hero in the eyes of the public for being the first Englishman ever to win the British Grand Prix. He also put up equal fastest laps on a couple of other occasions together with Fangio during the year. Bearing all this in mind, could he just have won at Aintree on his own merit? Earning the lap record that day only adds to the conundrum.

In certain sports car events the same year, Stirling drove a Mercedes 300 SLR, partnered by John Fitch or Peter Collins, and towards the end of the season he drove a Porsche Spyder with (Baron) Huschke von Hanstein, the driver-turned-Porsche team manager, in the nine-hour event at Goodwood. It was also in 1955 that Stirling drove a Mercedes 300 SLR in the renowned Mille Miglia road race in Italy. Starting from Brescia at one-minute intervals on 30 April in car number 722, and driving at unprecedented speeds on open Italian roads, fringed by spectators, at a record speed, averaging 97.96 miles per hour – miles, that is, not kilometres – over the 1,000-mile (1,600 km – the Romans used to use miles!) race, he led the field all the way round although he did not know that he had won until the very last car had finished.

Much has been written about this event and how Stirling's ingenuity produced a gadget, which was basically an open box, containing what can best be described as a type of toilet roll holder, around which were wound recce notes or pace notes. His co-driver, Denis Jenkinson, would read them out to him, or rather holler them out, as well as using his hands to confirm left, right or straight on, for the entire route. This was some feat, but as the SLR was an open roadster this was yet more complicated because they were open to the elements. Prior to the start of the event, Fangio, who was also competing in the road race, had given Stirling an over-the-counter amphetamine-based stimulant (which, at that time, was both totally legal and commonplace amongst rally drivers.) to help him keep awake. After 10 hours, 7 minutes and 46 seconds of total concentration by the end of the event, Stirling was so hyped up that, after the victory presentations had concluded, he drove all the way back to Germany and has always said that he could have easily driven home to the UK as well.

This was probably the most difficult test of Stirling's driving, stamina and concentration and also his greatest triumph ever but, although the event was against the clock, it was not a Formula One race. (His greatest race, as previously stated, was probably his last Formula One race at Monaco in 1961.)

Although Stirling admired Fangio greatly (the two of them always got on together extremely well) and the domination of Mercedes with the two of them driving had become awesome, somehow it did not sit too comfortably with him that he was driving in the number two position to Fangio in the Mercedes team. Consequently, when Mercedes decided to withdraw from Formula One racing at the end of the 1955 season, he switched horses yet again and inveigled his way back into the number one slot with the Italian official works Maserati team, effectively pushing Jean Behra down into the number two slot. Again, this was a somewhat different kettle of fish organisationally, but then, he had been there before. He also drove for them in sports car races that year and achieved even more success in those.

It was during 1956 that Stirling first drove a Vanwall, in which he won the Formula One race at the *Daily Express*-sponsored race meeting at Silverstone and broke the lap record in it.

Having driven and tested the Vanwall in 1956 and, despite certain reservations about its reliability, when owner Tony Vandervell invited him to become his number one driver in 1957, Stirling signed on with the all-British team. He could not have been happier because his continual quest to find and drive an all-British car, potentially capable of winning Grandes Épreuves, had, he thought, at last come to an end.

The hunt for a winning British combination of car and driver had constantly been in Stirling's sights. But, having made one mistake previously by not staying on with HWM, he had had hardly any other sensible chances of competing in such a perfect combination until now, even though he had previously had conversations about, and tested, the British-built BRM Formula One car.

His number two at Vanwall was to be Tony Brooks. As they were both unable to drive the car at Rouen that year, Stuart Lewis-Evans was called in to drive the Vanwall there and he subsequently joined them under contract the following year (1958) as the number three driver.

Stirling began winning in the Vanwall halfway through the 1957 season, the first Épreuve he won being at Pescara (on the east coast of Italy more or less on a latitudinal par with Rome on the west) and the second at Monza, much to the disgust of the Italians, who had become rather passionate about their home-bred cars winning on their home turf. He also continued driving for Maserati in sports car events and, during the third week of August, he went off to the Bonneville Salt Flats in Utah, where he set five new Class F records (cars of engine size 1100cc to 1500cc) in the specially built, stream-lined MG EX181, with a two-way average speed of 245.65 mph over the timed distance. This was 20 per cent faster than the previous record put up by Goldie Gardner just before the Second World War. Once again, Stirling never saw this as a 'big deal'. I asked him about it on one occasion and from what I remember, he muttered some-thing about driving on the salt in the right conditions, from which I gathered there was probably a lot of hanging around, which would not have suited his temperament, and this was because the condition of the salt was critical. Not too wet, not too dry…

At the end of 1957, he had married the attractive Canadian brewery heiress Katie Molson. It was, perhaps, her presence which might explain the reason why he only competed in more or less half of the number of races in 1957 than he had raced in the previous, somewhat frenetic year – but he certainly more than made up for this in 1958.

His first race of 1958 in Argentina was to prove, in all probability, the most tactical race of all his races when Stirling, in Rob's privately entered Cooper, managed to beat all the other works teams by a mere whisker.

It was a stinking hot day and everyone knew (or at least thought they knew) that Stirling's tyres would not last for the whole race and he would have to pit (make a pit stop to change them); towards the end of the race, his pit crew began to put out boards, indicating that he should come into the pits. Stirling would courteously acknowledge them with a wave of his hand and continue racing until everyone else realised, far too late, that this had been his strategy all along. He had played along with this for all it was worth, but he and his pit crew had managed to pull the wool over everyone's eyes. It was a masterstroke of trickery. Towards the end of the race, he managed to save the tyres by resorting to using some of the oil slicks on the track surface to help to prevent them from becoming totally threadbare.

No one would ever have conceived that Stirling could have possibly driven the whole race without pitting and, in the meantime, he had thoroughly enjoyed himself, playing along with the deception the whole time. He nosed past the chequered flag, 2.7 seconds in front of Luigi Musso in a Ferrari and Mike Hawthorn in third place, not far behind Musso. No wonder the crowd was on its feet that day.

Under the new rules for 1958, cross-ply tyres were the order of the day for Formula One racing and when Stirling's car was examined later, it was found that his Dunlop tyres were down to the canvas and would not have lasted another lap; they would just have burst. This was genuinely a masterstroke and a supreme piece of skilled and shrewd precision driving. On this particular occasion, it seems that Lady Luck had ridden along with him, all the while he was fighting off the rest of the field. Lady Luck often seemed to pass over Stirling during his time in motor sport and, although it did seem that she liked to flirt with him from time to time, he was never able to get her full measure.*

For all his straight talking, Stirling was very superstitious, a trait he inherited from his mother, and he always liked to race under the number seven (or at least have a seven in the number), which was the race number allocated to the RRC Walker Racing Team's blue Cooper Climax that he was driving that day.

The ensuing publicity, particularly in the UK, ensured that Stirling's surprise win in Argentina was generally considered to be one of the more startling results in his career, and yet he always made light of it. It certainly jolted the majority of those in motor racing into realising that Stirling was far cannier than anyone up until then had imagined, and this drive only reiterated the fact that he meant business and was someone with whom it was probably best not to tangle. It undoubtedly brought Stirling's name to greater prominence

---

* As a footnote to this race, he and his wife Katie had been skylarking about a couple of days prior to the fixture and she had accidentally scratched his eyeball, which needed hospital treatment, and he had only taken off the eye patch a few minutes before the start of the race.

with the general public and it left little doubt that he would be the man to watch in the future.

Stirling had put his marker down, fair and square, if nothing else. He had shown his mettle and everyone began to realise that he would stop at virtually nothing to win a race.

BACK TO REALITY

After the to-do of the Portuguese Grand Prix, Stirling had high hopes for the next 1958 Grande Épreuve at Monza in Italy, but it proved, once again, to be a great disappointment to him. He had to pull out of the race with mechanical problems and consequently was unable to add to his tally of championship points, not even the one (for fastest lap) that he desperately needed to be on more or less equal terms with Mike Hawthorn going into the last championship race of the season. Mike Hawthorn actually finished second to Stirling's team-mate Tony Brooks at Monza, so the cliffhanger race was to be the very last Grande Épreuve of the season in Morocco in October. It was to be an awfully long wait for both Mike and Stirling.

Shortly before the championship was to be decided, Stirling had experienced what he always described as his very worst accident in his racing career, which was whilst he was testing on the banking at Monza, Italy (banking being precisely that, a sudden, steep upwards curved slope generally made out of tarmac). The steering arm broke on his car and he shot up the banking at high speed; he really thought that he had 'bought it' on that occasion. All he remembered was taking his hands off the wheel, closing his eyes and thinking 'This is it'. It wasn't. When he opened his eyes again, the car had almost come to a stop; it had not gone over the edge of the banking and he found himself to be in one piece, fortunately. He always wondered 'Why?' Once he got back to the UK, he quickly brushed off the event as being just one of those things. But, he never once forgot what went through his mind at the time he was careering off. It made a very deep impression on him.

AN OLD BUCKET JUST ABOUT SUMS IT ALL UP

The race in Morocco would, as it turned out, be the last time that a championship Grand Prix would be held there. Unfortunately, Stirling had taken a real dislike to a high-ranking, self-important official in the Royal Automobile Club of Morocco, which was pretty unusual for him because he rarely took exception to anyone that strongly. He might not like someone very much, but he never normally allowed it to show whilst he was in their presence. I never found out what the man had done to upset him, but Stirling even refused to allow Katie to shake hands with the official in question. He could be extremely obstinate, particularly when his dander was up. Because he was leading the world championship at that stage in the year, for appearances' sake, Stirling was required to acknowledge the man in question, which he did, albeit exceedingly reluctantly, making his feelings about the man fairly plain to everyone present that day.

Normally, Stirling would not have been at all concerned about competing in this race, but the strain had begun to show even before he left the country because there was such a lot riding on it. In particular, he was desperately worried about whether his car would hold together because the condition of the surface of the circuit at Morocco was pretty rough and bumpy. In order to win the 1958 world championship outright, he had to win the race and put up the fastest lap; Mike Hawthorn would lose the world crown if he came anywhere other than first or second in this final race of the season.

A chartered flight had been arranged to take many of the racing personnel and their associates over to Morocco. Stirling always took flying in his stride and was generally very relaxed about it, but this trip was to be an exception.

First of all, he was under pressure, and understandably anxious about which way the championship would go but, to add to all his woes, the plane was a dreadful old bucket, which had seen far better days. Midway through the journey, the flight became exceedingly bumpy. At one stage, when the aircraft descended a few thousand feet in a very short space of time, the voice of one of his closest friends boomed out loud and clear, 'Will anyone join me in a hymn?' By the time the aircraft eventually arrived at its destination, everyone was feeling on edge and more than a little bit the worse for wear.

The circuit of Ain-Diab, near Casablanca, was a road circuit in the newly independent state of Morocco, whose head of state King Mohammed V attended the meeting. Stirling led the race from start to finish in his Vanwall, ably backed up by his teammate, Tony Brooks, until Tony was forced to retire with engine problems. The Ferraris consequently moved up a place, with Phil Hill, Mike Hawthorn's American teammate and a future world champion, lying in second place, albeit some way back. Mike Hawthorn was in third place, a fair distance from Phil. With some laps to go, the Ferrari pit signalled to Phil Hill to let Mike Hawthorn through into second place (which took some time), and with that place went Stirling's chance of winning the world championship. He won the race by well over a minute on his rival and he put up fastest lap, but even that was insufficient to win the world crown. There was absolutely nothing more that Stirling could have done. It was a real kick in the teeth to him and to say that he was mortified would simply be an understatement. If there was to be any recompense at all to the let-down, Stirling's win in Morocco ensured that Vanwall won the Manufacturers' Championship but, again, this would prove to be a somewhat hollow victory.

Grave misfortune had struck Stirling's other teammate during the race, Stuart Lewis-Evans, whose engine had blown up in a somewhat horrific manner. Whilst his car was skidding off the circuit, his overalls became covered in oil and caught fire. Although he managed to jump out, his burns were horrendous and he was immediately air-lifted back to the UK. Worse was to come though. Six days later, Stuart Lewis-Evans succumbed to his injuries and died.

Although Stirling's win in Morocco was described in various glowing tones, with one reporter even describing him as 'a perfectionist while all goes well', he was plainly a bit dejected when he arrived back in the office. He tried not to show that he was upset, but what actually mattered to him most was that he felt cheated. I have never known Stirling to be a bad sport, but he felt that he had driven flat out to win in all the championship events in which he had competed that year (and all the other events as well – because that was his mentality and how he was) and he had won four of them outright and had come second in another, whereas Mike had only won one single championship race outright. Tony Brooks had, incidentally, won three. Nevertheless, Mike had collected sufficient points from being placed in all the other world championship events plus one outright win to achieve what was undoubtedly the pinnacle of his career. Although Stirling was honestly truly happy for Mike, he was miserable about his own situation and he always thought that the system was immensely unfair. The way in which Mike won the championship severely wounded him as a principle – and always did – and far, far more than ever being beaten by any of the other drivers who went on to become a world champion during the years that Stirling was competing.

Yes, Stirling did feel that the way the system worked in 1958 was inequitable but, at the end of the day, those were the rules and he had to live with them.

TWO DIRECTIVES THAT SPOILT THE DREAM

As a point of interest, had the FIA not decided to withdraw the rule that, as from the start of the 1958 season, drivers would not be able to substitute or change places with another driver during a race, the outcome of the '58 championship would probably have been a very different state of affairs.

In all the years up until the end of 1957, after a driver had officially retired his own car, it was permissible for him to take over another driver's car that was still running in the race and continue in it as though he was driving his own car. At the end of the race, this 'follow-on' driver's race position would be attributed to the person who had taken over driving that car and who had crossed the finishing line in it.

Stirling had, on occasions, taken over cars in which he went on to win races and this win was always attributed to him. Many a time, he would take over a poorly placed car and work his way up to lead the pack, and this is what the crowd at motor events particularly appreciated watching. They relished a little excitement, and Stirling could generally be counted on to give them that – whether or not he won.

He gave them the thrill of battle and the thrill of the chase, but little did they know that it was he who enjoyed it most of all.

There are so many imponderables in all walks of life and especially in motor racing but, if the rules had not changed, Stirling would, in all probability, have been able to claim the crown and become the 1958 world champion. This is because, as mentioned, his teammate and number two driver at Vanwall, Tony Brooks, won three of the Grandes Épreuves that year.

As it was, he thought that this anomaly was an utterly absurd state of affairs and he would have preferred Tony to have won the world championship with his three wins rather than Mike with his one. Stirling always rated Tony as a driver and thought that everyone else underrated him. This was probably true because Tony was rather a reserved man and was never full of himself, as many of the other drivers were. It was not hard cheese on Stirling's part in 1958; he had always felt like this and always continued to feel that way. He did cheer up considerably, however, when he won the points-based British Racing Drivers' Championship Gold Star later on in the year, for the eighth time (in ten years). He went on to win a further two gold stars in the following three years.

Mike's world championship win proved to be somewhat of a pyrrhic victory. He announced his retirement from motor racing not long afterwards (due to a medical condition; unbeknown to the general public at the time, he hadn't been given long to live) and was killed whilst driving along the Guildford bypass in his private Jaguar, some three months later. Yet again, I was in the office on my own and Stirling was in the Bahamas, where he was building a house in the east end of Nassau, near to a friend of his, one Norman Solomon. The clamour for quotes from the press worldwide was quite unreal.

WITHOUT EXCEPTION THE PREREQUISITE OF WINNING IS THE DETERMINATION TO WIN WHATEVER THE COST

Stirling always said that he was a racer first and foremost. Although he never abused his cars, regardless of what other people might have thought, he enjoyed the chase and being able to beat someone fairly and squarely, using his skill and his intelligence. He was always proud that he never went over the given maximum rev limits, but he would be the first to admit that he would take the car up to any maximum that he had been given. People often used to say that he was a car breaker, most of the time meaning engines and gearboxes, but he was not. He took his mechanics and team bosses at their word and drove accordingly. He did his job and he expected them to do theirs. Namely, this was to give him a well-prepared car and as much knowledge about the vehicle as he required in order to do a good job for them – and for himself. After all, their mistakes would cost him – and them – not only in monetary terms, but also in prestige. He would always give the team feedback, after any testing before a race and, again, after the race. It was all about quid pro quo. Quite simply, it was a game of codependency.

Many years later in his life, Stirling would say that he knew that he was far quicker than most of the other drivers who have won the world championship and he never changed his tune. He considered that the be all and end all of 'the game' was, quite simply, to try to win every race in which he was entered and in which he took part, no matter how small and unimportant the race might have been. This took an enormous amount of concentration, quite apart from stamina and skill and if he had to drive at ten tenths for the entire duration of the race he would. For him, every race was there for the winning. Competing in a race just to tool round tactically and finish in anything other than first place was a non-starter for him, and much more so in any of the qualifying events in the world championship. Of that he has always been adamant. And in this aspect, he was unique. That is not to say that he wouldn't nurse his car when the occasion arose because he would, and a finish, to his mind, was better than a retirement. But, without a question of doubt, Stirling's attitude towards racing was definitely entirely different to most of the other drivers of his era. Winning was his sole objective. He was exactly the same in this respect in his private life as well. In essence, his was a completely different mind-set. He had to win at everything he put his hand to.

Without exception, Stirling was always in his element when he was racing. He was in a state of quiet euphoria when it came to competing against the rest of the field and, generally, it would give him a real sense of satisfaction when he was able to calmly demonstrate to everyone that he was the master at the wheel of any car he drove. Backing off and tooling round was consequently never an option for him. It would have been as farcical as him going for a quiet drive in the country on a Sunday afternoon. Unthinkable! And, quite apart from anything else, he would also feel that he would be letting the spectators down. In essence, they were the people paying him to put up a performance to the very best of his ability and he certainly wouldn't consider it honest to do anything other than that. It was a strange combination of personal achievement and giving value to those who made his way of life possible. Being honest to himself and being able to live with himself was ever important to him and, during the whole of his life, second best was never once an option.

Stirling was probably very fortunate that he started racing at the right time in the history of motor racing. He had been lucky to have been able to hone his skills at a very early age and, for a very long time, he was the youngest and most talented kid on the block.

By the end of 1958, Ken had left the BRSCC to go into partnership with Stirling's father, Alfred Moss, running a racing team called the British Racing Partnership (BRP), which was based in Highgate, North London. (Stirling was a sleeping partner, but he did drive for the team on occasions and made sure that he was well paid for doing so!)

The new club secretary, Nick Syrett, was a good mate of Hawthorn's and they both lived in Farnham, Surrey. I had come to know Nick fairly well because the telephone linkage between the two offices had not been disconnected when Ken left the BRSCC. Nick had a particularly dry sense of humour and was very much his own person. Unsurprisingly, he was absolutely devastated by Mike's death, to such an extent that I took him back for supper that night before he went on home to Farnham. Motor racing was quite a close-knit family, and particularly when the chips were down.

OUT IN THE COLD

A month after Morocco, Stirling would be off to Australia. However, before his departure overseas, one more disaster was to strike that year to pile up on all his woes.

Tony Vandervell, the owner of Vandervell Products and the Vanwall racing team, invited Stirling for lunch that autumn, and Stirling was actually very chuffed about it. As usual, he left the office immaculately dressed and went off without a care in the world, looking forward to the meeting at 'Old Man Vandervell's' house in Chelsea, but when he came back it was a very different matter. He looked ashen and decidedly dejected. Brusquely, I was instructed to get his father on the telephone immediately and Ken was also summoned to the office without delay.

It seemed to me that this was obviously a massive crisis but I was kept completely in the dark, unaware of what had taken place until after the meeting of the three of them when Stirling dictated his letter of thanks to Tony Vandervell for lunch and for his sponsorship for the last couple of years and mentioned his disappointment at being told at such a late stage in the season of Vandervell's decision to pull out of Formula One racing with immediate effect. This was dire timing because he certainly had nowhere to go for the following year and there weren't many people that he could turn to.

Stirling was the first person to be informed of this decision outside Vandervell's close-knit circle of confidants and he was really knocked sideways by this sudden edict, as was his teammate Tony Brooks, who was later informed of the decision. By this time, it was November, and the news meant that both Tony and Stirling were without drives for the 1959 season, as most of the other drivers had already signed and sealed their contracts for the following year. Tony subsequently went to Ferrari and did exceptionally well, finishing runner-up in the world championship in 1959, but Stirling was up a gum tree with nowhere to go. He had made a decision some years back never again to drive for Ferrari so, being the stubborn person that he was, that meant one less option for him. He'd had an atomic falling out with the 'Old Man' (as Ferrari was also known) and had made it known throughout the racing world that he would never ever consider driving for the team whilst Enzo Ferrari was in charge. That is not to say that he would not compete in a Ferrari of any kind, but he would never join the official works team. Stirling was a man of principle and principle is sometimes a difficult friend.

This was a particularly tense time in the office, with the three directors of Stirling Moss Ltd frequently huddled together, holding meetings to decide on strategy and into which basket Stirling should put all of his eggs.

And this is when Rob Walker stepped into the breach again. To cut a long story short, Stirling eventually decided to throw in his lot with Rob, for whom he had driven so brilliantly in Argentina earlier in the year. The little F1 Cooper Climax certainly wasn't the fastest car in Christendom, but it was British and Stirling was very patriotic.

There wasn't any need for a contract to be drawn up between Stirling and Rob; there was simply an understanding between the two men and a shake of the hands. However, many years later, Stirling was to find out that around the same time, Ken had arranged to manage Rob's racing activities for him on a very handsome commission and he felt extremely let down and deceived. In fact, he never got over it. At the time though, it was a case of where ignorance is bliss and he was happy enough with his deal with Rob, who always left Stirling pretty much to his own devices, liaising directly with his old Polish mechanic, Alf Francis. Alf had moved around quite a bit in the racing world since he first worked with Stirling at HWM (where I believe he didn't think much of him!) and by now he had become the chief engineer of the RRC Walker Racing Team.

As far as everyone was concerned in the inner circle, this agreement was a marriage made in heaven – although there would, inevitably, be a few flies in the ointment because nothing is ever *that* perfect.

Stirling's contract driving sports cars for Aston Martin was to continue for another year and he was happy enough with that, especially when he found out that an older British driver, Reg Parnell, had been newly appointed as team manager. Stirling knew and liked Reg Parnell and, as it happens, he had the most amazingly efficient secretary called Gillian Harris, who many years later married the Australian driver, Bib Stillwell. Gillian used to organise and produce movement, hotel schedules and timings in the most minute detail and was pretty handy with a stop watch as well. She was an unrecognised asset in the world of motor racing, as was Liz Michell, who worked for Rob Walker and later became the wife of David Piper, a true gentleman driver.

Aston would continue to enter three cars during the 1959 season and Stirling would remain as their number one driver, partnered by 'Jolly' Jack Fairman, who was considered to be a reliable number two to Stirling. The second car was to be driven by Roy Salvadori and the tall Texan Carroll Shelby and the third would be driven by the Frenchman Maurice Trintignant and the Belgian driver Paul Frère.

In Formula Two events, Stirling would drive a Cooper Borgward with considerable success, and he would also drive the British Racing Partnership's BRM in a couple of F1 races, rather than his Cooper, or rather Rob's.

Away from motor racing activities in 1958, Stirling had been invited to join the panel of the Miss World competition judges and he was looking forward to this enormously through the autumn. He felt that it was a tremendous honour and the prospect of seeing all the pretty girls in their swimwear was clearly the top attraction for him. He had been invited to be a judge of the previous year's competition, the timing of which had coincided with his honeymoon, so he had cut the honeymoon short to dash back to the UK to keep his commitment!

The 1958 pageant was held at the Lyceum Ballroom and there were only twenty-two contestants that year. Stirling did not actually agree wholeheartedly with the other judges about the final outcome, but an attractive brunette, Miss South Africa, was declared the winner. The runner-up was Miss France and third place went to Miss Denmark. The following morning, after the event, he was still grumbling in the office that, in his opinion, the best-looking girl had not won the competition and he genuinely felt quite peeved that she hadn't. Whether or not this was because he felt sorry for her that she hadn't won or whether it was because he had been unable to sway the opinion of the other judges, I am not too sure. On the odd occasions that I had driven with him during that first year, I had been surprised that he was always looking around and pointing out 'good-looking crumpet' that we passed. In my naivety, I thought that this was rather strange for a married man, but Stirling always appreciated good-looking women with curves in the right places. He often judged people from behind.

SURVIVED

Stirling and Katie were due to leave London towards the end of November and would, to all intents and purposes, spend the winter based in Nassau, which they both enjoyed. He loved the people and he loved the life that was on offer there, particularly the outdoor sports, such as water-skiing, snorkelling and swimming. But most of all he loved the sun, particularly when it was cold and drizzly in London. He was a born sun-worshipper.

He first visited New Providence Island to take part in Nassau Speedweek and he very quickly became a fan of the place, so much so that he bought a plot of land there and had started to build a house and was doing all the hard work on it himself. Apart from converting a Nash Ambassador into a type of camper van years before they came to exist, and all kinds of home improvements, the house was Stirling's first big foray into architectural design, the first of many as it turned out. (As a teenager, he had designed and built a concealed space in his room at the farm where he could secrete visitors in haste if need be.) He was always hankering to buy or to refurbish any property that he acquired.

There was quite a lot of preparation and there was much work to do before the couple left. As a result, in between Stirling's return from the race in Morocco and the time that they were due to leave (and in addition to all the hundred and seven other things that always needed doing and organising), Stirling had to tie up all the ends of his own plans and all the details for the next season with Rob and Alf and do some testing before he left the country. On top of this, he found time to personally sign over 800 Christmas cards, which I had to prepare for him. I was instructed to buy Christmas presents for all his godchildren after he had left the country and was entrusted with the company credit card for Harrods (who, with their own specific card, were very ahead of the times), where I was told to buy all the toys. He also had to coordinate a number of flights because he had decided to go on his own to race in Australia at the end of November and he would be going back to race in New Zealand in January 1959. In between times, he would have to fit in with Katie's plans as well. She was going to see her parents in Montreal over the Christmas period and Stirling would have to accompany her and do his duty as the 'perfect' son-in-law.

• • •

During this busy period before going away, Katie turned up at the office, as usual, without any warning, carrying a package containing what could only be described as a very warm, but rather unfashionable, dressing gown, which she suggested my mother might like. It was actually the type of dressing gown that Stirling's mother would have worn, if truth be known. It was an unwanted gift, but when Stirling heard her offering it to me to give to my mother, he was absolutely livid. Not because she had offered to pass it on, but because he felt she should have sold it – just like he did with many of his things that he didn't want any more.

This was the first real inkling that I was to have that Stirling could be a little tight with money. At the time, I was rather embarrassed, but Katie quickly stepped into the breach, calmed Stirling down and took the situation in hand. Passing the parcel over to me, she told me very sweetly that the dressing gown would be their joint Christmas present to my mother; whilst Stirling stood there looking a little ashamed and somewhat embarrassed. I may say that the gift was exceptionally well received and worn for very many years with love, affection and grateful thanks.

As the winter progressed, all the teams were busy preparing for the following season. The mechanics had to strip down and rebuild the cars and implement any changes in line with regulations that were coming into force for the new season. Consequently, there wasn't much demand for Ken's presence at his Highgate office and, because he was spending much of his time trying to raise capital for a new business venture that he felt had a lot of potential, the inevitable consequence was that he virtually took up residency in the office with me for the next three months. This somewhat put a damper on my newfound independence, which I was beginning to enjoy. The intrusion into my little world did not go down too well with me, particularly as he treated me as a complete nonentity, unlike Stirling, who was fairly accommodating and treated me with respect. The one thing that really cheesed me off was when Ken had the audacity to send me to the wilds of Surrey after work on Christmas Eve to deliver a turkey to his brother. It was very dark along the many unlit country roads and I certainly did not feel that acting as a delivery person out of hours was part of my remit. I was most unhappy about it. The fact that this meant I would have my own car over the Christmas and New Year period wasn't even any compensation because I had the use of our family car.

As it turned out, however, there was also quite a lot of Stirling's business that required Ken's attention, including new contracts that had to be drawn up and vetted by the legal eagles before being agreed and signed. Once we knew the racing schedule for the year, we could set to work looking at hotels, and beginning to organise the transport (subject, of course, to Stirling's approval).

By the turn of the New Year, I had survived working for Stirling for nine months and I was beginning to see the wood for the trees.

DESIGN PLANS

Early in 1959, we were given our marching orders by Her Majesty. The building we were in was leased. It was Crown Property and it was to be torn down in the interests of erecting a drab, 'modern', 1960s concrete-built 24-hour post office, which was still there until only recently.

Where would we all go?

It was decided to close the beefburger restaurant altogether just prior to vacating the building. It was a nice little business, but it was also high maintenance staff-wise, and no one had the time or the inclination to carry on running a new one in another area. At the time, sandwiches were becoming all the rage to eat at lunchtime and by then, some of Stirling's business acumen had obviously brushed off onto me because I urged him to start a small outlet somewhere. I even offered to make the sandwiches overnight myself, but he wasn't at all interested. So convinced was I that this would be a real money-spinner, I would have started an outlet on my own had I had the money, but I didn't, so I stayed put. Back then, Stirling only had a one-track mind: he was focused on motor racing and to a smaller extent, design, as well as researching new gadgets. He had inherited some of his father's flair for practical design and was particularly proud of the fact that Alfred had invented the Morrison Shelter (named after the Home Secretary at the time, Herbert Morrison), which was a simple refuge that people could use in their own homes (unlike the outdoor Anderson) for protection during the bombing in the Second World War.

To my mind, one of Stirling's best inventions, which the patent office would not permit him to patent, were blow-up, rectangular, plastic bags, which could be used in suitcases to fill air spaces to prevent things being damaged or creased in transit. He used to become really irritated when the things he had neatly packed in his suitcase had moved around and his clothes came out all crumpled. Rather than use a smaller suitcase (because the suitcase might come back full!), his answer was simply to put a blow-up bag on top to fill the gap between the clothes and the suitcase lid. These days, similar plastic bags are commonly used commercially when transporting heavy and delicate things, such as electrical equipment. Some ideas take a long time to develop. To my knowledge, Stirling applied for his patent in 1959/60, so it was clearly a long time coming.

Coincidentally, prior to this enforced move from William IV Street, Stirling had been negotiating to buy a small mews house in Mayfair containing a couple of maisonettes, so when he came back from abroad at the end of January 1959, he entered into more formal negotiations to buy the property and eventually he managed to obtain a mortgage and purchase it.

It was also around this time that I started to call Stirling 'Stirling' and one day, when Ken turned up unexpectedly in the office, he heard me do this and demanded to know who had given me permission to call Mr Moss by his Christian name. Having by this point learnt to lie on the telephone, telling people that Stirling was out when he was in, I coolly replied that it was Stirling himself. My gamble paid off, because Ken didn't dare to question his boss! That was finally settled, then. Game, set and match.

Many a time there were raised voices between the two of them in Stirling's office, but they generally ended up by agreeing, if only to disagree again, and they held a healthy respect each for the other. Apparently, Ken and Stirling had been very close friends in the early years of Stirling's career but, after their marriages, they had gradually drifted apart, particularly socially. I certainly never saw the apparently strong bond of camaraderie that had existed between the two men in Stirling's early racing years that I often heard about. I think the final straw for Stirling was probably Ken's marriage to his first wife, Anne, which was about a year before I joined the firm and shortly before Stirling's own marriage to Katie. Stirling definitely did not like Anne and, although he wasn't always a good judge of character, he certainly thought he had the measure of her this time, and he didn't pull any punches about his feelings. He told everyone that he didn't like her, including me. I think, at the time, that this was a genuine dislike on Stirling's part and not jealousy that someone else was going to have a demand on Ken's time and take Ken away from him. Although, that being said, Stirling could be very possessive. In fact, Stirling did not consider Ken's second wife a much better choice when she came along, and he did everything in his power to try to dissuade Ken from marrying her, including the failed strategy of telephoning a few of Ken's old girlfriends and suggesting that they should give him a ring to propose meeting up again! An ex of Stirling's, who Ken had always fancied as well, was also requested to play a part in this tactic.

Before Katie came on the scene, this was the only really long-term girlfriend Stirling had, and theirs had been a fairly long but tempestuous relationship, with neither of them remaining true to the other. After the initial 'honeymoon' period had waned, I gather that both of them went their separate ways. From what I could understand, she suited him very well in the bedroom, but it appeared that she didn't hold the same standards or high principles in life that he did and it was this that eventually was to become her downfall.

Stirling always alleged that she had stolen one of his Mercedes sapphire and gold cufflinks, which had been presented to him by the company, and he never ever forgave her for that. It was not so much the value of the cufflink that he minded on this particular occasion, but the sentimental value. I believe he eventually had another one made so he could use them as a pair to wear at official functions, but this incident was the final nail in the coffin as far as the relationship was concerned.

I only met the woman once when she wangled an invitation to

come along to the office to discuss going out with Ken, but I think she only swanned along because she thought Stirling would reignite their romance. But if that assumption was correct, she was to be very disappointed. Besides which, he was having far too good a time with his then current 'harem' to invite any more aggravation into his life.

• • •

Stirling and Katie returned home in February and I felt relieved that he was firmly back in the driving seat again.

It was to be a busy year for him and, strangely enough, a fairly busy time for me abroad as well because I landed up going to France twice on company-related business.

The strategic plan, now that the London property had been bought and paid for, was for Stirling and Katie to move into the mews house at 36/38 Shepherd Street during the summer of '59, but he was, of course, going to renovate it – and he was exceedingly happy that he had a project on which to work in London. However, now that he had to find another office, he decided to alter his original ideas and use the smaller of the maisonettes as an office; the upper maisonette would be enlarged by adding a studio on top. As always, where the council, architects and builders are concerned, the project kept on being pushed back, although it turned out reasonably fine in the end.

ON THE MOVE

Nothing really needed doing to the office side of the new premises that a lick of paint and a new carpet wouldn't fix. It comprised a very large room on the ground floor, which was scheduled to be divided into two, in a similar manner to the office at William IV Street, but this never happened. The room faced south-west this time rather than north – on the sunny side of the street! The office led into a long thin kitchen at the back of the building, which was ideal as I had become a coffee addict and had more or less begun to live on it throughout the day. I had even managed to persuade Stirling to drink coffee instead of tea, although he would continually complain about it and sometimes he used to nip upstairs on the other side to make himself a cup of tea instead.

There was a bathroom at the top of the stairs on the first floor of the smaller maisonette, and a couple of bedrooms, which Stirling and Katie were going to use as a temporary base until the upgrade of their maisonette 'next door' had been completed. Ken arranged to transfer the lease that Stirling had on his old flat in West Kensington to David Yorke, who had been the team manager at Vandervell (Vanwall) and, although the puzzle did fit together on paper in practice, it became rather nerve-racking trying to complete it all in the given time.

The second maisonette, starting on the first floor, was much larger and lighter, and Stirling intended to make this part an ultra-modern town house in which he and Katie would live. Not unusually, he had his own ideas regarding the layout (which sometimes clashed with that of his architect and, no doubt, his wife) and extending upwards meant that he had to have plans drawn up and submitted in order to acquire the necessary permissions from Westminster City Council. It also involved a lot more work in the office, writing off for brochures and samples, both in the UK and in the States, the States being far more advanced in terms of building technology, gadgets and so on, particularly where plumbing and electrics were concerned. The work entailed on this project meant that it had to be fitted in between all the other daily chores and activities and I often found myself staying on in the office long after the 9:30 a.m. to 5:30 p.m. official office hours.

One afternoon, Stirling turned up at the office door at William IV Street not looking quite himself. He wasn't. He had stuck on a flimsy, ink-black, false moustache to his upper lip and was wearing a trilby and a pair of black-framed spectacles.

'How do I look?' he asked.

He was always meticulous and the new look didn't exactly go with the rest of his dress: white shirt and a tie; smart navy-blue jacket; neatly creased, grey trousers and well-polished black moccasins. I wondered why on earth he wanted to appear different to normal and, being reasonably newish, I didn't want to hurt his feelings either. He quickly realised that my slight hesitation could be taken as a 'thumbs down' and, seeing the expression on my face, said, 'Well, on the other hand, perhaps I'd better not go dressed like this. It would be far too embarrassing if somebody did recognise me, disguised in this get-up. (Translation: it might get reported in the press.)

The reason that Stirling had thought about going out 'incognito' was because he wanted to pay a quick visit to the *Daily Mail* Ideal Home Exhibition at Olympia to pick up a few ideas for the new property. And crucially, he wanted to visit as many stands as he could in his normal, faster-than-light method of doing things, without incessantly being recognised and literally mobbed by fans and autograph hunters. His solution to the problem of constantly being hounded by fans, which I didn't realise at that time was quite as bad as it really was, had been to adopt a disguise so that he could get a little peace and quiet and privacy to himself. Celebrities always have to pay quite a heavy price for being in the public eye and, in particular, they suffer a loss of freedom and privacy plus an ever-increasing self-obsession, which was becoming apparent – even then – in Stirling's behaviour.

SWITCHING HORSES MID-STREAM

With the exception of the race in Auckland, New Zealand in early January (which was not a Grande Épreuve), the 1959 motor racing season really began in earnest in May with the F1 race in Monaco. Prior to this (and because of his change in circumstances with drives), Stirling had been busy testing a little more than he usually would have which, even so, wasn't that often. Cars to him were rather like lovers.

Harry Schell and Jo Bonnier had both signed up with BRM for the year and continued to appear regularly at the office whenever Stirling's back was turned. However, when Stirling was offered the opportunity of driving their cars whilst all three of them were coincidentally testing at Goodwood one day, he jumped at the chance, and he was very impressed with the BRM. He also tested Rob's Cooper at Modena because Rob and Alf Francis had agreed to run the car with a specially designed Italian Colotti gearbox that year, which they had bought for the team before Stirling had agreed to drive for Rob again. This gearbox was to become a bone of contention all year because it proved to be most unreliable, just the thing that Stirling did not need in his quest for the world championship title.

In fact, so impressed had he been with the BRM cars he had tested that day that, after the first two failures of the year in Rob's Cooper due to the Colotti gearbox letting him down, he thought that he might stand a better chance to score some championship points if he were to switch to driving a BRM. By this point, a couple of these had been acquired by the British Racing Partnership, and were being raced in their light apple-green colours, so he decided to pull rank. At times, he could be pretty callous. To some extent he was correct to switch cars because he came second in the British Grand Prix in the BRM but after his next outing in it (which was not a success), he decided to go back to Rob and drive the Formula One Cooper again, which he did for the rest of the year.

THIEF!

The old Charing Cross Hospital used to be just up the road from William IV Street in Agar Street before it transferred to its present site on the borders of Hammersmith and Fulham in 1973. It proved to be quite handy being so near, especially when once I broke the little finger of my right hand in the office, and rough sympathy was immediately meted out by Stirling. First of all, I was a 'bloody fool' (I'd been climbing the shelves to reach something), but he was also worried about the injury and suggested that I nip up to the outpatients' department in the hospital. By the time I returned, his sympathy had turned to exasperation because the finger was encased in a plaster cast and I was expecting to go home.

'Don't be ridiculous,' said Stirling, on hearing the suggestion, 'You can still type. You aren't *ill*. I am sure that you will be able to manage.'

And that, basically, was that. One soon learnt that one had actually to be dying before taking a single day off work. The same went for reading a newspaper. The first – and last – time he saw me reading a newspaper in the office, he went absolutely berserk and to this very day I still feel guilty about reading one during the day.

Shortly after the finger incident, I developed shingles and, again, I was expected to turn up to the office every day, which didn't do much for the shingles. One morning, he brightly suggested that his father could probably help me and he popped off to find him in his surgery. One of Alfred's numerous talents was that he claimed to be a hypnotist, so he was duly instructed to hypnotise me, which may or may not have been happening when Stirling suddenly burst into the room saying, 'For goodness' sake, haven't you finished yet? Get out of that chair and come along with me, Valerie, I have something I want you to do.'

His father was absolutely furious as I meekly followed his son out of the surgery like a little lost sheep.

Patience in day-to-day affairs was not one of Stirling's strengths. It was always a case of hurry, hurry, hurry. He would even chivvy me to keep up with him whenever we had to walk anywhere together.

By now, I was quite used to being told to nip out in the Aston to do Stirling's bidding and, once the season had begun in earnest and he was out of the country, I was allowed to use it to commute to and from the office, which turned many a head and a fair few male faces green with envy on the journey into town and back, which was fifty minutes each way. The young – and old – men of the day couldn't quite believe their eyes, seeing a mere teenager driving their ultimate choice of British sports car! Life just isn't fair sometimes, is it? It was also a great feeling to be able to put one's foot down and know that it would be plain sailing overtaking a line of virtually static traffic.

Increasingly, I began accompanying Stirling out on the drive to the airport if he was travelling alone. He would drop himself off and

I would either drive the car back to London and park it outside his flat or, if I was going to pick him up again out of hours, I would take it home with me. London Heathrow at that time consisted of a couple of Nissen huts, and the arrivals' lounge housed a few chintz drawing room sofas and matching armchairs for the use of those people waiting for passengers to come through customs.

On one occasion, in the early hours of the morning, I was woken by my mother shouting up the stairs, telling me that someone wanted to speak to me on the phone. I scrambled out of bed and looked at the time. It was 3 a.m.! A phone call for me? I stumbled down the stairs and grabbed the receiver.

'Valerie, is that you?' came the urgent voice at the other end of the telephone. 'Which car did you leave at the airport?'

What a strange question, I thought, as I pulled myself together, realising that it was Stirling.

'Well, the Pennant, of course, just like you asked,' I replied.

We also had a Riley at the time. It was exceedingly quick and would take other drivers completely by surprise because it had a specially tweaked MG engine in it and was one of several cars that we had on permanent loan from various manufacturers.

There was a long pause followed by an agonised groan at the other end of the phone.

'What's the matter?' I asked.

'Umm... I've picked up the wrong car, then,' came the rather shocked reply.

'I have just arrived home and saw the (Triumph) Pennant parked outside and I picked up a (Triumph) Herald that I saw in the car park at the airport. The keys were in the glove compartment, just like...' The voice trailed off.

'There's nothing for it, you will just have to come and pick up this car and drive it back to the airport very early in the morning,' he said.

Hmm. Me in Surrey, not him, in London, ah yes.

As it happens, we had been expecting a brand-new Triumph Herald to be lent to us by Standard Triumph to replace the Pennant that we had on permanent loan and when Stirling got back to his flat and saw the Pennant parked outside, he correctly made two and two add up to four.

The next day, I arrived at the time sparrows normally carry out their toiletries, picked up one 'stolen' Herald and apprehensively drove it back to the airport, after stopping to fill it up with petrol on the way. I thought that it would be a nice touch for the owner who would, to all intents and purposes, have initially thought his car had been stolen once he arrived back in the country and who may still be wondering to this very day why his car had been moved.

I don't think they would ever have imagined quite such an improbable tale.

A BRUSH WITH THE LAW

Life generally began to become far busier in the office, probably because of the knock-on effect that the previous year's cliffhanger for the world championship had created and the fact that now Stirling was the only professional *pilote de course* left out of the entire really top-notch British drivers. Many new drivers were beginning to come up through the ranks due to their ability and the fact that so many of the other top drivers were no longer around. However, Stirling was generally considered to be in another league altogether if his car was on song.

At one stage early that year, there was a lot of kerfuffle in the office because either Stirling or Ken had realised that Katie's Canadian driving licence would soon be out of validity and that she would not be able to drive in the UK. Stirling had tried – and failed – to get her special dispensation because she had not spent much time in the country in total since their marriage and we counted up the number of days that she had been. We did the same for him at the end of each year from his diary. But, this would not wash with the bureaucrats because 'rules is rules', and though it was a pretty spurious argument he obviously felt that it had some merit and was worth a try. When he didn't get anywhere with it, he accepted the authorities' decision and decided that it would probably be best if Katie had a few lessons with an official driving school because they knew the ropes and taught their pupils how to pass their tests. Initially, he tried hard to get one of the schools to sponsor her but no one took up the proposition so he paid for her to take some lessons. We booked an appointment for her to take her test in Kent and both of us – but him especially – sat on tenterhooks waiting for the call to come through to let us know whether or not she had passed.

There was an additional reason for Stirling to be nervous about Katie passing her test, and that was because some smart-eyed copper had spotted him infringing the traffic regulations in the Mersey Tunnel, and there was shock and disbelief when a letter arrived quite out of the blue saying that Stirling was going to be charged with driving without due care and attention. As there was every chance that his licence would be taken away from him for this demeanour, it was decided that it would be better to be safer than sorry in future, because much of the role of chauffeur would fall on Katie's shoulders if he lost the case. As it turned out, he was fortunate because, ultimately, he was only fined £10. Cue a huge sigh of relief all round.

Stirling had been absolutely furious when he saw the letter and let off steam calling the policeman all the names under the sun. Of course he also thought that he had been a paragon of virtue and had done nothing wrong. As it so happens, he was lucky to come out of it as he did. I actually remember discussing the incident with him and he simply wouldn't have it that he was in any way, shape or form in the wrong. But, he was!

In August, however, he was once again caught and charged for dangerous driving, this time in Chetwynd, near Newport in Shropshire, and he learnt about this infringement two days after his thirtieth birthday. This was to have repercussions far and wide and, again, Katie would have to become his driver if the case went against him. But, as the legal system grinds rather slowly in the UK, the case was not to be heard until the following April, precisely eight months after the 'happening' on 13 August 1959. Unquestionably, he was going to fight his corner, because he felt the charge was again totally unjustified and there was a flurry of correspondence and meetings with his solicitors, who were based in Central London.

FRIDAY THE 13TH

For some unknown reason, most probably work related, Stirling took me to practice with him for the *Daily Express* Trophy Race at Silverstone the following year. It was Friday 13 May and, during the Formula One practice, I was in the pits. The circuit was slightly damp and all was going well when very soon everyone began to realise that things were far from OK and that there was an ambulance out on the circuit. One learnt to dread the sound of an ambulance siren floating through the air in the uncanny stillness that appears to descend after an accident when gradually the noise of the cars racing diminishes and eventually stops altogether. This silence appears to be accentuated by a false distance and a vast amount of motionless space, no matter where it happens, and the wait is all embracing. What happened? Who is it? Who didn't come round? How bad is it? Why? All these thoughts crowd the mind in the stupor of one's ignorance, frustration and anxiety.

Harry (Schell) was driving the BRM that day and he had not brought his regular girlfriend with him, but another 'foreign bird'. Suddenly, Dennis Druitt from BP, who was in the pits, appeared by my side. Many regarded Denis as an upper-class toff; he enjoyed the gypsy life of motor racing as much as he enjoyed his gin and tonic and he knew motor racing and its characters inside out. He always had a cigarette in hand, even when he was in the pits – if he could get away with it. He generally wore a suit and a good-quality coat with the collar turned up to protect him from some of the gales at the more open circuits. I always thought that maybe he'd had an operation on his lips, because he always seemed to talk out of the side of his mouth, almost conspiratorially.

He told me the very worst news I could have heard. Harry was dead. He saw by the shock on my face how shaken I was and immediately asked me to go and find Harry's girl-of-the-day and take care of her and try to get her out of the way because they would be flying his girlfriend over and she would be arriving very soon. (Harry was also contracted to BP and, consequently, they were arranging her transport.) In a complete daze, I suppose, I did what I had to do until Stirling arrived on the scene and he immediately whisked me back to Castle House, where I broke down in front of him. After the initial tears had subsided, he took me by the arms and, looking straight into my eyes, said very quietly (and fittingly, given we were in the kitchen), 'Look, Valerie, that could just as well have been me out there. If you can't stand the heat in the kitchen, you had better get out. Now!'

It was the first time that I had ever thought about how fragile life can be and how vulnerable Stirling had been that day as well. Strangely enough, for some unknown reason, after that fateful day I never thought about it again for a very long time and it never once crossed my mind just how insecure and precarious my job was. Oh! To be so young and carefree!

Stirling wasn't being unkind or unfeeling or harsh; he was just being practical, as he always was. He was pointing out that I had a simple decision to make: in or out. Nothing was ever mentioned again over the years, but to anyone in the racing world death becomes an unfortunate fact, and there is very little point dwelling on it. Yes, it is sad that someone has died doing what he wants to do, and it is even sadder for his family. Those who knew him in the motor racing world would miss him but, to be brutal about it, there is always someone else in the shadows, waiting to grab a drive. There is absolutely nothing more that can be said and done about it. And, if we're being honest, that person will no longer be seen around. He is no longer on this earth. *Point final.* Motor racing is an extremely selfish sport.

BY THE SEAT OF HIS PANTS

Stirling always enjoyed driving at the Nürburgring circuit in the Eifel Mountains in Germany, with its 170-plus corners, including a long, right-hand parabolica (or long loop) immediately after the start. Each lap was 14.2 miles long and the 1,000 km classic sports car race was held there every year, attracting large crowds. Although Stirling won it three years on the trot, he did so with three different co-drivers: Jack Brabham, Jack Fairman and Dan Gurney. The year that he drove with 'Jolly' Jack Fairman or 'Gentleman Jack', as he was sometimes known, was a particularly memorable one.

Jack was like an immensely sociable, retired army Colonel-type, although he possessed an engineering background. He sported a neat moustache and wavy, greased-down hair and he, too, lived for his gin and tonics later in the day. As inferred by the second of his nicknames, he was always the perfect gentleman and, although a bit of a buffoon, was kindness itself. He was to Stirling what bread is to soup. More-over, Stirling considered Jack to be a 'safe pair of hands' and an excellent back-up and test driver, so he went off to Germany very optimistically, hoping that he would win the race for the second year in succession (in an Aston DBR1/300).

Stirling did, in fact, win the race, but when he dashed into the office the following day, he was stumbling over his words as he garbled, 'Valerie, you wouldn't believe it; you simply would not believe it but that bloody idiot went off the road and stuffed the car down the banking. Thank goodness it was Jack, though, because he had the intelligence to jump out of the car and run around to the back and push it out with his bottom. He managed to get it back onto the circuit, facing the right way, and brought it back into the pits in one piece. He had made a hell of a dent in the back of the car with his backside but I pushed him out of the way, jumped in and managed to finish the race in it. Lucky it was Jack, though,' he repeat-ed, 'because he's got the strength of an ox. And,' he declared triumphantly, 'we beat the bloody Ferraris!' (250 TR Fantuzzi Spyders, as it happens.)

TOOTHLESS AND TOPLESS

Early in June 1959, I received a telephone call from Stirling in France and he was in a terrible state. Apparently, what had happened was that he had been relaxing with some of the other drivers and their partners midweek, pre-race, by a river. There was the usual type of bank bordering it but, at one point, it rose steeply and he had jumped into the river from the top of it. Because the water below hadn't had a chance to warm up after the winter, it was icy cold when he hit it and he had automatically opened his mouth to scream and out had fallen his front dentures. Unbeknown to most people (including me) he had lost a couple of his front teeth in a crash at Syracuse some years before I joined him and his dad, being a dentist, had made him a very good set of falsies. Up until then, he never travelled with a spare set of teeth and he was desperate, amongst other things, to stop the other drivers in the party from teasing and laughing at him lisping. Katie had gone over to Le Mans with him and, consequently, there was no one else that he knew apart from me who could get a spare set over to him in double-quick time.

I was instructed to go over to his flat in Challoner Mansions as quickly as I could and pick up his spare set of false teeth from the top drawer of a chest in the bedroom and bring them out to him as quickly as I possibly could. By this time, I had been trusted to handle the whole of the petty cash and he instructed me to take some money out of it, and if there wasn't sufficient, to make it up myself (never considering that I might not have any money in my own bank account), buy an airline ticket over to Paris (Orly) and then take a train down to Le Mans, where he would meet me. Of course, he had already investigated train times and I was to telephone him from Paris just before I boarded the train to Le Mans to ensure that he would meet the correct train (this had nothing to do with my well-being, of course!).

I shot over to his flat in West Kensington as quickly as I could and, with the spare set of keys that he fortunately kept in his desk at the office, threw open the front door.

Stirling and Katie's bedroom was right opposite the front entrance and I immediately heard a gasp, followed by an 'Ooh!' and the sound of activity and people moving very rapidly.

I stood rigidly in the doorway and wondered what to do. Then I heard a woman's voice asking, 'Is that you, Val?'

'Yes,' I replied.

'What do you want?'

'Stirling's teeth.'

'His teeth?'

'Yes, his teeth.'

'Oh, where are they?'

'In the bedroom.'

'Well, come in and get them.'

I did, feeling most embarrassed because there was a man with the woman and both of them were sitting up in bed. I immediately saw the chest of drawers in the far corner of the room, pulled open the top drawer to find the spare dentures sitting neatly in a corner. I hot-footed it out of the building as quickly as I could and hurried out to the airport.

I don't know who had been more surprised, Stirling's sister or myself.

It was dark by the time I eventually arrived at the station in Le Mans and, sure enough, Stirling and Katie were waiting for me outside in a very posh tourer, which I later found out to be a Facel Vega, and I was bundled into the back.

'Have you got my teeth, Valerie?' Stirling demanded.

A pause.

'Valerie, have you got my teeth?'

'Err,' said I, scrambling about in my bag.

'Valerie, have you got my teeth?'

I continued to scrabble around in my bag but I was beginning to laugh.

'Valerie, have you, or have you not, got my spare teeth?' he asked, by now quite belligerently.

By this time Katie was beginning to look a little uneasy until she caught my eye and had cottoned on to what I was up to and we both burst out laughing as I brandished his teeth in the air. He immediately turned around and, snatching them from me, shoved them straight into his mouth. He was not at all amused. However, had I forgotten them, he would have been even less amused, but he would not have been angry and I would just have been sent back to fetch them. Although he was a stickler for detail he was, without exception, a pragmatist in a crisis and never became flustered and could instantly come up with the correct solution for the matter in hand. That is not to say that he would not be irritated and probably grumble for weeks afterwards, repeatedly bringing it up at opportune times. However, it was not to be on this occasion.

On arrival at the hotel, he told me that as I was there, there was little point in my returning to London immediately and that I might just as well stay on for the race, which I did. He looked after me better than he did his wife, who I guess knew the ropes by now. He took me shopping to buy a bathing suit (because he refused to let me tie a piece of material round me, sarong-like, as Katie had done) and some other necessities (which he even paid for!), so that I could join them and the others down by the river. And, during the long, cold night of the race, he, I and a driver/photographer friend of his, François Picard, played liar dice (which I never travelled without) in the early hours of the morning, whilst again, Jolly Jack Fairman was out doing his stint on the circuit. Stirling loved the competition of the game and was like a little boy, delighting in trying to pull the wool over both our eyes.

Stirling would generally leave a circuit as soon as his race was finished or as soon as he had retired but, at Le Mans this year, he felt duty bound to stay on after his car had been retired because the other two Astons in the team were leading the field and it was a tremendous achievement when, after twenty-four hours of nose-to-tail driving, Aston scored a one-two.

Immediately after the celebrations had finished at the circuit, Katie and I were scrambled and we drove back to Paris in double-quick time. We dumped the car at a garage and flew back to London the same night. Stirling never wasted a second of his precious time if he could help it.

• • •

Life for me in the office had suddenly notched up a point and a couple of months later, I was off to France again.

Ivor Bueb, a driver and close colleague of Stirling's, whose day job was working for Shell-Mex and BP Ltd, crashed and died in a British Racing Partnership car in a race at Clermont-Ferrand, Auvergne, and his personal touring car had been taken back to Paris and garaged there, awaiting collection. This was virtually the only time that I knew of Stirling actually becoming involved with the day-to-day running of BRP's affairs, apart from physically racing for them.

He knew that I had some very good friends in Paris, who were like family to me, and he suggested to Ken, whose job it was to see that Ivor's car was returned to the UK, that the cheapest way to do this was to send me over to Paris to collect it. He was sure, in his own mind, that if I was offered an airline ticket and the car expenses I would be willing and able to go over to France, clear all the necessary paperwork with the authorities (which was considerable) and bring the car back to the UK in one piece, without BRP having to pay for meals, hotels and other various hidden expenses. He also knew that I was a French speaker and, being a young woman, would get an easier ride with the bureaucrats – and he trusted my tenacity. He was correct on all counts. I jumped at the chance of seeing my friends and off I went to stay with 'my family', but the French bureaucracy proved to be, as the French might put it themselves, *incroyable*. Eventually, we managed to get the car, a Sports Lancia, out of the garage and along with my French girlfriend, Claude Flandin, we drove it for a couple of days around Paris until all the paperwork had been finally completed. Of course, we used it to go shopping and one afternoon we certainly attracted quite a bit of attention driving down the Champs-Élysées with the soft top down, particularly when another driver, craning his neck to look at us, crashed into the car in front of him. Because we were so young and unworldly, we just roared our heads off and continued on our merry way.

After these two trips to France life in the office became a bit tame but, once again, Stirling was off pursuing his dream and I was left to hold the fort.

If Stirling was going away for only a short spell, he didn't always take Katie with him and she would often phone in to see if I had heard from him and would also ask if anyone else had left her any messages which, if they had, I would pass on to her.

As it was summer, we left the front door open more or less permanently when it wasn't raining and I began to notice that quite a lot more visitors were beginning to pop into the office. It was always quite enjoyable meeting new people as well as some of the younger drivers, and it was pleasant to have someone to chat to from time to time because it broke up the day a bit, although I never really felt lonely being on my own because there was always too much going on.

PANDERING TO HIS ORDERLINESS

What with Stirling and Ken continually popping in and out of the office and the phone ringing all day long, there were loads of scrappy bits of paper with messages on them flying all over the place. In exasperation, I decided to institute a message book, which would be a foolproof record of everything, from logging all the calls which required actioning to all the chores that had to be done by one and all. This would ensure that no one would have an excuse for not doing anything that they should have done. Or, what's more to the point, being accused of not having done something because one hadn't been told! The first thing that I, Ken or Stirling would do, on arrival in the office, would be to check the message book to see what messages there were, and the beauty of it was that it would work without another party being involved.

Again, Stirling was very appreciative of this useful innovation and, if the truth be known, he was also probably a little narked that he hadn't thought of the idea in the first place, because the message book definitely pandered to his being in control of absolutely everything in his world. Previously, whenever he delegated anything, he would continually check and recheck to ascertain that it had been done and it used to drive me mad. 'Why would he keep asking me if I had done something when I had already told him that I had?' I would think to myself. In the end, I would tell him quite emphatically to stop asking me because I had already told him numerous times that I had carried out his wishes. He was the ultimate perfectionist control freak but, at least now, all he had to do was look in the message book to see if things had been done or not and/or leave his instructions. Messages would be dated and our initials were put in the margin so we could all see who was responsible for each item and, once the task had been completed, it would be ticked off by the person concerned.

I suppose it was around this time that I also began to totally ignore him when he began to go on and on about a specific subject when it really was inconsequential or inevitable. I would half close my ears and would merely grunt from time to time to show that I was listening when I wasn't. This also became a tried and tested method when he telephoned. Gradually, I learnt the knack of taking notice when it was something important. Otherwise, I would just get on with whatever else I was doing for the rest of the time. I was also beginning to realise that he was sometimes wont to tick on about rather insignificant matters (to my mind) and he would never let up. He would get a bee in his bonnet about an issue and go on about it until something else took his mind off it temporarily, but he would often revert to the subject off and on for some days.

My geography was also beginning to improve by leaps and bounds.

For example, I had never heard of places such as Catania, Avus or Riverside, let alone tried to arrange flights and accommodation for any of these places. Back then, accommodation was booked by telephone, letter, telegram or occasionally a borrowed telex machine.

In early August 1960, I received a very irate telephone call from Stirling. He was steaming with rage and there weren't any niceties when I answered the phone. One also had to be a partial clairvoyant to catch on immediately to what he was talking about.

'Get on to that bloody airline and tell them they have to get me to Karlskoga in time for me to race there,' he said bluntly down the line. 'I don't care how they get me there but tell them that if I do not arrive in time for me to race I shall hold them responsible for paying my start money. Ring them now and tell them that I am stuck in the wilds of I can't remember where and tell them to get me a flight out of here.' The phone went dead. I looked at the receiver in my hand, wondering where to start.

Karlskoga was one of those places I didn't know either and, after checking all the details of his journey, I telephoned the airline concerned with a watered-down version of his plight. The person at the other end of the telephone chose to act dumb, to put it politely, so I began to get rather agitated and, in the end, I demanded to speak to a manager. Another rather bored voice came on the line and when he heard what the problem was said, 'And what do you expect me to do about it?' to which I agitatedly replied, 'Get him there. I don't even mind if you have to charter a plane for him, just get him there.'

Such was his celebrity status, they must have pulled out quite a lot of stops because they did get him to the circuit in time and he arrived home one very happy bunny because he also won the race.

A CASE OF MISTAKEN IDENTITY?

The week after this happened, a girlfriend who I met at the secretarial college that I had been forced to attend, rang me up. She invited me to go to a party with her, which was being held in a chic mews house near Harley Street, and she also asked me to stay the night at her place in Queen's Gate afterwards, an invitation which I readily accepted.

The party was small and elite and was in full swing by the time we arrived. During the course of the evening, two tall men pitched up, one of whom had arrived very, very drunk and, as it turned out, he was rebuilding a 1930s Bentley in the back yard of a pub fairly near to where I was living in Surrey. Even though one was allowed to drink and drive in those days, this chap was in no condition to drive anyone home, let alone himself, so I walked him round and round the area for an hour or so, trying to sober him up. He was also rather fanciable, so I was quite flattered when he asked me for my telephone number, although I did think that after giving it to him he would probably lose it! At some stage during the conversation on the long walk, I must also have mentioned, amongst other things, that Stirling was driving at Roskilde Ring in Denmark that weekend. It was a short circuit and, unlike any other circuit, had banked corners and no real straight. It was probably one of the few circuits in the world on which the drivers had to drive anti-clockwise and, with an elevation of approximately forty-five feet (fourteen metres), spectators sat in amphitheatre-type stands above the circuit.

When I arrived home the next day, I was greeted with the words, 'Stirling wants you to phone him.'

I could hardly believe my ears because he would never have

telephoned me during practice or on a race day unless it was really something terribly important.

'Are you absolutely sure?' I asked, bewildered.

'Yes,' said my mother, 'your brother-in-law [who was Greek] took the call.'

I went and asked him where he had put the number.

'What do you mean, number?'

'Stirling's number; where is it?' I replied. 'Where have you put it?'

'Oh, he didn't leave a number.'

'Well, how am I supposed to ring him back if I don't have a number? Why didn't you ask?'

'I thought you'd know it.'

D'oh!

I gave a very big sigh because, frankly, I hadn't got a clue how I could begin to start looking for a contact number for him, especially as I wasn't in the office. Eventually, an incredibly helpful and sympathetic male operator at overseas directory enquiries managed to find the number for the circuit and rang it for me. Fortunately, most Scandinavians speak incredibly good English and, when they picked up the call, the man on the other end of the line told the operator that Stirling was out practising on the circuit but he would try to give him the message that I had rung. (I had made the call person-to-person, which meant that you only had to pay for the time spent actually talking to the person you wanted to talk to.)

Some forty minutes later or so, the telephone rang and Stirling was on the line. Before I had a chance to open my mouth he demanded, rather sharply, 'What do you want, Valerie?'

'I thought it was you who wanted me,' I replied, slightly miffed.

'Don't be so bloody ridiculous,' came the reply.

Hesitantly, I said, 'Well, my brother-in-law told me that you had rung and wanted me to ring you as soon as possible.'

'Well, it wasn't me who rang,' said Stirling.

Suddenly, I began to feel rather hot under the collar and wondered if it could possibly have been the young man who I had met the previous evening, having a joke.

The most surprising thing about this whole episode was the fact that even though he had been a bit brusque originally, Stirling really was quite affable and relaxed about being disturbed at the circuit. After clearing up the misunderstanding, we had a little chat about a couple of things and then he cheerfully rang off, leaving me somewhat flabbergasted that he had taken the incident so calmly. Once again, I had underestimated his mercurial character. And though I have my suspicions, I never did find out who called that day...

PATIENCE IS A VIRTUE

I was still working at William IV Street when my birthday came around and I thought very little of it and patently did not mention it in the office for the obvious reason that they thought I was older than I was but, all day long, enormous bunches of flowers kept on being delivered to the office. The delivery boys had managed to pass muster at the dentist's reception and were allowed out through the door onto the open walkway, and gradually the office looked as if it had been turned into a florist's shop. Eventually, curiosity got the better of both Stirling and Ken and they asked me why so many flowers kept on appearing, so I thought that there could be no better time than to own up and tell them the truth about my age. After a few mumbled words of congratulations, Stirling's first reaction was, 'Oh, we have been over-paying you,' and Ken immediately went to the safe where he kept the accounts to check whether the tax code he had for me was correct.

It was also around this time that Stirling decided to find someone to keep his press cuttings books. There were two main press cuttings agencies in the UK: Durrant's and Romeike & Curtice and he had been using the former. The cuttings had been piling up for years in large boxes and though he asked me to do them for him, it was one job I really did not want to do. The first reason was because it would be exceedingly time consuming getting them sorted and put in some kind of order and, secondly, I did not have an artistic temperament and would not have been able to make a good job of it. Like Stirling, I had very little patience. We asked around amongst his colleagues and friends and eventually Pam Boyd, the wife of the *Sunday Times* motoring correspondent, got cashiered into doing it and over the years she did a truly magnificent job.

Just before we moved offices, an American called Lloyd 'Lucky' Casner made an appointment to come to see Stirling at William IV Street. He was a good-looking, smart, clean-cut, attractive and immensely charismatic man. Not only could he charm the birds off the trees (me included), but Stirling as well, which took some doing. Fittingly, his favourite song was Frank Sinatra's 'High Hopes'. He certainly had some.

Casner owned a Birdcage Maserati sports car (so called because of its looks) and he wanted Stirling to drive it in sports car races, under his team name of Camoradi. We tried to find out about Lucky's background but, short of knowing that he had been an airline pilot, we could find out very little about him. Somewhat recklessly and totally out of character, Stirling finally agreed to drive the car for him in sports car races. He drove it in a couple of races in America but his first outing in Europe was a complete and utter disaster. The car had been cobbled together out of all sorts of odds and ends and was literally hanging together by threads. Stirling had been simply horrified and made his feelings known all round in no uncertain terms. Lucky's charm, though, always won through and he managed to calm Stirling down and steer his way successfully through this particular bit of choppy water. Much to Stirling's delight, though, he later won the Nürburgring 1,000km race for the third consecutive year, driving the Birdcage with the American Dan Gurney as his co-driver – even though they had dropped back to fourth place after a five-minute pit stop on lap twenty to replace a broken oil pipe. But, at the end of the day, Stirling was chuffed and Lucky's charm had prevailed yet again. Lucky and I also became firm friends until his death, when he crashed during filming at Le Mans in April 1965.

PART TWO

BUILDING HIS DREAM

FOREVER THE HANDYMAN

All the while, Stirling was trying to do a fair amount of the refurb work at 36/38 Shepherd Street himself, but was continually frustrated about the length of time it was taking for the workmen to finish all their tasks. He had envisaged being able to move into his personal part of the house well before he left to winter in Nassau and then parts of the Southern Hemisphere, but unfortunately that was not to be. David Yorke, who had decided to take over the lease of the Challoner Mansions flat, had been very tolerant of the situation, but even his patience was beginning to wear a little thin because he had given in his notice to the landlord of the place where he was living and it was now becoming urgent for him to be able to move in somewhere else. It was decided, therefore, as there wasn't long to go before Katie and Stirling would be going away, that they would move into the smaller of the two maisonettes and 'make do' with it for the few weeks before they departed, and Ken and I were to move the office into Shepherd Street whilst they were away during the winter.

By this time, I had decided that I wanted to break loose from living at home and had started looking for a flat that I could afford to rent in Central London.

Just before the couple left, Katie very thoughtfully asked me if I would like to stay at Shepherd Street whilst they were away. Naturally

I jumped at the idea, so she told me not to say anything, but she would 'work on Stirling' and tell him that they needed someone to look after the place whilst they were away. And that is precisely what happened. I remember at the end of the first week that I moved in, I cooked a meal for six of my friends, never having cooked anything before in my life. On the advice of the barrow boys at the other end of Shepherd Street, who turned out to be really helpful and accommodating in so many ways, I consulted the butcher in Shepherd Market, who told me how to cook the meat and, of course, the barrow boys told me how to cook the vegetables. Surprisingly, everything turned out rather splendidly, which stood me in good stead for the future.

Shepherd Market at that time was a friendly yet somewhat sleazy little village within a very large city, full of nooks and crannies; it was bordered to the north by Curzon Street, to the south by Piccadilly and to the west by Park Lane, which had not yet been converted into a dual carriageway. It was known as being one of the renowned red-light areas in the capital, so we, in Shepherd Street, were surrounded by brothels. In fact, we got to know quite a few of the 'girls' over the years and became quite friendly with a couple. Men roamed the area morning, noon and night, waiting to be propositioned or vice versa. It wasn't really very nice for a woman who was not 'in the business' to walk alone, even during the day and, because I was so young, I felt rather awkward and embarrassed, but I soon learnt that the only thing that seemed to make the men quickly scuttle off was the unacceptable form of the phrase to go away involving the F word. It was frightfully undignified way back then, but it really did work every time.

THE BOMB GOES UP

After competing in Australia that winter, Stirling went on to New Zealand and was there when the official announcement was made that he had been awarded the Order of the British Empire (OBE) in the 1959 New Year's Honours list. Crowds came out to cheer him and he had never before seen so many fans attend a motor race; there were well over 70,000 spectators, nearly the same capacity as Calcutta's Eden Gardens. (The new stadium at Wembley 'only' holds 90,000 people.) After New Zealand, Stirling went on to Buenos Aires and Cuba, after which he wasn't expected to come back home until early March.

At Buenos Aires the Scottish driver Innes Ireland proved the new Lotus to be exceptionally quick, which seriously concerned Stirling, who immediately got in touch with Rob Walker. The upshot was that Rob ordered one for Stirling to compete in for the second Grande Épreuve of the 1960 season in Monaco. This was fitted with a Coventry Climax engine.

By now, the William IV Street office had been packed up and moved over to Shepherd Street. I still hadn't found a flat because, quite frankly, I hadn't bothered to look for one, but I was becoming increasingly irritated at being ordered around by Ken in Stirling's absence and had begun to think about moving on, jobwise. I had already been with Stirling for two years and, although I didn't have anything specific in mind, I felt that the experiment had served its purpose and the call of greener pastures, whatever or wherever they may be, were beginning to look rather more attractive.

As I was dithering about in this state of affairs, I was invited by a boyfriend to spend the weekend with him and his family. They owned a farm in Sussex and, whilst there, I decided to tap them for their advice on the situation. The upshot was that they agreed: if I wasn't enjoying the job it would be better all round if I left, and they advised me to bring matters to a head as soon as possible – but to wait until Stirling was next back in the country.

Late on the Sunday night, Ken telephoned the farm; we used to leave our contact numbers in the office whenever possible if we were going away. He summoned me to attend the office sharp at the unusually earlier hour of nine on the Monday morning, adding, 'On no account be late.'

As if I would. It was more than my life was worth! I was absolutely incensed. That was it… the last straw to break the camel's back and, in high dudgeon, I caught the train from Haywards Heath up to London early next morning, determined to hand in my notice as soon as I could.

As I put my key into the lock at 36/38 and opened the door, I heard a voice yell down the stairs, 'Valerie, please would you come up here for a moment?'

I could hardly believe my ears. It was Stirling's voice. What on earth was he doing home? And, more to the point, where was he? I had left the bedroom in a hell of a mess when I had left for the farm on the Friday night.

I climbed up the stairs to find him lying in 'my' bed.

'Morning!' he said, quite cheerfully.

'Good morning,' I replied, emphasising every syllable.

'I want a word with you, Valerie.'

'And, I want a word with you as well,' I said, emphatically.

'OK, you go first.'

'No, you can.'

And, sitting quietly on Stirling's bed, I was told the news that he and Katie had split up. I simply could not believe my ears, but when it did sink in, tears began to trickle down my face.

'Don't you start,' he said, 'or you'll make me start. Now, what is it you wanted to tell me?'

I looked at him, lying there, trying to put a brave face on things and I couldn't for the life of me bring myself to tell him that I was going to leave him in such a plight.

'Oh, it's nothing,' I said, shaking my hair away from my eyes.

'Oh, yes it is.' he replied gently. 'Just tell me.'

Hesitantly, I said, 'Well... er... I was going to hand in my notice but it doesn't matter now.'

'Yes, it does,' he replied. 'What aren't you happy about. Have I done something?'

'No,' I replied. 'It's... er...'

I then explained the situation to him and he told me that he would sort it out, but if I really wanted to leave then I must.

Under the circumstances, I felt duty-bound to stay and see how things worked out. Stirling had obviously been knocked for six and I could always leave, once he had found his feet again. All I had to do was give a week's notice.

Our conversation was never mentioned again, but from thereon in, things in the office did begin to improve for the better. Living in London had freed me from the constraints of living at home and it was to become a very hectic time in my life, with increased pressures all round, both workwise and socially.

COUNCIL OF WAR

Once Ken arrived in the office, we held a council of war. Stirling did not want the press to get hold of the story of his split with Katie and neither did he want them to point the inevitable finger at me as being the 'other woman' because (a) there wasn't 'another woman' and (b) he didn't think it was right that I should be victimised and have my name tarnished by something that had absolutely nothing to do with me. At that juncture, I was not aware of quite how dogged and deceitful the press could be. Neither was I aware, at the time, of the stigma of being named as the 'other woman'. How things have changed.

Ken's first marriage had also come to grief some months earlier and he had moved into a large, raised ground-floor apartment in the upper part of the Earl's Court Road, near Kensington High Street, and it was ultimately decided that Ken should leave his flat and move in with Stirling *pro tem* at Shepherd Street. Although it would be a bit uncomfortable for him, he would be able to keep an eye on Stirling and keep him company during this crisis. Stirling was never any good in his own company and, many a time on a long flight, he would initiate a conversation with a fellow passenger just for something to do. Strange, really, considering how shy he normally was. It was also suggested that I move into Ken's fairly luxurious bachelor pad in Kensington and, looking back, I definitely got the best end of the deal – there was never any question at the time of telling me to find something for myself, let alone asking me to pay for Ken's place.

Due to the unforeseen timing and the nature of the break-up, and because there was no other woman involved, probably for the first time in Stirling's life, he was completely and utterly at sea. This was the biggest crisis in his life that he had ever had to face and, to an extent, it was magnified by having to keep it secret.

This type of musical-chairs housing situation worked very well at first and it was a case of all hands on deck. Obviously, Stirling's first priority was to get a bedroom fixed up in the larger maisonette as quickly as possible so that he could move into it, and I soon became his housekeeper, secretary and personal assistant all rolled into one – but never the lover! I suppose it was fortunate that neither of us fancied the other although, as Stirling once said a couple of years later, 'If we had, we would have been perfect for each other.'

As a result of this crisis, I was on a roll. I had my own company car and I had my own flat and, if the price of this was losing a little bit of independence, I could cope with that. I would arrive at Shepherd Street between seven and eight in the morning, cook both Stirling's and Ken's breakfasts and, as the days went by, I would take care of Stirling's laundry, the shopping and the hundred and one other things that required doing in a house, as well as getting down to the day job.

Stirling had always preferred to do all his own cleaning at Challon-er Mansions, rather than pay someone else to do it (including during his marriage), so he became Mr Mop again at Shepherd Street, and he never failed to clean his own shoes – probably a leftover from his days at school at Haileybury.

This *ménage à trois*, as it were, rolled along tremendously har-moniously for quite a while and this period also helped to heal any wounds between Ken and myself. However, before he could say any-thing about going back to his own flat, our cover was blown.

UNDER SIEGE

Somehow the press had got hold of the story of Stirling's separation and they started door-stepping at Shepherd Street. And, of course, Stirling was absolutely correct that they would regard me as being the 'guilty' party because I was the only female in the frame at the time.

Early on the day in question, I arrived at Shepherd Street in my car to find hordes of journalists and photographers hustling together outside the front door. I parked the car and tried to push my way through them. I nearly fell through the front door as I opened it, with some of the press guys hot on my heels, but I just managed to force it shut and went to find the boys upstairs and we held yet another council of war. Stirling had already asked the 'posse of press men' to go away before I had arrived to no avail so, once more, he went downstairs to talk to them but, try as he might to explain that there wasn't a story, they would not listen to him – let alone believe him – and neither would they go away. And so it continued on all week. There was no let-up, morning, noon or night.

I used to make cups of tea and offer them to the press corps at intervals during the day, with Stirling's full approval, because I felt sorry for them. They were always very gratefully received and, for once, Stirling didn't grumble about the cost because he also felt sorry for them, having to hang around in the cold outside, knowing full well that they would never get a word from us. After a couple of days, things did begin to calm down a little, but a hardened core still remained loitering around the front door, much to the annoyance of the other neighbours in the street. Similarly, by then we knew that even the journalists knew that they would not get a story from us, but it was not going to prevent their editors ordering them to stay put. On a couple of occasions, Stirling went out to reiterate that there was absolutely no point in them continuing to hang around but, of course, they had no alternative but to remain. It would have been more than their lives were worth if someone got a scoop because they had decided to shove off to the pub and have a drink. Once it did finally dawn on the powers that be in their ivory towers that they had got the wrong end of the stick and that they were onto a losing wicket, they called their boys back to Fleet Street and decided to jump to the wrong conclusion anyway. Of course, I felt pretty self-conscious when they inferred that I was the 'other woman' when it wasn't true and, at the same time, it was absolutely infuriating.* I felt a sense of utter helplessness because they would not listen to the truth. In fact, I remember walking down the street one day, thinking, 'I don't really care what people think about me because I know the truth and that's all that matters.'

It still holds good for today.

MUD PLUGGING

Once our cover was blown, there was little point in continuing our own charade and Ken, understandably, wanted to get back to his own

---

* There was a certain stigma to divorce and it was very difficult to obtain a decree until the laws were changed in 1969 and actually came into practice in 1971. One 'acceptable' reason for divorce, before the law made it easier, was adultery, which was generally a set-up affair but not always. Usually, the male party concerned in a divorce, irrespective of whether or not they were the guilty party, would ask a woman to spend the night with him in an hotel and she was generally paid for the 'service'. A private detective would dash into the unlocked bedroom at a pre-arranged time and would later testify in court as to what he had seen, namely two people of the opposite sex in the same bed together in the middle of the night, one usually being the husband of the two parties involved in the divorce. It was a total charade but pretty much always accepted by the judiciary.

pad. By now, Stirling had moved into one of the bedrooms in the larger maisonette and I was to move back into the bedroom over the office *pro tem*. One good thing that did come out of the crisis was that I did not have so far to travel to do the early morning chores before getting down to the office work. The strict, 'I am the boss and you are only the secretary' bond had frayed, but Ken always found it very difficult to let his hair down. However, because we had initially been thrown together so much and because London really was just like a large village back then – when you couldn't poke your nose outside your own front door without bumping into someone you knew – some of Ken's friends became my friends and vice versa. And, of course, the same went for Stirling as well.

I remember once being in Trafalgar Square when a motorcyclist, clad in leathers and an all-enveloping helmet, cruised by and shouted out, 'Hello, Val!' In that guise, of course, I hadn't a clue who it was, but it turned out to be one of the professional Grand Prix motor racing cyclists of the day, Bill Ivy, who was also to die a few years later at Sachsenring, practising for the East German 350cc Grand Prix (for motor bikes, although he did try his hand at motor racing, as did the likes of Mike Hailwood and John Surtees, who was not only world champion on motor bikes but also in cars and who was never, I may say, knighted for his twin achievements).

Gradually, Stirling's state of mind began to improve and he would soon be off out of the country again, racing and living out of his suitcase.

Before that, though, I became involved in one of many forays with him. We were on our way back to London together on a country road when he quite unexpectedly turned into an extremely muddy field, which had a small gradient to one side. I could see quite a lot

of people standing around looking as though they weren't doing anything in particular and who also seemingly appeared to be very cold.
As soon as our car came to a halt, a cluster of officious-looking people
surrounded it. Once Stirling had managed to struggle out of the car,
he seemed to be transported by them at shoulder height, somewhat
surreally, rather like a boxer leaving the ring, towards what appeared
to look like a rather mud-splattered, black, open-topped tourer. I
followed the flow, as was my wont by now, and before I could take
stock of the situation, Stirling had jumped into the driving seat of
the tourer and was beckoning and then chivvying me to get into the
passenger seat.

'Now Valerie,' he said, 'I want you to bounce up and down in the
seat when I tell you to, like this…' and he gave me a quick demonstration, pushing himself up in the air, rather like a jack-in-the-box.*

Dressed in a skirt, I tried, but he yelled, 'No, no, you bloody fool,
like this…' and he gave me another demonstration. I decided that
there was nothing for it; I would have to hitch my skirt right up.
Then, he started the motor and we took off along a short and very
muddy track, which led to the even muddier hillock. He immediately
shouted directions at me and I did my best to carry them out. Slip-
ping and slithering all over the place, we struggled to drive the car
to the top of the hill, up quite a sharp gradient. We arrived at the top
without stopping or getting stuck in the mire and he seemed quite
satisfied with his performance. Presumably he was satisfied with my
performance as well because I wasn't shouted at. Down we went and
started all over again. In fact, we had three runs and I don't think

---

* I've never really understood what all the bouncing up and down was in aid of, but I imagine
  it had something do with weight distribution to ensure the car didn't get bogged down in the
  mud, perhaps why it was called 'mud plugging'…

that I disgraced him at all because he didn't comment any more on my contribution to his efforts; always a good sign. Telling me that I had done well would have simply been an anathema and quite out of the question!

Apparently, we had just taken part in what turned out to be a trials event, better known as mud plugging. We left in the normal rush, as we had arrived, immediately after the third run.

It was to prove to be a pretty unsuccessful season for Stirling in 1960, although this really had little to do with his personal life, but for me, living back over the office again, it actually turned out to be exceedingly useful because there was so much additional work to get through during the day. I became completely self-motivated when Stirling was away and, just like him, I managed to cram an awful lot into my little pint pot, as it were. If I had a lot of office work to do, I would stay on late and finish it and then, when I packed up, all I had to do was climb the stairs, have a bath and go to bed or, if I went out on a date, I would go out and then finish the work off when I got back to Shepherd Street.

CHALK AND CHEESE

I had never met Stirling's best friend, David Haynes, before this crisis but, David being David, he made it his business to get to know me around this time. Quite out of the blue, he rang me up, introduced himself and suggested that we should go out to dinner, and from then on our friendship flourished. If neither of us was doing anything very much and Stirling was at a loose end, we used to join forces and all go out together. Having known Stirling for a long while, David knew that Stirling would start dating again quite quickly because that was the nature of the beast but, because of the somewhat delicate situation, when Stirling did start dating again, David and I would often make up a foursome to allay the suspicions of the press until such time as they began to back off and become bored; eventually, they understood that, at least for the time being, they were going up a blind alley and it wasn't Stirling who was leading them there.

The pairing of David and Stirling was a strange one. David was the antithesis of Stirling and the only thing they had in common was their love of cars and women and, fortunately, their tastes (particularly where women were concerned) were entirely different. David was an aspiring saloon car driver, but he was certainly not in Stirling's league. One word could describe David best: 'square'. But he did have an excellent sense of humour, which of course Stirling did not, and he was never afraid to have his say – and frequently did.

David was typically British, having been to a minor English public school (as indeed had Stirling). He was about six foot tall, but was never the type of person who would look good dressed casually and he would generally sport at least a jacket and a tie, although he would try to dress down a bit more at the weekends, but he never looked natural doing so. He was quite good-looking. His longish, straight black hair was always neatly parted at one side and slicked down with a pomade (à la Denis Compton). His eyes seemed permanently half closed and he appeared to screw them up and blink hard two or three times, every few seconds. However, he certainly looked good in his light blue racing overalls (who didn't?) and, initially, when he first met Stirling socially at a party given by the well-known TV presenter McDonald Hobley and his stunning wife, Noel, he did not have two ha'pennies to rub together – and neither did Stirling for that matter.

FORCED TO REARRANGE THE CHORES

It never rains but it pours and, in April 1960, to add to all Stirling's woes, he was summoned to appear in front of a court in Shropshire to answer his dangerous driving charge. The eight months that it had taken for the case to be heard in court had been action packed and the case seemed to come upon him all of a sudden. He drove over to Shropshire from London, accompanied by Ken and his barrister, who pleaded his case, but to no avail; he was handed down a £50 fine (the equivalent of over £1,000 in today's money) and a one-year suspension of his driving licence. And, on whom would fall the onus of being his chauffeur? Yes, of course, one Valerie Pirie.

When he arrived back in the office, I don't know whether he was more annoyed about the suspension or the fine. Just to be on the safe side, he took out an American competition licence (he already had an American road licence) and would compete under that because the FIA/RAC had never had cause to rule on whether a driver who had lost his own national road licence could drive competitively on circuits, which were generally not considered to be public roads. Nürburgring, Le Mans and Monte Carlo were three of the larger exceptions, although they were closed on race days. It just wasn't worth the hassle.

This wouldn't be the first or the last time that I would have to drive Stirling around everywhere, but it was to prove exceedingly time consuming and ate yet more into the day – and the evenings as well. My hours were becoming ever longer, what with running the household, the office and now the driving, and something had to give. Because he could no longer drive, I was at his beck and call morning, noon and night, and it always seemed to take ages to settle into the job in hand when we arrived back in the office, rather than being able to work right through the day more or less uninterrupted. And then, whenever he had to go out on an appointment during the day, I would have to hang around in the traffic until he came out of wherever he was, and obviously, if there were traffic jams, journey times would take even longer. Being out and about more, I began to see that some things were beginning to slip.

During my time with Stirling so far, I had learnt that, if I wanted to achieve any positive outcome with him, the best course of action was to bide my time until the 'right moment', which sometimes could be days, and this was one of those times! I thought that it would be far better all round if Stirling were to employ a proper cleaner, in order to free up more of his time and mine, but I didn't want him to go ballistic when I mooted the concept because, if he did, we would never get one at all, either in his lifetime or mine. At last the day dawned when I judged him to be in the right mood and I broached the subject. Amazingly, he immediately concurred and busied himself wording a small advertisement, which he subsequently telephoned through to the *Evening Standard* himself. I was stunned – and delighted at the same time – to have scored such a direct hit. Obviously, cleaning the office and the house was getting to him as well, although he would never have admitted it. I will say this for Stirling, it was always all hands on deck when we were really busy and he would muck in quite readily and happily where he could. There were no airs and graces; he would just get on with it, trying to accomplish everything at breakneck speed in the time available. Ken was quite the opposite. As Stirling wasn't going to be around very much at this particular juncture either, he had to squeeze in seeing the applicants for the job at very odd hours to fit in with their schedules and his.

We never ever mentioned in the advertisements that we placed for jobs who they were for, because Stirling would never use his name in this way and he and I used to be at odds as to the wages he would offer, which were always, in my opinion, decidedly on the low side for the work required, let alone when the applicant found out how pernickety he would be. The surprise on their faces when they first came in and found out that they might be working for such a top personality always amused me, but in this instance Stirling met his match. Being, as they were, down-to-earth ladies, the cleaners would always fight their own corner when it came to pay, with many really first-class potentials stepping out of the fray because they felt that the money that he was offering was not up to their own expectations. I never failed to be embarrassed when it came down to discussing this subject, but Stirling never was. He genuinely thought that he was offering them 'a really excellent deal'.

AN INCENDIARY IDEA

By this stage, Stirling was negotiating to acquire a twenty-five-foot frontage on the old bombsite at the top end of the Shepherd Street cul-de-sac, just behind what was to become the Hilton Hotel and two or three doors up from where we were, with a view to building a brand-new property for himself on the site. It was to be ultra-modern and, once again, it would incorporate his office so that he wouldn't have to waste time travelling to work. Of course, he had grumbled at first when we had to move from William IV Street to Shepherd Street but he had found it so convenient having his office within his house that this would be a mandatory requirement in the new one as well.

Once again, an enormous amount of research was to take place as to which were the most up-to-date, modern designs and appliances available on the market to suit his taste for the new place. Now that he had more or less switched horses mid-stream, as it were, he became entirely focused on the new building site, and work on 36/38 virtually came to a standstill, although the studio at the top had to be roughly completed and approved by Westminster City Council so that he would be in a position to sell the property when the time came. He now spent all his spare time working on the plans for his new house.

Whenever he wanted to buy a particular oven, faucet, basin or even a roll of wallpaper he would contact the manufacturer direct – and ask if they would provide the products free of charge in return for the use of his name in publicising them once the house had been completed, and he used to spend hours on the telephone, negotiating with all the various companies. Occasionally, if he really did want or need an item and if the chosen manufacturer wouldn't play ball with him, he would suggest paying a proportion of the cost or, if this failed, he would go and find an alternative supplier, if there was one, who would play ball. Again, I never felt comfortable with this but Stirling didn't have any qualms about it whatsoever. Neither did he have any qualms about returning goods that he had bought, although most of the time muggins here was generally sent to do this chore. I loathed it and always felt most embarrassed. Thankfully, I always felt it to be a little easier to be able to say, 'A friend of mine bought this and...' (Legislation was not as it is today.)

In his constant quest to obtain cheaper prices on certain items for the house that he was unable to negotiate personally, he decided to form a couple of companies so that he could legitimately obtain trade discounts. One such company was called Designs Unlimited Ltd and he asked the printer to supply the headed paper on thin wooden sheets of paper. It was perfectly fine to type on, but the difficult part came when one tried to fold it without the grain splitting or breaking.

Stirling had managed to persuade the *Sunday Times* to agree to sponsor a couple of features on the house once it was finished (little did they know how long a wait that would be) and this was the bait he always used in his negotiations, but this was of little use when negotiating with companies in America, from where he brought in a tremendous amount of hardware and electrics.

Once the land on the bombsite had finally been acquired, he had to find an architect who would work with him, and I put it that way because that was how it would be (though that is not really how it turned out). Stirling had already designed the house he wanted to build on the site, but this had to be translated into a viable working proposition and the plans had to be submitted to and approved by Westminster City Council.

Norman was the appointed person. A short man, very full of himself, which did not bode well, although initially the pair hit it off very well indeed. However, the relationship soon began to deteriorate when Norman told Stirling that he was not prepared to be at his beck and call morning, noon and night, and it finally resulted in Norman often refusing to answer his phone. I remember one day being sent round to Norman's office in Notting Hill because of the lack of communication between the two. This balking was, of course, frustrating for Stirling because of his limited time in the country, but he would never accept that Norman had his own business to run and other clients to attend to and that he ran his business on a 9:30 a.m. to 5:30 p.m. basis like most ordinary mortals, and preferred to keep the evenings to himself.

THE DICKIE VALENTINE CONNECTION

During one of Stirling's visits abroad, a couple of the musicians from Radio Luxembourg's *Dickie Valentine Show* (which was always recorded at their London studios, the back door of which opened out near us at the top end of Shepherd Street), asked if they could park their cars on his bombsite whenever they came to record the show. Parking regulations had recently come into force and a breed of traffic wardens had sprung up overnight, who were being somewhat overzealous in performing their duties. I couldn't see any reason why they shouldn't use the land, so told them that it was OK by me and that they could go ahead. As far as I was concerned, the land was doing nothing and was no use to us, and we knew exactly where they would be if, for any reason, we required them to move their cars. It was a no-brainer.

Once Stirling found out about this arrangement, many weeks later, he was infuriated.

'How much are they paying?' he demanded.

'Nothing,' I replied.

'Nothing?'

'Yes, that's quite right, nothing,' I confirmed.

This conversation could have gone on for ages, but I cut it short by telling him that they were keeping the weeds and grass down and, basically, this contribution was well worth them being there on occasions during the summer. I had, by now, learnt to think very quickly on my feet to be able to come up with satisfactory and plausible answers to many issues. I had thought up this particular excuse on the spur of the moment in order to satisfy Stirling that he was getting something out of the deal. Naturally, the musicians realised that they would have to find somewhere else to park their cars once building started on the site but, as yet, it had not. As time went on, I became great friends with them all, including the leader of the band Geoff Love (who also operated as Manuel of the Mountains) and of course Dickie himself (until his death in 1971) and his agent David Bryce, who everyone told me was his brother, though I never knew if he really was or whether they were all just pulling my leg. If they were, David played his part very well.

One day I had to go over to Garrard's, the then Crown Jeweller to pick up some Goodwood trophies, which they had been rhodium plating for us and which were going to be put in the studio of the new house. As I cruised up to park on the corner of Regent Street and Air Street I saw a parking meter man lurking in the shadows. Luckily for me, I then spotted David Bryce coming towards me so I quickly jumped out of the car, which happened to be a little NSU bearing the number plate M7, thrust the keys into David's hand, quickly gasped out the situation to him and asked him to take care of the car for me whilst I ran into the jewellers. When I dashed out again, he was smiling broadly.

'What are you laughing about?' I asked.

'I was just asked for my autograph,' he replied. 'Obviously the chap thought I was Stirling so I signed his name and he went away as happy as Larry!'

Once I arrived back at the office, I told Stirling about it and he couldn't believe his ears.

A PERSONAL DEMONSTRATION OF SKILL

Looking back, it was really amazing quite how much was accomplished in the office. There never was any let-up. Stirling had to fit everything in between his motor racing commitments and, by this point, Rob Walker (Stirling's patron) had acquired a Ferrari Berlinetta for him to drive in GT (grand touring) races, which he really loved. He took me out in it with him at Silverstone and showed me how he could spin the car on the spot on the straight. Later, he took me round Brands Hatch on a couple of laps, explaining what he was doing at each corner and why. He would show me which was the best line to take, understeer and oversteer, which gears should be used and so on and so forth. I have to admit as we approached the first corner at Brands after the start (Paddock), I closed my eyes but, as we exited it, I opened them again going up to Druids, the second corner, because I thought to myself, 'This is Stirling Moss driving, and he is hardly likely to be trying to kill me, let alone himself!' During the rest of the drive, he was explaining braking and accelerating and throwing the car into the corners as quickly and as smoothly as he could. It was an exhilarating – and educational – performance.

The Ferrari was a beautifully designed car and he looked good driving the sleek, dark blue bullet, in his smart white helmet and pale blue overalls, as he powered it through corners like a knife slicing through butter – cleanly and efficiently. Earlier in the year, he had driven a Porsche in F2 events and had won both of them. By the time the first European Grande Épreuve in Monaco came along at the end of May 1960, Rob Walker had managed to get hold of a Lotus 18 for him to drive. The Grand Prix there is always run on some of the ordinary roads in Monte Carlo, which tend to be rather twisty – uphill and down dale – and there were very few places where it is possible to pass, least of all the long dark tunnel. Stirling was in his element in the new car. As usual, he drove to win, and he did. He seemed to be getting right back in the swing of things and it was as though he had more or less got over the upset of his marriage problem, because a little normality was returning to his life – and mine. It wasn't much, but we seemed to have got ourselves into some kind of a routine, which happened to work to his satisfaction.

The next championship race was to be in Zandvoort, Holland, where the straights were much longer and, consequently, much faster for many of the other cars with more powerful engines, and he knew he would be up against it and wouldn't really have a cat in hell's chance of winning unless all the Ferraris broke down. True to form, he certainly made a good race of it, but had to make do with finishing in fourth place. The following week he went off to compete in the Belgian Grand Prix at Spa-Francorchamps.

CRUNCH TIME

Early on the Saturday evening, practice day, quite out of the blue, I received a telephone call from Ken telling me that, as a result of Stirling's suspension breaking during practice, he had crashed and had sustained severe injuries and was being airlifted back to London. It turned out that Stirling had broken his nose, both legs and cracked a couple of vertebrae in his back. He would be undergoing some revolutionary new treatment for broken bones at St Thomas's Hospital in London, under a consultant specialist, one Mr Urquhart. This treatment excluded putting any part of the body in a plaster cast. We arranged to meet at the hospital early on the Monday morning.

Next day there was even worse news. Two of the other Formula One drivers were killed during the race at Spa; Alan Stacey and young Chris Bristow, who I knew well and whose sister, Sonya, I also knew and who would become a lifelong friend. Yet another new talent had appeared on the motor racing scene at Spa, a young man who was to become a two-time winner of the world championship, Jimmy Clark, in only his second appearance, driving a Formula One car (Lotus). He finished fifth, winning his first ever world championship points.

When I arrived at the hospital on the Monday, I was directed down hundreds of corridors to reach Stirling's private room, which was in the West Wing on the ground floor at St Thomas's. Ken was already there and Stirling was feeling very sorry for himself so we did our best to cheer him up, although we knew that he would be out of racing for quite a considerable period of time, despite the fact that he would try to make his recovery as speedy as possible. He was always a pretty impossible patient, always wanting to push himself too far, too soon.

The door then opened and in walked the great man himself, accompanied by a bevy of reasonably attractive nurses. Stirling visibly brightened as he cast his beady eyes over them. Mr Urquhart examined his patient without asking us to leave the room and then told Stirling to sit up and swing his legs over the side of the bed. Ken and I raised eyebrows at each other. Good as gold, Stirling did as he was told and was left with his legs dangling in mid-air.

'Now,' said Mr Urquhart addressing his patient, 'I want you to gradually push yourself down off the bed so that both your feet are resting on the floor.'

Once this had been accomplished, which had obviously taken a fair amount of effort on Stirling's part, if his face was anything to judge it by, Mr Urquhart quietly asked Stirling to place his weight gently but equally on both his feet and to move forward, a step at a time. Somewhat perturbed, Ken and I glanced at each other again. Stirling considered what had been asked of him, took a big intake of breath and very gradually transferred the weight of his body onto his feet and, second by very slow second, he tried to shuffle across the floor towards Ken and myself. We could see that the pain and the effort was excruciating and, after three, falteringly slow-motion steps, he began to collapse into a heap. The nurses rushed forward to help him; Stirling rallied at this and was soon helped back into bed. Very few people ever believed that Stirling had been made to walk on two broken legs, two days after the shunt. Everyone thought that they must have been cracked (which is presumably what they were!), but 'seeing is believing'.

Satisfied with what he had seen, Mr Urquhart turned and informed his patient that he would come back to see him again later in the day, and left the room.

Once Stirling had been settled back into bed by the nurses and they had departed, assuring him that they would pop in and out to check on him regularly during the day, he started telling me what he wanted brought in from the office to work on. The list was endless. After a while, he needed to pee. We rang for a nurse, who produced a white, china bottle but, could he go? Ken and I began to laugh. We put on all the taps and he still couldn't go and, in the end, we resorted to blowing between our teeth and, at last, eureka! By this time we were all hysterical, including Stirling, who was trying to protest all the while through his laughter.

Shortly afterwards, I left to go and collect all the paperwork and files that he required and he spent the next few days making himself at home, running his office from the confines of the hospital bedroom's four walls. Naturally, there was an influx of additional mail and telephone calls to deal with, and I think we arranged to have a special telephone line put into his hospital room for him to use on a temporary basis (remember: no mobiles!). In between times, he was falling in and out of love with quite a few of the ten or so nurses who were looking after him and that was all he could talk about in the evenings when I used to visit him, after holding the fort all day long at Shepherd Street and dealing with the flood of sympathetic – and some not so sympathetic – letters which flowed into the office.

The accident at Spa had absolutely nothing to do with the fact that Stirling's marriage had come to an end at the beginning of the year (the accident was due solely to a mechanical failure). All the same, I later found out that Katie had telephoned him at the hospital to find out how he was and whether he would like her to come over. But, as there was to be no change in their relationship, Stirling decided that it would only make things worse if he saw her again at that stage. Incidentally, I believe that Stirling had at no time thus far been involved in an accident due to an error on his part in an F1 race; it had always been due to a mechanical failure (although a certain amount of mystery still surrounds his final accident in a Formula One car).

After what seemed like a lifetime to both Stirling and myself, he was allowed home, and this was to present even more problems. One of the first things he did when he got back was to arrange an outing for all the nurses who had looked after him. A minibus and driver were hired for the night and dinner and a show were booked. When he left hospital he was given a pair of crutches, but initially he had to use a wheelchair most of the time and I had to don L-plates again.

Convalescence was a pain, for me, not necessarily for him, although he resented not being able to drive competitively. He literally wanted to run before he could walk in his desire to get back in a car on the circuit and, after a couple of weeks, I even had to go cycling with him in London (to strengthen the muscles in his legs) as he would never go anywhere alone if he could avoid it. He arranged for a bicycle manufacturer to supply us with the bicycles. I was rather plump at the time and I didn't appreciate even the smallest incline, let alone Stirling shouting at me to 'keep up' all the time. He sat at his desk in his office becoming very bored and thinking of where he could go next to amuse himself, such as driving down to Dorking in Surrey to see his mechanics. I would have to load the wheelchair into the car and then take it out of the car at the other end and then reload it once he decided to return home.

Once, after he went back to hospital for a couple of days, he was even photographed leaving, carrying the mountain of box files that had accumulated during the time he had been incarcerated. He never could go anywhere without being pestered by the photographers for 'just one more'!

BACK ON COURSE

Thankfully, he was given the all-clear to take part in the Portuguese Grand Prix at Oporto in the middle of August, some eight weeks after his shunt at Spa, and we were all back in business again. Unfortunately, he was disqualified there, strangely enough for the same infringement that the organisers had tried to disqualify Mike Hawthorn for two years previously. Talk about still trying to get their own back! This meant that he did not have a hope in hell of becoming world champion that year but, even so, it did not deter the racer in him and, as usual, he went all out, putting on a good show.

The final Grande Épreuve of the season was at Riverside, USA, in November, which Stirling won. But his two wins, plus a third and a fourth, just weren't good enough to win him the world championship, which that year was won by the Australian Jack Brabham in a Cooper.

RELEGATION FOR GRAHAM HILL

Fairly soon after I had assumed my job as chauffeuse the first time round, we were coming back into town along the A1 on a Saturday or Sunday afternoon from the north, and as we approached the area of the suburbs of London known as Mill Hill, Stirling told me to pull off to the left. I did as I was told and drove along a morass of small roads until I was told to pull up in front of a house. Unbeknown to me, Stirling had been invited to a small afternoon birthday party for one of Graham and Bette Hill's daughters and he had just remembered it coming back into town (strangely nothing had been written in the diary), so he thought he might as well pop in to say hello. We didn't stay very long. There was a whole load of kids playing games in the garden, which was certainly not Stirling's thing, but thereafter we began to give Graham lifts in the car out to the airport if Stirling and Graham were competing abroad in the same race. Graham was trying to make his way in motor racing (and subsequently he hit the heights), which was particularly difficult for him initially, what with the expense of a wife and two small children (Damon was yet to be born). So he would always check with me to see what was happening and, if we were driving out to the airport, he would make his way over to Shepherd Street by tube and we would all go on from there. And yes, even when Stirling was unable to drive the car out to the airport himself, Graham was not permitted to drive it and was bundled into the back.

Initially, for some unknown reason, Graham thought my name was Daphne. Many other people in the racing world soon became aware of this, including Stirling, who even thought it was quite amusing. He would try to remember to call me Daphne whenever Graham was around, putting the emphasis on the first syllable, and it was almost a year before someone had a quiet word with Graham and told him that he was being 'had'. Graham could be absolutely hilarious, with his extremely caustic wit and, aware of Stirling's usual lack of fun, he actually appreciated his involvement with the in-joke.

Graham would sometimes hitch a lift back with Stirling in his Facel Vega (which he kept on the Continent) if they were both attending the same race meeting and, on one occasion, after I had accompanied Stirling to a race at the Nürburgring in Germany, we gave Graham a lift. Because there was only an excuse of a seat for a passenger in the back and they had slung their bags there, I had to sit at the front in the middle, between the two of them, with each leg astride the centre console. It was a bit of a squash, because every time we went around a left-hand bend, I was thrown towards Stirling and the screen washer, which was a rubber push button on the middle console, would spray water onto the windscreen. Stirling didn't mind me leaning over onto him, but what really infuriated him was the washer going off and he threatened, in no uncertain terms, to throw me out of the car if it happened again. Of course, I ignored him, but Graham really believed that he might sling me out so every time the car lurched to the left, Graham would quickly grab me and clutch me close to him, little realising that when it came down to it, Stirling would never have dared to have done such a thing, even in fun. He knew that the repercussions would not be worth it.

Stirling hated conflict and when he heard through the grapevine that Graham had fallen foul of Lotus team boss, Colin Chapman, which could have led to a court case, he decided, off his own bat, to do something about it. The one thing that he did not want was for the sport of motor racing to be dragged through the courts either, because he cared for his vocation and all that it entailed. After one practice session at Silverstone, I watched him covertly take the two men aside and engage them deep in conversation, which ultimately resulted in Colin and Graham rather grudgingly shaking hands. No one ever found out precisely how the particular dispute between the two men had been resolved so quickly, but it was one of those fairly rare occasions when Stirling preferred to surreptitiously keep a low profile and fade into the background.

Another time Stirling decided to keep very much behind the scenes was after he had given a specially equipped van to a young man, Paul Bates, who had contracted polio whilst serving in the forces in Malaysia. Paul was confined to lying on his back twenty-four hours a day hitched up to an iron lung, with the prospect of living the rest of his life never being able to see anything other than the four walls of his room, the very thought of which totally appalled Stirling. After becoming aware of Paul's plight, Stirling personally organised for a van to be especially kitted out so that Paul would be able to be moved from his room into the van and be able to obtain a change of scenery from time to time. Stirling was absolutely adamant that there shouldn't be any publicity about this, but the day that the van was delivered, he did sneak off to be the first person to drive his invalid out into the countryside. Stirling's cover was eventually blown in April 1959 when he became the subject of the well-loved BBC programme *This Is Your Life*, hosted by Eamonn Andrews with the big red book, which was always presented to the personality in question at the end of the show.

UNDERGROUND WORK

Work started on the bombsite towards the end of 1960, and whilst digging the foundations the builders hit the same underground river that the constructors of the Dorchester Hotel had when it was being built very many years before. But, of course, the inconvenience and expense incurred at the Dorchester was on a much larger scale and I believe eventually resulted in the constructor, McAlpine, taking over the development of the whole project, including the subsequent operation of running one of London's premier hotels until 1985 when it was sold to foreign investors. 'We' were forced to take strong and costly measures and this put the Shepherd Street project back considerably, making a total nonsense of Stirling's building and living accommodation schedules. Norman and Stirling resumed their feud – and I ducked. But I wouldn't have been at all surprised if Stirling hadn't blamed Norman for this as well!

Coincidentally, Stirling's other lifelong friend, Norman Solomon from Nassau, arrived to spend the summer in London with his family and he often used to pop into Shepherd Street. He was about the same height as Stirling and had a much thinner, tanned face with an aquiline nose and twinkly eyes, with his thick, mousey hair, bleached blond on the top by the Nassau sun, slicked back from his forehead. He was great fun and it was interesting to see how animated Stirling always became in his company. In fact, I had never before seen Stirling so elated. I used to look forward to Norman coming around every so often and he even persuaded Stirling to let me go off to a matinee at the theatre with his family one afternoon 'Because it would let him off the leash and he could spend a little more time with Stirling.' That was some feat!

Norman obviously had news of Katie, who was living permanently on New Providence Island, and had been in contact with her but the news was not good, as far as Stirling was concerned. Norman confirmed what Stirling dreaded to hear. There would be no going back. But, even then, he continued to live in hope.

Luckily for Stirling, a wealthy businessman had approached him to see if he would be interested in selling 36/38 Shepherd Street because a mutual friend had told him that it might be on the market in the not too distant future. After a lot of discussion, Stirling agreed to sell the maisonettes to him, on the proviso that the purchaser would wait until his new house was ready for him to move into. This obviously helped the cash flow somewhat as well. Little did the purchaser know at the time how long he would have to wait to move in but when he did, he got the property at a very cheap price! The market had moved on.

BEAUTY IS IN THE EYE OF THE BEHOLDER

Now the serial dating began in earnest. Girls flocked round Stirling everywhere he went and he was never averse to asking an attractive bit of crumpet (as he would refer to women) for her telephone number wherever he was, whether it be in a night club or a restaurant or even if he was out with someone else. Although Stirling never drank during his racing career, he never minded buying his date a glass of wine or offering her half a bottle at dinner, but that would be the limit. But, being on a date would never prevent him chatting up any good-looking bird either, whenever and wherever the chance took him. His one real aversion was if any of his bits of crumpet were to put on make-up in public rather than going to the ladies'. Even lipstick after a meal was a definite no-no.

It could never be said that Stirling was an intellectual because he was always so focused on his life of satisfying his own whims, such as winning, building/design and crumpet, but, around about this particular time, there was going to be a general election and I asked him about his voting intentions. He looked at me absolutely surprised and wide-eyed.

'Me? Vote? You must be kidding,' he said. 'I don't know anything about politics.'

'Well,' I replied, 'you should be ashamed of yourself. I don't care what political views you hold but it is your duty to vote. If you don't vote, you cannot possibly hold an opinion on anything the government does.'

This point hit home as he reflected on my words and he immediately asked me to find out who the candidates were for his constituency and he promised me faithfully that he would go and vote, come the day, which he did. He actually went up South Audley Street to the polling booth to cast his vote. Thereafter, I arranged a postal vote for him.

Stirling tended to have fads, and one of these involved taking out a subscription with the Arthur Murray School of Dancing in Leicester Square, where he would try to get to grips with some of the South

American type of dances, such as the tango and the salsa. He would also try to enlist his friends to join in and go along, totally oblivious to the fact that most of them had normal 9 a.m. to 5 p.m. jobs so they would not be able to pop along quite as easily as he could during the day. The reason for recruiting his friends and colleagues on this particular occasion was mainly because he would be given free, extra lessons as a form of 'discount'. Whether it was really his desire to learn the dances or the attraction of the female teachers is a moot point, but this craze became quite short-lived after he received a rebuttal from one of them, but by then he had learnt enough to put the experience to good practice with some of the crumpet that he did take out.

Once, when he was racing in Monaco, he espied an especially attractive girl in the crowd and decided to give her a wave every time he passed her. After he had won the race and had finished with the prize-giving ceremony, he headed off into the crowds to find her and, I gather, they spent a wonderful evening together. He never seemed to have any qualms about chatting up anyone and any shyness would certainly desert him on such occasions. On the other hand, some girls would more or less throw themselves at him and he always felt that it would be a little indelicate, in such situations, to say no if they were his type!

Many of his conquests were exceptionally glamorous and, initially, there weren't many blondes in the horde. The majority of the girls tended to be foreign and were models – or part-time models – there was plenty of modelling work available in the '60s for tall, thin, good-looking birds – and it would be rather unusual if he didn't pick up a 'piece of crumpet' somewhere along the line whilst he was away, but he rarely brought one back with him to the UK. They were generally dates for the duration, although he would keep in touch with a few of them afterwards on a just-in-case basis. It was always handy to have a contact in another country and even handier if it was a piece of crumpet.

The greater part of his companions simply wanted to be seen out with one of the world's most well-known celebrities and, I may add, quite a few of them thought that it might advance their own careers if they were to be photographed with him. He was continually trailed by a clique of photographers wherever he went. It would bug him slightly, particularly if they would not take no for an answer, but he generally used to bargain with them: he would agree to one photograph being taken if they would then guarantee to give him a break and let him enjoy the rest of the evening *à deux* without being pestered again. His little black book that he kept before his first marriage – and which he never threw away – started filling up once again with the names of every girl that he took out, accompanied by all the details of their vital statistics – and much more.

Personally, I could never see what they saw in him, but then I suppose beauty is in the eye of the beholder. Even so, many had an eye on the main chance and loved being able to drop into conversation that they had 'been out with Stirling Moss'. Stirling was never a particularly good conversationalist, mainly due to his lack of interest in current affairs, unless he was talking about cars and mechanics but, because he loved to dance, he would generally take his date out to dinner in the West End of London when he was in the UK, preferably to a place which had a small dance floor, where he had the excuse of being able to hold his 'piece of crumpet' close to him. He would dance the night away until the early hours of the morning without having to talk very much. He had apparently always been a night owl and he always was, until age caught up with him. After the band had packed up for the night, Stirling would whisk his piece of crumpet home 'for a coffee', as was customary in the '60s, and they would listen to some light music on his new stereo equipment; I don't imagine that he ever took the bird in question home. It would have been difficult without his licence anyway. However, he did not like any crumpet lingering on at the house in the mornings, although some air hostesses, who were flying shifts, for example, and who were only going to be around in the UK for a couple of days before they were off again, sometimes did stick around, even though they normally had their own first-class hotel accommodation. He would always make it perfectly clear to those concerned that he would not be available whatsoever during his working hours and that they would have to take care of themselves. This devotion to duty ruined a couple of potentially very good relationships.

IN THE DRIVING SEAT

Rather naturally, I got to know many of Stirling's dates well, especially when he was unable to drive himself around. Stirling would ask me to drive them wherever they were going in the evening and, many a time, I would agree to pick them up again later on, but not if I had a date or if it was too late or if it really was inconvenient for me to do so. Of course, Stirling expected his crumpet to pitch up at Shepherd Street for a drink or a cup of tea before he took them out because he had such a wonderful excuse that he could not collect them from their own homes. He reconciled this in his own mind as giving him more time to 'work' and that he would waste less time doing such a run of the mill chore like picking up a date. Frankly he would never have dreamt of going to collect them in the first place unless he was really serious about them which, at the time, he never was, and he certainly would have shied at taking a taxi – or rather, paying for one.

Strangely enough, he was a romantic at heart and once, when someone had caught his eye, he went to extraordinary lengths to find out who they were and where they lived. He then arranged for the florists Moyses Stevens to deliver a single red rose to the lady in question for six consecutive days, accompanied by the message: 'From your secret admirer'. On the seventh day, 'the secret admirer' sent a bunch of red roses, suggesting a meeting place and time. Now, who could resist turning up on such a date?

All this night-ferrying continued until Stirling received his licence back in April 1961, but it frequently threw us all together socially as well. He and I often found ourselves attending the same functions and shows, particularly those of the top American stars who were coming over to London in their hordes, such as Frank Sinatra, Sammy Davis Jr, Judy Garland and Peggy Lee, the latter appearing on the stage of the Pigalle in Piccadilly one evening 'totally out of her mind'. It was actually highly embarrassing.

We would all arrange to meet up beforehand and go out together for dinner either before or after the show, but preferably afterwards.

One evening, a group of us, including Stirling and his current date and me with one of my boyfriends, decided to go to see Spike Milligan in *Son of Oblomov*. It had received great reviews (depending on Spike Milligan's mood of the evening). There was a basic script, but,

Spike being Spike, he used to ad lib an awful lot. We were sitting in the front row of the stalls when, at one point, Spike Milligan was mending a bicycle on stage and suddenly, without looking up, he ad-libbed, 'What are the correct tyre pressures please, Stirling?' Stirling was totally overcome with embarrassment. He cringed and wished a hole would open up in the ground in front of him, but the audience loved it.

Ferrying Stirling around in the evenings did have its advantages on occasions, the main one for me being that it gave me a great 'get out of jail' card if I did not want to go out on a particular date, which was very handy. All I had to say was that unfortunately I couldn't go out because I had to drive Stirling somewhere that evening and that was that. The bane of my existence was young men backing me into a corner at parties to talk about cars. It became so bad that at one stage I even changed my name to avoid that particular trap. And, another thing that really annoyed me was when people would airily say that they did not like Stirling Moss, almost as a throwaway line.

'Have you met him?' I would demand and, if the answer was 'No', which it inevitably was, I would say, 'Well, don't you think it is particularly harsh to judge a person before you have even met them?'

One morning, when I arrived in the office, I found Stirling very put out because I had, unbeknown to him, used him as an excuse not to go out with someone. Unfortunately, the chap in question had accidentally bumped into Stirling the previous evening and Stirling was none too happy about being put on the spot.

'I was caught completely off guard,' he grumbled, 'but I managed to carry it off, I think, without him knowing, but never, ever, do that to me again, Valerie. In future *always* let me know if you use me as your excuse.'

RATTLING ALONG

It was around the early '60s that we realised that American team owner Lucky Casner and Stirling seemed to have similar tastes in women and had many a mutual girlfriend – although not generally at the same time! On Lucky's suggestion, Stirling and I went over to stay one weekend with him and his then live-in girlfriend, who was also an ex-girlfriend of Stirling's, in his Munich apartment for the renowned beer festival. After a good lunch on the Saturday afternoon we decided to go to the cinema. Heaven only knows why we didn't check to see what was on first, although Stirling and Lucky probably did and chose the film from its title, *The Train*. Unsurprisingly, it turned out to be a black and white film about a train, which rattled along non-stop, seemingly going nowhere in particular. And it rattled along for rather a long time and, after about half an hour of this mind-blowingly boring nonstory, completely out of character, Stirling began a slow handclap. I was absolutely astonished but it was obviously time to go. Stirling's threshold of boredom was none too great at the best of times and, although he absolutely loved going to the cinema, this was a film too far for him.

SKATING ON ICE

One particular Monday morning, Stirling arrived triumphantly in the office saying that he had heard that all the Sloane Rangers of the day went skating at the ice rink in Queensway on Monday nights and he asked me if I wanted to go along with him that evening.

I looked at him rather suspiciously.

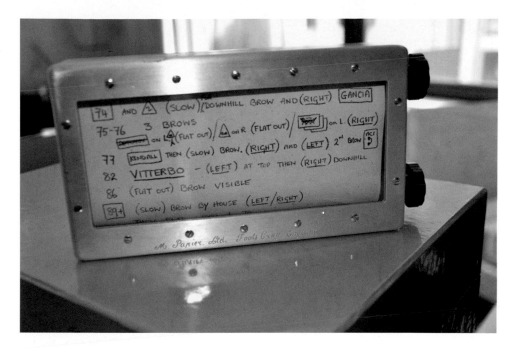

74 AND △ (SLOW) DOWNHILL BROW AND (RIGHT) GANCIA
75-76   3 BROWS
on L (FLAT OUT)/ △ on R (FLAT OUT)/ 🚗 on L. (RIGHT)
77 KENDALL THEN (SLOW) BROW. (RIGHT) AND (LEFT) 2ⁿᵈ BROW ACI
82 VITTERBO — (LEFT) AT TOP THEN (RIGHT) DOWNHILL
86 (FLAT OUT) BROW VISIBLE
89+ (SLOW) BROW BY HOUSE (LEFT/RIGHT)

M. Panier, Ltd. Fools Cray, Gurvan

ABOVE Stirling's
ingenious gizmo to
track the course for
the Mille Miglia, 1955.
© MIA FORBES PIRIE

LEFT An iconic
shot of Stirling
c. 1956: he always
went completely into
a world of his own
on the grid before
the start of a race.

ABOVE Winning is still the name of the game! The expressions say it all. Liar dice at 3 a.m. Le Mans, 1959. Stirling, waiting for his turn at the wheel, with myself and François Picard. PHOTO BY MAXWELL BOYD/ ANDREW BOYD

YOU ARE A

-but you're cute

HAPPY ~~BIRTHDAY~~ MONDAY

Stirling

LEFT The 'You are a VIP(ER)' card, which Stirling gave me one Monday morning, c. 1961.

After his accident at Spa in 1960, Stirling would join a group of us at our local in Belgravia on Sundays. Pictured chatting outside 36/38 Shepherd Street before we left are Stirling, Paul Jantet, Sue Pilsworth and myself. The bikes weren't used that day but Paul's little Renault was. (The bikes were for exercising his broken legs.)

Dear Stirling,

"For Valerie, a nice wee kid
    Quite gladly I'll subscribe a quid.
Or, as in parts she's nicely round
    If you prefer, we'll say a pound.
Maybe we could buy one cheaper
    But Stirling boy, you've got to keep her!

                Gooding. 1962"

        Yours,

        John

John Gooding's rhyme to Stirling in praise of my worth (after I had once again given in my notice), 1962.

At Shepherd Street, in our Frederick Starke-designed overalls, myself and Sue Knights with Stirling in 1963.

Stirling came to support me whenever he could whilst I was qualifying for my racing licence in 1964. Competing for a signature to acquire an international racing licence included running against the finest. I was No. 75 in this race and I knew my place!

EVENT 2

GRAND TOURING CAR RACE
for Grand Touring Cars complying with Appendix 'J' (1964)
Group 3 to the International Sporting Code, with an engine
capacity not exceeding 1600 c.c.

10 LAPS

START 3.05 p.m.

NO.	ENTRANT AND DRIVER	CAR	C.C.
Class A—1151 c.c. to 1600 c.c.			
64	The Chequered Flag—Team Lotus (Dvr.: M. H. Spence)	Lotus Elan	1594
65	The Chequered Flag—Team Lotus (Dvr.: J. Y. Stewart)	Lotus Elan	1594
66	Ian Walker Racing Ltd. (Dvr.: P. Arundell)	Lotus Elan	1594
67	Team Elite (62) Ltd. (Dvr.: C. Hunt)	Lotus Elan	1594
68	Chris Barber (Dvr.: M. Beckwith)	Lotus Elan	1594
	H. Jones	Lotus Elan	1594
	D. R. Fabrications (Dvr.: J. Oliver)	Lotus Elan	1594
71	R. J. Crosfield	Lotus Elan	1594
72	Surbiton Motors Ltd (Dvr.: L. G. Arnold)	Lotus Elan	1594
73	M. J. Wayne	Lotus Elan	1594
74	Harry Stiller Racing Ltd. (Dvr.: H. Stiller)	Lotus Elan	1594
75	S.M.A.R.T. (Dvr.: Miss V. Pirie)	Lotus Elan	1558
76	J. McKechnie	Morgan 4/4	1498
Class B—Up to 1150 c.c.			
77	J. Harris	Austin Healey Sebring Sprite	1098
78	M. E. Garton	Austin Healey Sprite	1098
79	Brian Bennett Racing Partnership (Dvr.: B. Bennett)	Turner Climax	1098
80	Team Fife (Dvr.: T. D. Simpson)	Marcos GT	997
Reserves:			
81	R. T. Nash (1st reserve)	Marcos GT	997
82	Harry Stiller Racing Ltd. (Dvr.: D. Marriott) (2nd reserve)	Lotus Elite	1216
	C. Sturdgess (3rd reserve)	Lotus Elite	1216
84	W. A. Jones (4th reserve)	Lotus Elite	1216
85. J. Gordon		LOTUS ELAN	

Grid and Lap Chart on page 25

RESULTS:

OVERALL RESULTS:

1st **65**   2nd **66**   3rd **68**

4th **64**   5th **73**   **71**

Winner's Time **9·32**   **9·5**

Fastest Lap: Car No. **65**

Time **55·2**   Speed **88·04** m.p.h.

CLASS RESULTS:

Class A—1151—1600 c.c.

1st **65**   2nd **66**   3rd **68**

Winner's Time **9·32**   Speed **84·85** m.p.h.

Fastest Lap: Car No. **65**

Time **55·2**   Speed **88·04** m.p.h.

Class B—Up to 1150 c.c.

1st **78**   2nd **77**   3rd **80**

Winner's Time **10·34**   Speed **76·56** m.p.h.

Fastest Lap: Car No. **78**

Time **61·12**   Speed **78·41** m.p.h.

The distinctive Stirling
Moss signature helmet,
borrowed – without
permission, of course!

Brands Hatch 1964,
before my wheel nearly
ditched me.

© KEYSTONE/STRINGER

Me with Sir John
Whitmore in Hugh
Dibley's Mews c. 1964, after
the bureaucratic nightmare
of getting the racing
Porsche out of Customs.
© DOUGLAS MILLER/
STRINGER/GETTY IMAGES

Going to the church on time. Herb Jones, Stirling, Sally Ducker and myself off to a wedding c. 1964.

Keeping up with the fashion: Stirling with sideburns at my wedding, 1975. © ESTATE OF NORMAN POTTER

Property hunting,
south London, c. 2000.
© MIA FORBES PIRIE

Relaxing in the pool in
Florida: Stirling and
his wife, Susie, in 2009.

A couple of maestros
comparing notes at
Monza, 24 April 2015.
Stirling once said that
Lewis Hamilton, after
trying one of Stirling's
F1 cars, had told him
that he had found the
car quite difficult to drive.
© MAURIZIO RIGATO

Stirling interviewed by my daughter, Mia, in 2016. © MIA FORBES PIRIE

Lady Moss and myself, joint partners in crime, always with Stirling's best interests at heart, 2018. © MIA FORBES PIRIE

'Why would you want *me* to go with *you* other than to drive you there?' I asked. 'I would only hamper your style, and anyway, I can't skate.'

'Neither can I,' he said, 'so we can hold each other up.'

'I know you, you won't do that,' I replied, rather indignantly, 'you will just go off and find some other bird and leave me on my own.'

He argued his case and as I had nothing better to do that evening I decided to string along with him – he could be exceedingly persuasive when he really wanted something. Naturally, he did go off and leave me to struggle on my own but he did have the grace to come and find me at the dance intervals and we would wobble off the ice on our skates and go into the café where all the other young people would congregate.

Stirling had a superb sense of balance due, no doubt, to his horse jumping activities in his youth and the fine balance that is required when motor racing, and he took to skating like the proverbial duck.

After this first Monday, we continued to go skating 'together', because it was fun and it was sociable and he did pick up one or two bits of crumpet there.

On one particular evening a young, sweaty 'Hooray Henry' with a rather wide girth, who was sporting a blue and white striped shirt, white collar and red tie, pushed his way through the milling crowd towards us in the café and eyeballed Stirling. Neither of us recognised him. Stirling looked to me as if to say, 'Who is this git?' and I just shrugged my shoulders.

'Stirling, old boy,' the chap said, 'what do you think of the new 246? Wot! Wot! Wot!'

Stirling looked him up and down and queried, 'The new 246?'

'Yes, the new 246, old boy.'

Stirling looked at me once again and, again, I shrugged my shoulders because I didn't have the faintest idea as to who the chap was or what he was talking about. I was always helping Stirling out because he had a memory like a sieve, as far as faces, names and issues were concerned, unless they were business colleagues or, of course, one of the few people in his intimate circle of friends.

Stirling took his time before addressing the chap in question again.

'The new 246, *old boy*?' he said very slowly and deliberately, the emphasis being on the 'old boy'. 'I don't know what you are talking about.'

The young man gave a horsey, if somewhat embarrassed laugh, and slowly moved away.

It transpired that he was talking about the new Ferrari. And, from that day onwards, any Hooray Henrys that we came across were always codenamed as 246-ers.

Incidentally, years later, for some unknown reason, Stirling also began to use the phrase 'old boy' in conversation with men, whether he knew them very well or not. It just seemed to develop over a period of time after his accident, although his father frequently used the phrase.

DRIVING FORCE

Everyone always asked me what it was like to drive Stirling around but, for me, it wasn't any different from driving anybody else around – except that it had to be done at breakneck speed. Naturally, it was always accompanied by a running commentary about all the other 'idiots' driving on the roads plus instructions to me, which I might, or might not, take any notice of. As for driving out to the airport, I could almost do it with my eyes shut because he was flying abroad pretty regularly and at least twice a week for about half of the year. Sitting beside me in the front passenger seat, Stirling made a fine back-seat driver and I had already become used to all his little quirks, the greatest of which was never to alter the position of the driving seat. Ever. So, whenever I had to officially run him around I was used to being forced to drive with my arms outstretched and my toes barely reaching the pedals. He was always the same and would moan like hell if anyone moved the driving seat so one just learnt to live with it.

We used to rush around town, at his instigation, as if our lives depended upon it. I would frequently dart in and out of the traffic, mainly on his instructions; often when I was driving, he would half open the passenger door to block any other car trying to come up from behind when in dense lanes of traffic and overtaking, or rather, undertaking. Ultimately, whenever we drove each other, it would be as though there was an imaginary line drawn down the middle of the car and I would take charge of my half and he would take charge of his half and we would give each other instructions. We trusted each other implicitly.

Stirling had already taken the Institute of Advanced Motorists' driving test whilst we were at William IV Street, and he made me take it as well. In the end I passed on my second attempt, having failed first time around because I was unable to do a racing change, which I had never heard of before, and the examiner showed me how to do it. (Basically, this involves changing gear without moving one's foot off the accelerator.) Stirling just sniffed when he heard about this, but I very much doubt if anyone else was expected to make this change on their advanced test. I equally doubt whether any ordinary driver would have known how to do this either.

TIME IS OF THE ESSENCE

Another of Stirling's quirks was punctuality. Time meant everything to him. He even had a time stipulation written into his contracts. If he was being paid to put in an appearance somewhere, he would only stay until a given minute of a given hour. After that, he would either leave immediately or he would insist on being paid overtime. There was never any argument about it. Similarly, if I was driving him about, I had to pick him up at the specific time he gave me and if I did not turn up on the exact minute that he had suggested that we should rendezvous, there would be merry hell to pay, and I would be put under interrogation as to the whys and wherefores! London traffic has always been bad, particularly in Soho, and it either crawled or came to a dead stop, but worst of all would be a lorry or a dray delivering barrels of beer to the cellars of the pubs. There would be no alternative but to switch off the engine and sit and wait, often for twenty minutes or so. Even then, most of the streets were one-way in Soho, so one couldn't turn around and go back the way one had come. Whenever practical, Stirling would get out of the car and walk to his destination. If not, he used to postulate and curse under his breath non-stop until the lorry lumbered away. It didn't help either that I did not own a watch, so he decided to remedy this by buying me one when he was in Scandinavia and he gave it to me once he arrived home so that I would never have another excuse for being late again. Of course, this generosity was completely one-sided, because it would ensure that he could live his life according to his own stand-ards and expectations. It certainly complicated my own.

Stirling had ensured the time clause was written into his contract with BP in that when he went along to officially open garages for them, which he did quite often, particularly in far-flung places in the UK, he would only guarantee to stay and meet and greet and sign autographs until a specified time. Thereafter, he would only stay on longer at the agreed rate in the contract, but this did not cover any delays at the start.

He was, therefore, absolutely livid one day when he arrived at the Battersea Helipad from where he was to be flown to open a new BP garage in the south-west of England only to find that the helicopter, which was to take him there, had not arrived. He stormed back to the office and shot off a letter of complaint to the person at BP who had organised the tour then, having partly relieved his frustration, tore off again back to the helipad. Not knowing any better at the time, I typed up what he had dictated, as per his instructions, signed on his behalf and posted it that evening after I had left the office.

He received his answer a couple of days later in the post in the shape of a confidential package of… ping pong balls! You should have seen the expression on his face when he opened it. It was a total mixture of frustration, irritation and, yes, actually a glimmer of ad-miration for such an 'amusing' and original reaction.

On another occasion, Stirling had arranged for us both to have lunch with a friend and sometime driver, one Kinny Lall, but I had to drive down to meet them from North London and had warned Stirling that I might be late because the traffic through Cricklewood and Kilburn was always dire.

Kinny had turned up at the office early and Stirling was just giving him the usual dressing-down for this misdemeanour (in his book) when he heard my car roaring up Shepherd Street, exactly on the minute of half-past twelve.

'See,' said Stirling, moving towards the switches by the garage door and pointing to the large hand on his watch, 'Viper is always on time.'

With that, he punched the switch for the automatic garage door, which came crashing down on the bonnet of my car and gave it a resounding thud.

THE VIPER

Viper. That was his special nickname for me and he didn't like anyone else using it. The way it came about was this.

It had become the fashion in the very early '60s to abbreviate names as a way of giving nicknames to friends, and it became very popular to add 'er' or 'ers' onto a name. For example, my surname of Pirie developed into Pirrers and Caroline into Carrers, and so on. I went around for a long time as Pirrers (although at one time Stirling also called me Button) until one day he began muttering to himself, over and over again under his breath, 'VP; V-Per,' from which he triumphantly came up with the word Viper, which was something completely unique; and, as he said at the time, I acted like one as well. Thanks a million! From henceforth, I was always Viper to him, and he really got quite annoyed if anyone else tried to call me that.

I was quite surprised to see him on another Monday morning sitting at his desk, looking particularly pleased with himself. He had arrived back from America the night before where, as it turned out, he had bought a birthday card, which he thought would be particularly

apt for me but, because he couldn't wait to give it to me until my birthday, he had placed it in the plain white envelope provided and put it
on my typewriter, where I would immediately see it first thing when
I came in. It read:

You are a

V

I

P

And, on opening up to the next page it read:

E

R

Happy... and the word 'Birthday' had been scrubbed out and he had
scribbled in 'Monday' instead.

WHAT IS HE DRIVING AT?

Stirling always organised his own life to be just as he wanted it to be
and he became exceedingly irritated if it went awry. This, naturally,
included the running of the office. He would also become completely
exasperated if he couldn't find whatever it was that he was looking for.

Again, early one morning I turned up at the office only to find
Stirling rummaging through the filing cabinet by my desk. Thank
goodness my filing was up to date – it frequently was not and this
would irritate him.

I was greeted by, 'Valerie!' (The use of my full name always meant trouble.) 'Where the hell have you put Bert Reece's letter? I have been looking for it since last night.'

Rather thrown by such an implicit accusation so early in the morning, I asked who Bert Reece was.

'Bert Reece works for Pan American Airlines,' came the somewhat vexed reply. 'And,' he continued, 'I have looked under "Airlines" and I have looked under "R Miscellaneous" for Reece and I have also looked under "P Miscellaneous" for Pan Am, so where the hell have you put it?'

'B Miscellaneous,' I replied instantly in quite matter-of-a-fact way.

'B Miscellaneous?' he repeated. 'B Miscellaneous?' he exploded, 'Why the hell did you put it under "B Miscellaneous"?'

I looked at him and shrugged my shoulders. I couldn't see why he was getting so het up about not being able to find a letter which, to my mind, was of such little importance.

'Because I only know him as Bert,' I replied.

Stirling was absolutely speechless for quite a few seconds and then he burst out laughing, quite an unusual thing for him to do at that time in his life (being the rather serious young man that he was), and he kept on repeating in wonderment, 'B Miscellaneous... B Miscellaneous... I simply don't believe it.'

Stirling was so dumbfounded by this Bert story that he actually remembered it for the rest of his life and it became one of his party pieces.

Such was his compulsion for neatness and order. Everything had to have its place where *he* could put his hands on it. This would prove to be quite a bone of contention because I often did not have the time to do everything that was required of me during the day and the filing, which I loathed doing, would very often be left for many days before I would get around to it, such was the abundance of paperwork that was created.

Another time I arrived at the office after he had been rifling through my desk drawers and had found some clear plastic folders, which I had bought out of the petty cash. I had never seen anything like them before on my travels and they had cost 1/9d (about 8p) each at the local stationers in Shepherd Market. I realised that he would think they were rather expensive so I had taken off the price tags and put them away in one of my drawers, intending to produce them later in dribs and drabs.

Once again, I was accosted by Stirling first thing in the morning. He was holding up the files saying, 'These are rather good, Viper, how much did you pay for them?'

Before I had time to prevaricate, I found myself saying, 'One and nine pence.'

'For the lot?' he asked.

'No, each.'

'One and nine pence each? One and nine pence each?' he repeated. 'That is daylight robbery,' and, thrusting the files towards me, he continued, 'take them back to wherever you bought them and ask for the money back.'

Handing the files back to me, he asked where I had bought them and I told him that it was the stationery shop in the market. However, I did not have the slightest intention of returning them and decided to produce them again at some future date, which I did.

'How much did you pay for these?' demanded Stirling, examining them minutely.

'Oh,' I replied breezily, 'just over a bob.'

'I told you they were bloody robbers down the road, didn't I?' he grunted, highly delighted that he thought that we had saved some money. He then swept the complete set up from my desk and happily began using them for himself.

TIME IS MONEY

Unsurprisingly, Stirling's intolerance included other road drivers on frequent occasions (whether or not he was driving), and he would give a running commentary about this one being an idiot and another being a bloody fool and so on. He particularly loathed pipe smokers and those who put a St Andrew's Cross or simply 'Écosse' on the backs of their cars instead of 'GB'. (Remember, this was fairly early days for travelling abroad again after all the hostilities.)

I remember on one occasion, down in the East End of London, Stirling was following a man who was dithering around all over the place and, annoyingly, whatever Stirling tried to do, he could not get past the man safely. At last, some traffic lights stopped both cars in their tracks and Stirling quickly opened his car door, leapt out and ran up to the other driver's door. The man was petrified. Stirling indicated that he should roll down his window so, very gingerly, the man did as he was told and it scrolled down an inch or two. Stirling pulled out his clip of bank notes that he always used to carry in the back pocket of his trousers, peeled off a £1 note and thrust it through the crack in the driver's window, saying, 'Here, take this and get yourself some driving lessons,' before running back to his own car and driving off.

THE ORIGINAL STEERING WHEEL

Shepherd Street was just around the corner from an exclusive members' club for anyone associated with motor racing. Known as the Steering Wheel, it was owned by John and Haysie Morgan. John was also the secretary of the BARC (the British Automobile Racing Club, which was also responsible for running races in the UK) and the Wheel was a magnet for all the drivers who descended upon London.

Members could bowl up to have a chat or they would arrange to meet over a drink or a meal. It was in an ideal spot, being centrally located in Brick Street and just around the corner from the old British Racing Drivers' Club (BRDC) offices in Down Street and Les Ambassadeurs (Les A) and Helene Cordet's Club in Old Park Lane. Next door was Baron Studios and, Baron being the court and society fashion photographer of the day, it is not difficult to guess the Wheel's twin attractions for Stirling. Even though he didn't drink back then, the motor racing fraternity and the opportunity of bumping into glamorous models outside Baron Studios – who he could chat up – were of dual interest for Stirling.

There was a semi-circular bar in one corner of The Wheel, which was large enough for about eight to ten people to stand around. The remainder of the room was devoted to an open sitting area, where people could chat and have a drink and/or a snack, and it was dotted with small, dark wooden tables and dark, British racing green leather-studded tub chairs. There was a dado rail round the walls, above which were items of motor racing memorabilia, such as paintings, trophies and photographs, many of which had been signed by their subjects, and, immediately below the rail, on two sides of the room ran matching dark green leather bench seating. Off the main room, to the left of the entrance, was an open dining room up a flight of three or four steps, which overlooked the main seating area, where people could eat more formally at small tables covered with immaculate white table linen, silver cutlery and condiment sets and a small flower arrangement, just like any other restaurant in London. The food was excellent and not expensive, and it was extremely popular because members could entertain guests there to lunch or dinner without any outside hassle – and it was even handier for Stirling for a while after he bought the property in Shepherd Street.

Peggy Sandberg, who took care of the daily management of the club, always welcomed everyone on the same terms. She ran a tight ship, aided and abetted by her two stalwarts, Frank and Ernest. Frank, the barman, was jovial and very friendly. He had an exceedingly large frame and always wore a freshly laundered white shirt and black bow tie under a maroon jacket with black lapels. He had a moustache and wore thick, dark-framed spectacles, with one eye constantly looking at somewhere other than in your direction. Ernest was aptly named. He was in charge of the restaurant. It was mooted that the two were brothers but they were like night and day. Ernest was much shorter than Frank and looked altogether like an Italian spiv. He took life rather seriously and, indeed, he took himself altogether too seriously and never seemed to let his hair down, only rarely enjoying a joke. Peggy could be stern yet she could be exceedingly kind; she was excellent at socialising and ran the club with just the right amount of discipline.

The first time Stirling took me in there, he pointed out a new driver, who had just arrived on the scene from New Zealand: Bruce McLaren, who was endeavouring to get into single-seater motor racing in Europe. Bruce was sitting in a corner on the banquette leather seating with his fiancée and they were hugging half a pint of beer between them. Stirling told me that they were as poor as church mice and that Bruce was really struggling but that he would make it. He also added that the pair were probably hanging around trying to make some contacts, although it didn't look like it to me! At the time, I thought it was rather strange that someone would come such a long way without so much as a halfpenny in their pocket, but I was so new to the game way back then and I didn't realise quite what people had to put up with to get into big-time motor racing. Come to think of it, I suppose Stirling was no different.

THE ANTIPODEANS

Bruce had won New Zealand's 'Driver in Europe' award and had also caught the eye of the Australian driver Jack Brabham, who was already racing in the UK, and it was he who was subsequently responsible for introducing Bruce to the Cooper Car Company. Bruce turned out to be not only a good driver but also an excellent engineer. Tragically, his career was cut short when he died testing one of his own cars at Goodwood in 1970. He was an exceedingly pleasant man, with twinkling eyes and a round face, who, to me, always exuded a certain aura of calm.

Jack, on the other hand, was the original quiet man. He had even less conversation than Stirling, and I experienced this first hand when I was sat beside him at the British Racing Mechanics' dinner one year.

It was whilst everyone was having pre-dinner drinks there that

Stirling came to find me and told me that John Kennedy, the President of the United States of America, had been shot. For once in my life, I thought he was joking and, try as he did, it took quite a long time for me to believe him. As they say, everyone remembers where they were when they heard that particular piece of news.

Jack was a lovely man but very hard work, conversationally. He certainly made up for it one particular evening, well after he had retired, when he and his second wife joined John Surtees and his new wife for dinner along with myself, Susie and Stirling at Shepherd Street. The conversation was dominated by the elders' recollections and anecdotes about the good old days (!), to which none of the wives could contribute. Jack became increasingly animated during the conversation, so much so that his wife cut in to remark that, all of a sudden, Jack's 'diffness' (deafness) seemed to be improving by leaps and bounds!

During their careers, neither of these two world champions seemed to be very sociable and neither was Jack's fellow countryman (yet another world champion), Denny Hulme. One year, after one of them had won the world championship, they were to be found sitting quietly together on an upturned oil drum, having a natter as if the rest of the world did not exist. All the hubbub and acclamation was as nothing to them.

It always fell to my lot to be seated next to difficult people because Stirling knew that I could always talk to anyone, whatever their rank or circumstances. I remember one really boring birthday bash of Stirling's, when I had the misfortune to be seated next to (Lord) Eddie Montagu, whose great collection of old automobiles is housed near the New Forest. He had to be one of the world's most crashing bores, and that night I truly deserved an Oscar! Good old Viper, indeed!

GREAT BRITISH VALUES

Stirling's parents had taught him many of the fast-disappearing, great British values, such as honesty, politeness and respect for other people and, once he started to make a name for himself, he realised that it was better to be seen to be modest – or perhaps it just came naturally? – rather than let success go to his head, and to act like any other normal human being, which of course would not have been difficult for him, due to his natural diffidence.

All his younger life, it had been drummed into him that it was utterly pointless to just hang around not doing anything; that nothing comes easily in life and that he would have to work hard to achieve and pay for whatever he wanted. Rather naturally, he was always proud of his achievements, which resulted in a strange mixture of dignified modesty. It had also been made abundantly clear to him in his youth that money did not grow on trees and that whatever one wanted, one had to work and save hard for until it became affordable. If this meant selling personal effects, such as records, bicycles and the like, so be it. Consequently, nothing he did was on an impulse. He would think long and hard about whether or not he really wanted or needed to acquire anything.

Time and again in his youth, Stirling was told to stand on his own two feet. His father had even taken him to boxing lessons at the tender age of three so that he would become physically fit and would be able to protect himself should the need arise.

Whenever he was in the area, Stirling would generally call into his parents' farm at Tring, Hertfordshire, where the family had moved after the lease on their twenty-acre or so Bray property had expired in 1950. Coincidentally, the farm was fairly near Silverstone, but I never knew him to stay there overnight during the time that I was around, although obviously he did in the early years of his career, under the eagle eye of his parents. Initially, they were very much against him racing.

Whenever he was in England and had a Sunday off from competing, he would often pitch up at the farm, after making his own prior arrangement with his parents, for roast Sunday lunch. This was his favourite meal by far and his preference was for roast lamb, roast potatoes, cauliflower cheese and all the accompaniments, such as mint sauce and/or redcurrant jelly. His mother, Aileen Moss, was an excellent cook but never seemed to be very happy when he brought anyone else with him and if ever Stirling took a girlfriend along, it could be positively embarrassing because Mrs Moss had no qualms whatsoever about letting the girl in question know that she would prefer her to be anywhere else other than with 'her boy'. She could – and would – be downright rude to many of his friends. She would only tolerate those who were of use or close to Stirling, such as Ken and David, and she certainly did not like me, even though I was of some use. I suppose, to be charitable, she was probably rather jealous that 'her boy' had to rely so much on me after the breakdown of his marriage. The feeling of antipathy was entirely mutual and my hackles used to rise whenever I would go round, but then, I had been brought up in a totally different environment, in which it was deemed best to always be charming on the surface and to try to overlook any such rudeness. Also, I felt that I couldn't very well let Stirling down when he was relying on me for transport and he didn't particularly like anyone else driving him.

Knowing how I felt about his mother, he did telephone me when she died to see if I would like to attend the funeral but added that he would quite understand if I did not want to go along. Similarly, when my mother died, he asked me if I would like him to come along to support me. It was a lovely thought and, quite frankly, it amazed me that he would have put himself out to do that for me. As it happened, it was not necessary.

His father Alfred, on the other hand, with his eternal cigar gripped firmly between his teeth, which was more often dead than alight, would be charming to everyone, but he could be a deadly business-man. In addition to his dental practices, BRP and other property businesses, Alfred Moss specialised in breeding White Cloud pigs at the farm (of the same name) in Tring. He also bred a particular species of pure white rabbit and even tried his hand at rearing mink for a while. Ever the businessman, Alfred ensured that virtually every single part of the rabbit was sold, including the paws, which were used in the manufacture of 'decorative' lucky rabbit's foot key rings. Later on, Stirling also bought some rabbit skins from the 'Old Man' – there was no question of them being given to him.

Stirling had inherited Alfred's business acumen in certain ways but, because he was so single-minded about his racing, he never really pursued anything other than that until after his near-fatal acci-dent when he officially retired from racing.

If he didn't go to Tring for Sunday lunch, Stirling, David and sometimes myself would have lunch in a naff-ish chain restaurant of David's choice just off Leicester Square and, for David's sake, Stirling would put up with the limited menu and the utilitarian, sparse decor. After lunch, we would generally wander over to the Odeon cinema in Leicester Square, where we got to know the manager pretty well, or we would go to the Curzon in Curzon Street, just around the corner from Shepherd Street. Going to the cinema was one of Stirling's three favourite pastimes (the other two being design and crumpet), but he would never have dreamt of going on his own.

In all the years that I knew Stirling, he would never use his name to try to obtain preferential treatment in public. However, I did ask him on one occasion if I could use his name and, after I explained why, he gave me an alternative option. He was always particularly quick-witted and would never fail to find ways round any problem, which meant that I had to learn to do the same.

I had promised faithfully to take a couple of Saudi children who had limited time in London to see the *Lawrence of Arabia* film, which had just been put on general release in 1962 to much acclaim, and was being shown at the Odeon in Leicester Square. So popular was it that droves of people were being turned away every night, with the queues for it tailing back to the Charing Cross Road. Once Stirling understood the delicate situation I found myself in (because a promise is a promise), he suggested that I should persuade the official on the door to let me in to see the manager, explain the situation to him and, because Stirling knew that he would instantly recognise *me*, he felt sure that, under the circumstances, he would help me out, which is precisely what the manager did, and we were allowed in. The children were obviously over the moon.

Incidentally, Elliot, Stirling's son, once told me that Stirling used to joke and say that there wasn't any value in his name. Naturally, he was being facetious because it related to the mis-spelling of it with an 'e', as opposed to 'Stirling'. He also said that the 'Craufurd' part was always spelt as in 'turd'. Clearly, self-deprecation came high on his list of banter whilst his son was growing up.

TRUE TO HIS WORD

People were constantly approaching Stirling Moss Ltd with business schemes, many of which didn't see the light of day, but, when someone approached Stirling wishing to start a travel agency, he quickly pricked up his ears. He contacted his father immediately (and, of course, Ken), and after protracted negotiations, they all backed the proposition.

Harry Myers was Stirling's kind of man because he was quiet and exceptionally polite and efficient. He never became flustered. When he made his first approach, Stirling's immediate thoughts were that he would be able to obtain cheap, discounted flights for all his travel. Wrong! That was the one thing that he would not be able to do if he became a director of the company. There were very strict rules about investments in travel agencies and what Harry was looking for was financial backing and the guarantee that Stirling, Alfred and Ken would put all their business through the agency and encourage their friends and acquaintances to do the same. The deal was eventually concluded with Stirling's name only appearing on the stationery, as far as I can remember, as 'S. Moss'. From then on, Harry would take most of the burden off our shoulders by making Stirling's travel arrangements. It would be Harry who would in future carry out the majority of the research for us, into details such as all the waiting times between connecting flights, where applicable, and then come back to us with the choices before finally checking the details with us once more to make the final bookings. For obvious reasons, Stirling's itineraries could be very intricate and Harry was an absolute life-saver and could dance on the proverbial sixpence, never failing to come up with the goods. He certainly took a lot of responsibility off my shoulders and made my life a whole load easier, but I still had to do the usual things, such as contacting friends and business acquaintances, hotel bookings and tying up any other loose ends.

Before investing in the travel agency business, Stirling preferred to travel Pan American Airways (now defunct) whenever possible, because they did offer him incentives for flying with them which, of course, he could never resist. Neither could he resist the temptation of the exclusive hospitality on offer, including being surrounded by the very many attractive hostesses the airline employed, who welcomed members to the Clipper Club, which Pan Am had established in many airports round the world and was the forerunner of today's hospitality lounges. Stirling would often chat up the attractive air hostesses or female members of the ground staff that he came across on his travels, and especially when he was abroad if he hadn't made any prior arrangements.

Once, when I was waiting with Stirling in a special lounge at the new terminal at Heathrow – Stirling always wanted me to stay and talk to him right up until he was collected by a hostess, who would take him straight to passport control – we were joined by a tall young man, who was bemoaning his fate because he'd had a dust-up with his young lady, the fairly well-known actress, Janette Scott, the previous day. He could talk of nothing else. Imagine our surprise when a member of staff came up to him a little while later and apologised for not being able to find him any hairspray.

Hairspray? Stirling and I looked at each other and raised our eyebrows whilst the young man began to explain to us that he was expecting to be met by a posse of photographers when he left the aircraft in New York and he didn't want his hair to be blown all over the place.

Whilst they were being ushered out of the room, Stirling muttered to me under his breath, 'I'll let you know,' to my unspoken question. By this stage, we had begun to understand each other so well that some words and phrases were totally unnecessary.

True to his word, Stirling reported back that there was not a single photographer in sight when they arrived at the then Idlewild Airport in New York (now JFK). And, the young man in question turned out to be the Footlights member and subsequent TV inquisitor, who was pursuing some political story, just as he later did with Nixon and the Watergate scandal. He subsequently succeeded and did go on to make quite a name for himself. The man in question was David Frost.

Stirling was once grilled by the tough interviewer and the fore-runner to David Frost, one John Freeman, who hosted the very popular *Face to Face* series on television, in 1960. Although John always put the interviewees through the hoop, he did it in a slightly more gentlemanly and penetrating way than, say, the likes of Jeremy Paxman or Clive James. It was regarded as being an exceptional honour to be invited onto this programme and I think that Stirling always regarded it as being one of the highlights of his non-racing career at that time, presumably because it was so prestigious. Underneath everything, Stirling did secretly enjoy the trappings of being who he was.

The business that Stirling was least pleased to be associated with was one that was inadvertently headed up by someone who turned out to be a crook, whichever way one looked at the situation, even though I understand that the background checks on him had been glowing.

Express Coachcraft was a brilliantly conceived idea by Ken Gregory, aided and abetted by Alfred Moss, but it was brought to its knees by this one totally dishonest individual who ran off not only with all the funds in the company bank account, but with Ken's first wife as well! Stirling lost a considerable amount of money in the business, as did some of his friends and colleagues. Because he could see its potential and, being the scrupulously honest person that he was, he had also persuaded many of his close associates to invest in it, and that is why he felt so particularly let down when it all went west. Once the company had collapsed all around them and Stirling finally realised that it was going to be impossible to save it, he was terribly bruised and constantly brooded in the office about having persuaded people to part with their money to invest and back a company in which he had given his blessing and, to all intents and purposes, been personally involved. Ultimately, he was persuaded that, even though those backers had put their faith in him, they had done so voluntarily and that it was, in the final analysis, a business decision which each of them had taken and that they could in no way hold him responsible for losing their money. Even so, he was not a happy bunny about the situation and he rang up every single one of them to apologise.

After that bitter experience, he more or less decided that he would keep to what he knew best, driving fast cars quickly and accurately and to the best of his ability. It goes without saying that his sole objective was to always be first in the frame. He had the ability and self-belief and he never really thought that the cards were stacked against him. No one did at the time.

THE CHINESE CONNECTION

Whenever I had to trundle out to the airport to pick up Stirling, it was usually pretty late in the evening and nine times out of ten on the drive back he would suggest going for a meal at the Lotus

House Chinese restaurant on the Edgware Road, which stayed open until three in the morning, seven days a week – practically a unique phenomenon in London. It was popular with other night owls but, generally, we could sit there quietly and not be bugged by any autograph hunters. Unusually for such a late-night restaurant, it was a peaceful place with subdued lighting where Stirling could relax, as much as he ever could, and unwind from the hustle and bustle of his life and come down from the satisfaction of winning his last race or brooding over why he hadn't won it (and ultimately thinking about what more he could have done if he hadn't retired for whatever reason). Unusually, he would do most of the talking after I had updated him with office affairs and it was always about the mechanical stuff on his car, such as the suspension, or he would sit there, having cleared a space for himself on the pristine white linen tablecloth to work out which gear and axle ratios he would need for his next race and the like. It was all absolute double Dutch to me, but he liked to use me as a sounding board, albeit an ignorant one. I didn't know anything at all about the mechanics of a car and never would. I wasn't the slightest bit interested. That's what mechanics were for! And, as for those dreadful boyfriends, huddling me into a corner to talk cars... I was my own person and wanted to be accepted as such. One thing I could never understand was the higher a gear the lower in the gear range it was. (I later gathered it rather depends on whether one is talking about the driving gear or the driven gear. Lower gears achieve a higher torque for the same power. When a car first sets off, first gear is selected because the car needs more torque. First gear is the shortest ratio and, as the car speeds up, other gears with longer ratios are used. So, there you have it!)

Happily for him, I didn't answer back or argue with him because

I really did not understand a word of what he was talking about. He used to scribble away quite contentedly on scrappy little bits of paper and work out whatever was necessary and he would be in his element, as happy as the proverbial pig in clover. We were in there eating shortly after I had applied for my provisional racing licence (because a boyfriend was going to buy me a saloon car to race) and he went to endless lengths to show me how to take the right line for some of the corners on the various circuits by drawing out the 'track' and marking it up. He also wrote down the appropriate gears I should select for the bog-standard car I would first be driving on the various corners and straights.

FORGING ABROAD

In the meantime, Stirling's social life was becoming busier and busier and, as some of his friends became mine and vice versa, we spent quite a bit of our spare time in each other's company. It had become a huge joke amongst my friends that I could write Stirling's signature as easily as if I was writing my own and no one would be able to tell the difference. In fact, a new, cheap, fun restaurant in Bayswater popped up which was very popular, and one wall had been covered in vivid red hessian, on which people were initially encouraged to sign their name with a black marker pen. Don't ask me why this proved to be so popular but it was. The wall was virgin territory when a group of us first visited the place and I was encouraged to inscribe his name at the top of the wall, much to everyone's amusement, including Stirling himself. No one could tell the difference – not even Stirling.

Soon after we had been to this restaurant, Stirling bounced into the office early one morning and asked me where my passport was.

'Upstairs,' I replied.

'Good,' he said. 'Run up and fetch it and get the car out, we're going to the airport.'

'What, now? I asked.

'Yes, now.'

I did as I was bidden and off we went.

I never ever bothered to question Stirling's motives because, invariably, being the practical person that he was, he always had a reason for whatever he did, however obtuse it might seem at the time. We parked in the airport car park and rushed through passport control with hardly a word being spoken and it wasn't until I was on the plane that I found out that we were off to Switzerland for the day. (One could easily swan through immigration and catch a plane within thirty minutes of arriving at the airport back then.)

Once there, we took a taxi to the outskirts of the town, where the driver dropped us off and Stirling began to look around him. We started walking along a broad pavement and soon large snowflakes began to float down like swarms of cabbage white butterflies and the road and pavement soon became ankle deep in snow. We were not kitted out for such weather and I started to shiver and grumble but my complaints fell on deaf ears. Stirling, who had all the time been carrying a couple of small, blue Pan Am cabin bags, continued to trudge on, with me hopping along beside him trying to keep up. He was concentrating on his surroundings. Eventually, he stopped outside a modest-looking building, looked up and hesitated slightly before deciding to go inside. I followed in his footsteps, somewhat relieved to get out of the snow and cold. He went up to a counter, had a fairly long discussion with a man behind the glass and, once the discussion had concluded and he had signed some paperwork the clerk had given to him, he shoved one of his Pan Am bags over to me and opened the other. He took out a book of travellers' cheques and began countersigning them. Suddenly, he realised that I was standing there doing nothing and barked (one of his favourite words), 'Well, get on with it, then.'

I looked at him blankly.

He pointed to the other Pan Am bag and said, 'Don't just stand there doing nothing, start signing.'

And so, the two of us stood at the counter, countersigning all the cheques in his name in front of the teller, whose face remained totally impassive for a good half-hour or so.

On arrival back at London Airport, we walked through the quick, hand-luggage-only 'nothing to declare' channel (where there weren't any queues as not many people knew about it), with a couple of very empty-looking bags and would have been back in the office before 'official' closing time had it not been for the difference of time between Europe and the UK.

Knowing about the fast-track exit came in rather handy for me a couple of years later when I had to pick up Stirling from Heathrow one Monday morning. I had also spent the weekend abroad and had rolled up at Marseilles Airport early in the morning to buy my ticket back to London, only to be told that the early flight to Paris was already full (there weren't any direct flights then). Disaster! What was I to do? Even if there had been some way of getting hold of Stirling he would have been most unsympathetic, to put it mildly. However, I did manage to pull a few strings and I eventually landed at Heathrow some twenty minutes or so ahead of Stirling's estimated time of arrival. As I only had an overnight bag with me, I immediately headed over to the same fast-track channel that we had gone through coming back from Switzerland and sailed through. I quickly found the car in the car park and drove it straight round to 'Arrivals' just as Stirling was emerging from the exit.

'Had a good weekend, Viper?' he asked.

'Yes, thanks, and you?'

That was a very narrow squeak indeed.

TIME ON HIS HANDS?

Stirling's workload was becoming heavier and heavier and, after his split from Katie, he never really took what he would call another proper holiday during his career, although one would be forgiven for thinking that his life was one big holiday – heaven forbid! He was the busiest man I have ever known, most of it self-inflicted. Perhaps I should also say, he was the most fidgety and fretful when he wasn't in the driving seat. Certainly whilst he was racing abroad, he had plenty of time on his hands (although he would never have admitted it) and, hanging around in the many outposts and big cities that he did in the world in equal measure, he would try to make the best of it. He would also be on the constant lookout for new crumpet whenever and wherever he was in the world. If he was stuck in one particular place abroad, he would while away his time, shopping, having haircuts, getting his clothes tailored and possibly taking part in some kind of sport or being taught new ones, such as learning to fly in New Zealand. Being so famous didn't help either. The pressures on his time became all the greater and the increasing number of overseas races considerably extended the racing calendar each year, making motor racing virtually a year-round sport.

One year, he flew back to London quite unexpectedly the day before New Year's Eve quite simply because he was fed up being on his own and was missing London, which he always considered to be the greatest city in the world.

Although he had obviously not organised to do anything special for New Year's Eve, he immediately began to ring round some of his friends and contacts to find out what they were up to. One group invited him to join them at the Carlton Towers Hotel in Sloane Street off Knightsbridge and, as the Rib Room was one of Stirling's favourite haunts because he liked the food there, he accepted their invitation to join them. When he found out that I wasn't doing anything either that evening, he asked me to go along with him. We drove over to the hotel in the Mini because (not drinking at that point) he never had to think about being booked for drink driving and, when we left in the early hours of the morning, we found our car looking like a white humpback whale. There had been a two-inch flurry of snow whilst we had been seeing in the New Year and, without any fuss whatsoever, Stirling clad only in his dinner jacket just brushed the snow off the windscreen with his arm and scrambled into the car, telling me to get in and stop fussing about my shoes being ruined. Then off we sped up Sloane Street, leaving the rest of the group stranded and looking very cold indeed, waiting for virtually non-existent taxis to take them home. It would never have crossed his mind to offer anyone a lift.

Quite often, Stirling would initiate an almost one-sided conversation with me as to where the best alternative would be to situate the office if it wasn't London. I never knew why, but the answer he regularly came up with was always the same – Hong Kong. During his racing career he stayed with friends who, when he first went to HK, had a cute five-year-old daughter, and she was so adorable that he declared that she would, one day, become his future wife. Everybody laughed at the time, but in fact she did some twenty years later.

BLIND DATE

Around this time I was going out on a lot on dates but there was no one special in my life and I was continually bugging Stirling to introduce me to some gorgeous fellow who would sweep me off my feet and carry me away. Stirling's thoughts were divided on the issue because he didn't want to lose me, but neither did he want to be seen as if he wasn't doing anything. However, a new driving talent had emerged on the scene during the year and Stirling thought, as we were both Scottish, that we might just hit it off together and suggested to the young man in question, Jim Clark, that he take me along to the BRDC Annual Dinner in early December. Although we became lifelong friends until his death in 1968 racing in Germany, he wasn't for me or me for him. He was even shyer than Stirling, in fact, painfully so. He was a quiet, unassuming man, extremely bashful, but with a prodigious talent. He had a totally split personality because he loved his farming just as much as he did his motor racing. He owned a 1,200-acre farm in Chirnside, Berwickshire, and coincidentally by that time my mother also owned a house in Chirnside. Consequently, we fraternised quite a bit with many of the other people from the Borders who were involved in the motor racing scene. The local garagiste and a leading light in the Border Reivers Racing Team, Jock McBain, owned a Doughty speedboat and, whatever the weather, mad fools that we were, we would all go water skiing in it in Berwick Harbour. Certainly, Jimmy used to come out of himself much more in his own surroundings and amongst his Scottish friends. He also enjoyed the odd sherbet, so we would arrange to meet and catch up from time to time when I was up in the area and have a quiet drink and a natter together, usually in what Jimmy would call the Queen's Legs in Berwick High Street, though the pub was actually called The King's Head on the other side of the border.

Stirling felt very relieved when he saw that we were not attracted to each other, but he was equally content that he had been seen to be trying to get me hitched up. He never really tried again. During his racing career, Jimmy tended to drift into long-term relationships, but he did tell me at Hugh Dibley's first wedding that he would never get married until he had stopped motor racing, and of course, he never did.

One day, I decided to pop into Jimmy's about ten o'clock in the morning and the housekeeper answered my knock at the door and said, hands on hips, in a rather intimidating manner, 'Muster Clark's no' up.' She looked at me accusingly and added, 'He went to a wedding in Newcastle yesterday.'

'Well,' I said undaunted, 'please would you tell him I am here anyway?' and a little while later Jimmy came down the stairs somewhat sleepily in his stockinged feet, looking slightly the worse for wear, and we started chatting about the lambing and general farm business.

As an aside, later that day I went to see an ancient aunt who, on hearing that I had seen Jimmy that morning, asked what time I had visited 'Mr Clark'. When I responded just after ten, she sat ramrod straight and said, 'Calling is between three and four in the afternoons.'

PART TWO

ACCIDENTS HAPPEN

I also looked slightly the worse for wear when I went to collect Stirling at London Airport (what Heathrow was originally called when it was the only one serving the city), where he was arriving from Amsterdam after racing in Zandvoort one weekend. Driving back to London from Berwickshire in a white Renault Floride, which was on loan to us from Renault in Acton and which wallowed all over the place, I came off the road on a reverse camber right-hand bend near Jimmy's farm. I had hurt my leg and was particularly worried about what Stirling would say to me about the car, so another racing friend offered to drive me out to the airport to pick him up. I waited somewhat nervously for Stirling to come around the small wooden semi-circular screened doorway into the very tasteful waiting area in the new modern terminal, and was rather shocked to see him emerge accompanied by Juan Manuel Fangio and Jimmy (Clark). Hopping towards him, I told him what I had done and Fangio (who was never known as Juan) and Jimmy visibly blanched and held their breath, waiting for the explosion which never came. Stirling only looked me up and down, saw that I had been injured and said, 'Valerie, if you had told me you had a cold I would have been less surprised.'

As soon as we arrived back at the office, he immediately got on to Harry Myers to book and pay for me to go on one of the first package holidays to Spain for a couple of weeks and simply closed his ears to all my protestations.

Due to his rather parsimonious background, this was very generous of him because he was normally rather stingy, a case in point being his constant moan about the amount of petty cash I spent

183

buying coffee. This really got to him and he would never let a chance go by without ticking on about it, even mentioning it once in a quote to the press. Naturally, I took no notice whatsoever.

GENEROUS TO A FAULT

Stirling would never waste his money on what was deemed as frippery because it had been drummed into him so many times in the past about wasting money and this doctrine would carry him through most of his racing career – and beyond. In part, it also contributed to his stubbornness, because he had been taught that money was not a given in life and that one had to earn it and be careful with it. During his teens, Stirling's sole aim in life was to become a *professional* racing driver, as opposed to being a part-time racing driver, even though he was encouraged to learn the hotel business, having been employed as a general dogsbody at the Eccleston in London in the early days when he was trying to juggle both careers virtually simultaneously. However, once he had tasted the flavour of success, his sole object in life was to become a full-time racing driver and to succeed in whatever else he put his hand to – which would not be the hotel business.

As a matter of fact, it was hardly surprising that he did watch all of the pennies in the business because he was the sole breadwinner and he had to support his small entourage, with its quite substantial outgoings (although he was the main contributor and the major expense all rolled into one!). On occasions, he could be extremely generous when the mood took him. Sometimes, he might lend money to close friends and, later, members of his own racing team if he was asked to do so, but he would only do this if he knew the person sufficiently well and felt sure that he or she would pay him back whenever they could. He would always make the terms of the agreement crystal clear from the outset and occasionally would have a legal agreement drawn up. I think at least three, if not four, of his employees have him to thank for having been able to begin to clamber aboard the property ladder.

I would also prop up his perceived generosity without being asked or told. I took it upon myself to send flowers or fruit to people 'in sympathy' or who were ill – sometimes to people he didn't know at all – all of which contributed to the overall picture of him being 'a very nice chap'. On occasions, if he arrived early for work and was opening the mail, he would be totally surprised to receive a word of thanks or a 'thank you' card. He hadn't the faintest idea what it was about and would generally ask – and promptly forget it – but he never once queried the *raison d'être*, probably because, by this time, he trusted me implicitly. One motoring journalist who had told me about a certain family crisis was absolutely overwhelmed after his wife told him that she had received a bunch of flowers from Stirling and thereafter he never had anything but a good word to say about him.

Stirling was also an absolute stickler for paying *precisely* that which he felt he was responsible for. For example, when he was out with a crowd of people having a meal, he would insist that everyone paid for what they had specifically consumed rather than taking the somewhat easier option of paying an equal share of the bill. I remember on one occasion, there were no fewer than twenty-eight of us eating together at a very long table near Nürburgring, Germany, and, when the bill was produced at the end of the meal, Stirling took it upon his shoulders to dissect it, item by every single item, to establish what each person had eaten and drunk, which he did meticulously, although it did take rather a long time! He absolutely refused to simply divide the bill by twenty-eight. Shades of the Rector of Wicken!

A more altruistic example of his generosity was after a race when he had lapped Mike Hawthorn, and he began to feel rather sorry for him. He realised that he was almost belittling Mike and his abilities so Stirling decided to lift his foot off his accelerator and drop back behind Mike's car so that it would at least be recorded for posterity that both drivers had finished the race on the same lap. This didn't cost Stirling anything but a little bit of his own pride and it was an unusually kind and thoughtful act to do in a competition, albeit un-usual and a one-off. However, by this time, he had already made his point in the race and he didn't feel that it was worth rubbing it in anymore and further diminish Mike's abilities. I doubt very much that Stirling would have been so kind to some of the up-and-coming drivers in the '60s. I am positive that his attitude would have been that they would have to learn the hard way, coming up through the ranks like he did.

On another occasion when it was pouring with rain and Stirling was practising at Brands Hatch, I decided to take the scooter out (which had been acquired principally for Stirling to drive around London more quickly) to go up Park Lane to collect his Remington razor, which was being repaired at their outlet near Marble Arch. It had been on my to-do list for quite a long time, and I was tired of him complaining that I hadn't yet had it fixed. When I arrived back at 36/38 Shepherd Street, the phone was ringing in the office and it was Stirling. I thought it was a bit strange but it turned out that he had the foresight to try to prevent me from finding out that a good racing driver friend of mine had been involved in a serious accident.

However, prior to his call to me he had asked Ken Gregory, who was also at Brands that day, to drive back to London to take care of me, just in case. This was quite out of character for him, but he knew that I would be absolutely devastated if this driver died because we had started going out together and Stirling wanted to ensure that I would be OK and would not be alone.

Another year, and I have no idea why, Stirling offered to pay for me to accompany him to the Brussels Grand Prix, so I agreed. Presumably it was because he didn't have a girlfriend to take along with him, although he always swore that he never ever made love before competing competitively. Anyone who accompanied him, though, would have to keep well out of his way at the circuit and be able to take good care of themselves because he never liked anyone fussing over him on race day, and neither did he like being disturbed from his thoughts.

It wasn't a very important race meeting but most of the top drivers had committed to participate and, when it came to it, it was not to be Stirling's day either. With just under half the race left to run, we saw from the pits a pall of black smoke rising in the distance and, because Stirling had not come round when he should have done, we all thought that he had been involved in an accident. Fortunately, he had not crashed. He had sustained a mechanical failure near that part of the circuit almost instantly after the other incident and he was not at all a happy bunny. His mood continued.

When he was checking us out of the hotel the following morning and I was waiting patiently beside him at the check-out counter, he turned to me and sharply told me to pay for my own accommodation. I was absolutely staggered and told him precisely what he could do with that suggestion and, to give him his due, he did back off immediately. It was a good try, although not quite good enough. Even I, for once, was astonished at the paucity of his generosity!

CRUMPET

Gradually, it seemed that Stirling was steadily getting over his break-up with Katie and was soon becoming increasingly infatuated with quite a few young women, with monotonous regularity. He was like a little boy, telling me all about those that he had met on his travels.

Whenever Stirling and any of his girlfriends decided to call it a day, he would always try to keep on the best of terms with them so that neither he nor the girl in question would house a grudge, with a couple of very notable exceptions. Apparently, he would tell them right from the onset of the relationship that their chances of marriage with him were nil so he was never embarrassed if he ever bumped into any of them when he was out with another *amour* on his arm. Life was all very civilised so there were never very many upsets in that department. Both parties would just move on in their own separate ways and if their paths crossed again, each would be quite happy to see the other, with no hard feelings entering into it whatsoever. It was, after all, the Swinging Sixties.

I suppose at one point before we moved up to 44/46, I did get a bit jealous for a couple of months but, looking back, I think it was a form of protectionism because even though most of his bits of crumpet were really nice, a few of them were very badly behaved, even more so when I had to drive them about in the evenings together when he couldn't. Stirling would never sit beside his girlfriend in the car – he would always park himself quite happily in the front passenger seat, watching the traffic with his piece of crumpet assigned to the back.

One day, I was driving him in the area of White City, a most insalubrious part of the world back then, when Stirling espied a bit of tottie walking towards us in the distance. He had fantastic eyesight.

'Look, look at that piece of crumpet, Vipes,' he said, pointing.

I quickly glanced over in the direction he was pointing and I was certainly not impressed by what I saw.

'Slow down,' he said, 'slow down.'

I didn't take a blind bit of notice of him.

'Slow down, I said, slow down,' he said accusingly.

We drove on and whilst approaching a zebra crossing straight ahead of us he yelled, 'Stop, stop...' and as we sailed past the woman in question he turned to me, hurt, and said, 'You have just ruined my entire love life. I was going to marry that girl.'

'She was a scrubber,' I responded disdainfully, without taking my eyes off the road or my foot off the accelerator.

Five seconds later, we both burst out in laughter.

DRIVING HIM MAD

One weekend, I had to drive him to Brands Hatch with one of his lovelier girlfriends sitting in the back of the car. We had left the house rather late. The quickest way for us to go to Brands entailed first driving through endless miles of the sprawling suburbs of south-east London and then there was always a bottleneck at Swanley, in Kent, before the authorities built the bypass round it. Traffic would back up and it could take ages to get to the circuit. Stirling did not stop complaining about how late we were (his fault, not ours!) and for me to get a move on, so I decided to literally and deliberately take him at his word. Approaching the circuit on a downhill piece of road before a roundabout, I pulled out, making a third lane, which was only just possible if there was a tight, single lane of oncoming traffic.

'No, no, Valerie, you can't,' he said from the passenger seat. (He was serious because he was using my full name.)

'Oh, yes I can,' I replied. 'You told me to get a move on and I am.'

'I didn't mean quite like this,' he started to protest, just as a man in one of the oncoming vehicles stuck his head out of the window to yell some exceedingly rude expletives.

There was a squeak from the back of the car from our rather shocked passenger; Stirling looked lost for words; the man in the other car then recognised him and couldn't quite believe his eyes and we continued on our merry way. Consequently, Stirling decided it would be far wiser for him to keep his mouth firmly shut for the rest of the trip because he knew me too well by then.

We did make it to the circuit on time, nonetheless.

MAKING ANOTHER MOVE

Once the skeletal house at 44/46 was virtually finished (i.e. the concrete structure had been built), the only way for Stirling to be able to keep a constant eye on the builders every single minute of every day was to move into the half-finished offices and work from there – and did the workmen ever love that! I was fairly nonplussed by now because I had become fairly used to taking my own portable typewriter on journeys with Stirling and typing wherever we landed up, most of the time on my lap in the car.

Immediately the bare concrete shell of an office could be secured safely in the new premises and the built-in office fixtures and fittings had been more or less completed, we began to move all the files and office paraphernalia we had at 36/38 Shepherd Street up to 44/46. All the desks, filing cabinets, hidden cupboards, glass-fronted book shelves and so on in both offices, all to you-know-who's design, were inbuilt and made from teak.

Stirling had allocated himself the last two numbers in the street as his official address even though it was a single dwelling.

The council soon made their objections known about the numbering. They considered it to be exceedingly high-handed of him to assume his official address without at least consulting them, but eventually they gave way on the grounds that there were two front doors (one of which, number 46, was to be used as his office address and the other number, 44, was to be his private address). However, at some future date, the house would become registered as a private dwelling. Although there was a considerable amount of bureaucracy at the council, it was nothing like it would have been today, when I doubt that he would have got his own way.

In actual fact, Stirling moved most of the office himself, aided and abetted by a couple of the builders. 'Much cheaper, you know!'

'His' desk was extremely innovative and practical because it was a two-in-one desk, where two people could sit more or less diagonally opposite each other. From his own fairly conventional-type, rectangular desk, a conjoined second desk veered off at an angle, where I eventually ended up sitting with my typewriter (by this time a new one!) facing the small garden whilst he looked towards the front office. All the teak desks were topped in utilitarian 'wooden'-looking Formica, which was very easy to keep clean.

Stirling's taste in wood had moved on from the 'other Shepherd Street', where he had favoured silver-coloured driftwood, and now it was all to be teak from the Orient – apart from the room at the top of the building (which was referred to as the studio), and the basement.

Quite apart from there being nothing on the bare, plastered walls, the concrete floor was rough, and dust and rubble lay everywhere. The offices could hardly be described as comfortable – far from it – and once we were ensconced, Stirling and I had rather a massive fight, to put it mildly, about the lack of heating. Eventually, he condescendingly brought in a one-bar electric fire. I took one look at it and refused to work in such cold and inhospitable conditions. It wasn't until I handed in my notice for the umpteenth time that he ran down the road and brought back a fan heater, which he ostentatiously put on in my room. I was not averse to blackmail when it was warranted.

He took the one-bar heater into his own, larger office and tried to make his point but failed miserably, sitting hunched up over his own desk wearing a very heavy overcoat and scarf, thick socks and shoes and trying not to show that he was shivering. Nothing else in the building was operational so if we wanted to go to the loo, we had to run down to 36/38.

TAKING NO NOTICE

It became fairly common knowledge in 'the Trade' that I was wont to give in my notice on occasions and, once, when it had not been rescinded for a couple of days, Raymond Baxter (commentator and BBC journalist), who must have called the office, and a couple of trade associates sent letters or little rhymes to Stirling in support of my cause.

Here is another such ditty addressed to him from John Gooding of BP from when I was trying to get a raise in salary and I had given Stirling an ultimatum. We were at loggerheads and we were both being stubborn. I had obviously chosen the wrong timing!

> *For Valerie, a nice wee kid*
> *Quite gladly I'll subscribe a quid*
> *Or, as in parts she's nicely round*
> *If you prefer, we'll pay a pound.*
> *Maybe we could buy one cheaper*
> *But, Stirling, boy, you've to keep her!*
> Gooding 1962

Now Stirling turned his attention to trying to sort out the rest of the construction and how the interior of the house should look and what furniture he would require. It was enormously time consuming and he became totally immersed in chasing up this, that and the other (the 'other' generally being his crumpet!) and I was left to run practically everything else.

Of course, he and Norman the architect had long since parted company, soon after the underground river debacle, and Stirling began to employ his own medium-sized contractors to finish a lot of the interior work – and that wasn't working out too well either. He was not impressed with the quality of the work, let alone the lack of it. In the end, after his blood pressure had gone haywire almost every day that he spent in London, he decided to get rid of the contractors and to employ his own direct labour because, quite apart from anything else, he felt that it would be far cheaper. He never thought about the impracticalities of his being away so much of the time, but he had made up his mind and that was to be that. He was not for turning! Consequently, we would be constantly advertising in the *Evening Standard* for plumbers, carpenters, painters and so on, generally interviewing them 'after hours' if the prospective employee bothered to turn up at all. Because we didn't mention who the job was for, yet again, the surprise on the applicants' faces when they first walked through the door and found out that they might be working for 'the great Stirling Moss' had to be seen to be believed. They were always taken aback and most even more so when they heard about the decidedly low wages that were on offer. It has to be said that most of the would-be employees had a somewhat different take on what they were worth to what Stirling thought they were worth. If they did eventually reach a mutually acceptable compromise about pay, once they began work there would be further issues because Stirling would constantly interfere in what they were working on or he would change his mind when he arrived back from racing and no workman, however competent they may be, likes to be told his trade. Stirling simply could not understand what their problem was because he only ever saw things from his own perspective, and he would only accept an absolutely perfect job, which is generally a bit of a tall order, particularly as far as the building trade is concerned.

BAD RELATIONS!

The turnover of self-employed workmen was horrendous – most only lasted a week, just long enough to collect their pay and move on. I had strict instructions, on pain of death, never to pay any of them until the end of the week if anyone wanted to leave whilst he was away. Personally, I couldn't see that it was any cheaper to employ direct labour either (rather than employing decent contractors), particularly when one took into consideration all the hassle, turnover and expense of advertising and interviewing people. But he wouldn't have any of it; he always had to be right.

Life was all very Stirling-esque. One worked as one could in cramped and cold spaces, surrounded by concrete dust and workmen shouting and banging, whistling and singing all day long. Despite his grumbling, Stirling was in his element, running all over the place, making decisions, complaining a lot and trying to sort out the inevitable snags, which were not of his own making, naturally (!), and which perpetually crop up when having any work done by outsiders. But, he had to leave his building worries behind him when he went off to America, Nassau, South Africa and the Antipodes, where he was racing over the Christmas and New Year period. David Haynes was going with him to keep him company, taking along his own tins of Heinz baked beans and can opener that he always travelled with when he flew abroad – and not even Stirling could prevent him from so doing. David absolutely refused to eat anything other than good, solid English food when he was out of the country, so if there wasn't anything plain and wholesome on the menu, rather than eating any of that 'foreign stuff' he would open up a can to ensure that he wouldn't spend most of the night and the next day in the bathroom, listening to a moaning, totally unsympathetic companion shouting at him and telling him what an idiot he was. Stirling was fairly fussy about his food but he would never resort to cans of baked beans. He always grumbled about French food because he preferred good solid

English fare (apart from crêpes Suzette) and, when in France, could never get a steak as he would like it, which would be cremated.

Things droned along during the winter months whilst he was abroad and I didn't pay any particular attention to the building side of the operation because I wasn't frightfully interested in building at that time and didn't really know much about it. It was not exactly on my list of priorities and I would generally tell Stirling every time he telephoned that things were going OK, if rather slowly, which was the truth.

All the while, many of the new American drivers used to bowl up to the office. They had begun to migrate across the pond to Europe in quite a fair number to try their hand at international racing rather than their own kind, which was run under different rules. These included the likes of Phil Hill, Dan Gurney, A. J. Foyt (four-time winner of the famous US Indianapolis 500 race at 'The Brickyard' in the States), Augie Pabst and many others. Even the lovable and by then retired Argentinian world champion, when he had nothing else to do, used to drop in, often when Stirling wasn't around. Fangio was a simple, very natural, charming, courteous gentleman, in the real sense of the word, and he always held a particularly special place in Stirling's heart – and mine. Whenever he appeared in Stirling's absence, he would always be accompanied by a young Argentinian driver called Bordeo. They would generally invite me out to dinner and ask me to bring some of my girlfriends as well. We had some great evenings together and, even though Fangio spoke very little English, he was a fun person and if ever he wanted to tell a joke, it would take him simply ages. The telling of it in a mixture of 'Spenglish' would always be far funnier than the joke itself.

Stirling admired and liked Fangio tremendously because, over and above his driving prowess, he was such a lovely, warm-hearted person. He was kind and polite and he had this quiet but unique sense of humour. He even helped me out one day when I telephoned him in Argentina to ask him to help a girlfriend of mine who suspected her husband of making a whole load of hay in the Argentinian sunshine! Fangio actually rang up the hotel in question to find out if the husband had stayed there with his bit on the side, and he had.

Once Stirling arrived back from wintering overseas and saw what little progress had in fact been made on the house, he was absolutely beside himself. As always, I was blamed initially for the lack of progress but when he found out that he couldn't do any better himself, he was left feeling utterly frustrated – and impotent. Tolerance was not one of his greatest virtues, particularly when dealing with other people, if only because their brains were incapable of keeping up with his. I had to continually try to keep the peace between him and the workmen. One felt totally inadequate and completely out of control and it was mentally draining for both him and me. He was at odds to understand the lack of progress but, however hard he stamped his foot, the builders continued to work at their normal snail's pace. No amount of huffing and puffing would help – in fact it tended to make matters worse.

CADGING A LIFT

It would be some many months before the offices alone would be finished properly because, quite apart from anything else, we were waiting for a massive black and white A-Z map of London to be printed, which was to be pasted over the entire front office side wall including a quarter of the circular staircase, the back part of which protruded into the front office.

The concrete staircase was one of the first things that had been constructed off-site; it was delivered and put in place before the outer shell of the house had even been completed. He had found this type of staircase to be the solution to the lack of space there would otherwise have been in the house because, when he acquired the land, he could only afford to buy a 25ft frontage of the parcel on offer. He for ever after rued the fact that he had never been able to afford to buy the entire plot. However, he had the surprise of his life, many years later, when he was informed that the mortgage, which had been taken out on the property, was a 'with profits' mortgage. This meant he had come into a fair amount of money that he hadn't had a clue about and which, naturally, had not been put into the original equation. Had he known back then what he later found out, we probably would have had even larger problems on our hands!

Stirling thought that his idea regarding the A-Z map was brilliant – of course all his ideas were (!) – and that it might just keep some of the visitors quiet whilst they were waiting in my office to see him because he guessed they might be rather more interested in seeing where different areas within London are rather than chatting to me and 'wasting' my time. Again, the use of eye-catching wallpaper to deflect attention. In actual fact, the map proved to be incredibly useful to us as well on many occasions. We were always making frequent forays into uncharted territory, as it were, in the outskirts of London, to collect bits and bobs for the construction. It made life so much easier being able to plan the route and make notes from the large map rather than consulting the small print in the A-Z guides where, nine times out of ten, the destination was either on the crease of two pages, or the route continued overleaf or even several pages overleaf.

We had hurriedly looked at the map before dashing down to the East End of London to look for a satin chrome mat well (you may well ask) when we found ourselves in probably what turned out to be one of the most hilarious situations in which the two of us were ever involved.

Again, it was a bitterly cold day and we were glad of the warmth inside the tube train. As we approached our destination, Stirling asked me at which stop we should get off, Mile End or Bow. I said I thought it was the former but he rather thought it was the latter and one of those situations developed when we both wanted to please the other – and not be wrong – but eventually we decided to get off at Mile End. We made our way to the exit and as we emerged into the daylight outside the tube station, I immediately saw that (a) it had been snowing very heavily since we descended into the depths of London and (b) that I had made a mistake and that we had indeed got off at the wrong station, which was furthest away from the small industrial estate that we were going to visit. I apologised profusely and immediately began to dive back into the underground station when Stirling held me back.

'We'll walk,' he announced.

'No, it's too cold and there's too much snow,' I protested.

'Don't be so ridiculous,' he said dismissively as I was very unwillingly pulled along the pavement.

Now, I hate walking, so I had no intention of marching all the way down the street with him but, by this time, we had fortunately arrived at an intersection and all the cars in the main road, travelling in an 'easterly direction', as Mr Plod would have put it, were stopped at a red traffic signal. I espied a man sitting alone in his car and said to

Stirling, 'I'll ask him to give us a lift,' and before he could prevent me from so doing I had pulled open the back-passenger door of the car and asked the driver if he was going to go straight down the road. He said he was, so, quick as a flash and without more ado, I jumped into the back of the man's car, trying to drag Stirling in along with me. The lights began to change to green just as Stirling managed to tug the last part of his coat inside the car; he pulled the back door shut and the somewhat startled man drove off with the rest of the traffic. I began to tell the driver how terribly kind it was of him to give us a lift in such atrocious weather as Stirling sat quiet as a mouse, but the man just continued to drive down the road without saying a word. After about half a mile, just as we were approaching some more traffic lights, Stirling looked at me and nodded.

As the lights turned red and the car slid to a stop, narrowly missing the car in front, we jumped out, thanking the driver profusely as we disappeared giggling together into a rather small and dreary industrial site.

The driver never spoke a word to us the whole time and he never turned around. The poor man was probably terrified that he was going to be attacked or kidnapped and was obviously relieved when he wasn't. We might have been in the East End of London, which was the realm of the notorious Kray Twins, but I don't really think that either of us looked as if we really belonged to that part of the world.

CARPETED

As far as the new house was concerned, Stirling's next priority was, once again, to move into the guest bedroom (which was a small

en-suite double room at the rear of the house) as quickly as possible, irrespective of the condition of the rest of the property. This
would enable him to move out of 36/38 completely, improve his cash
flow and keep an eye on the rest of the house whilst it was finished
around him. There was still a mountain to climb and it would take
very many long months of hard work to complete the house, to say
nothing of the irritation and annoyance he would cause amongst the
workmen, being on site twenty-four hours a day whenever he was in
the country.

Black Friday was when 'we' hit a major design snag. One of the
workmen who was working in the back bedroom came and found
him and told him that there was insufficient space between the spare
bathroom door and the door into the bedroom from the small land-
ing outside. Unwilling to admit that there was a flaw in his design,
Stirling immediately sprinted up the rough concrete stairs to the
third floor, expecting to tell the workman that he didn't know what
he was talking about but, when he saw the problem for himself, he
was stuck for words. The workman was quite correct. But, by now, it
was far too late to alter the concrete structure of the bedroom and the
en-suite bathroom. Most of the plumbing had already been installed
and knocking down a couple of walls was simply out of the question
at this stage in the development. Stirling was beside himself, being
thwarted, as he was, every inch of the way – and now this. It was quite
beyond him to admit defeat and, if the truth be known, the most
bitter pill to swallow was probably his disillusion in his own design
capabilities. And there was no Norman to blame! He quickly came
to the conclusion that the bathroom door would have to be a sliding
door but even this was not feasible because, once again, there was
insufficient space for it to slide back into a recess. I thought that he

had given up the hunt for an answer, but I should have known rather better than that because some weeks later he came back from America triumphantly lugging a folding, concertina-type plastic door with him, which was erected after he managed to obtain approval from Westminster City Council. Yet another hurdle jumped, but there would be plenty more.

As far as the wall coverings were concerned, he was equally triumphant when he managed to find some attractive Swiss wallpaper which incorporated in its manufacture a form of thin metal which enabled the paper to be actually scrubbed with a brush if necessary and he thought that – if hung properly – it would be extremely practical and would last for a very long time without having to keep on renewing it.

Meanwhile, the workmen continued to drag their heels and I was becoming sick and tired of Stirling continually moaning about them. I felt that things couldn't go on as they had been for very much longer so, more in desperation than anything else, I suggested to him that we should get some carpet laid in the bedroom, where the carpenters were taking an inordinate amount of time putting in some units and, of course, the folding door to the bathroom. Fortunately, the carpet had already been delivered and was sitting somewhere in the depths of the building, still in its wrapping gathering dust, so it would be just a matter of getting someone to lay it.

Looking back, the main problem with the whole of this Shepherd Street project was that there was never a written schedule of any kind for any of the work that had to be carried out, and consequently, there was almost no coordination whatsoever. The men wandered around the building doing a bit here and a bit there so nothing was actually completed. Stirling being away so much of the time didn't help either and, of course, being the total control freak that he was, he was unable to delegate anything very much. Everyone had to meet *his* standards, which is pretty difficult at the best of times when trying to satisfy a pedant, and many dropped by the wayside. He even insisted that every single screw that would be visible in the house should be in alignment and as I was absolutely positive that the builders wouldn't be prepared to do this I took to walking around the building with a screwdriver, to adjust the screws as and when I saw they were not in parallel. It was just not worth the hassle of asking someone else to do this who you knew would either give you a right mouthful or simply wouldn't bother to do it anyway. I am afraid to say this is one habit that has never left me to this day!

'What's the point of laying the carpet?' asked Stirling practically. 'The workmen will only make it dirty.'

'Oh, no they won't,' I replied, vehemently. 'I will put a notice on the outside of the door telling anyone who wishes to enter the room to remove their shoes.' (No one ever removed their shoes in houses in that era.)

He looked at me disbelievingly and said flatly, 'It will never work.'

'Oh, won't it!' I replied grimly. 'Let's give it a whirl.'

And give it a whirl 'we' did from then on. I used to monitor everyone who wanted to go into that portion of the house, including Stirling, by keeping the key to the lock in the office and doing spot checks. Initially, he refused point blank to take off his own shoes until I told him quite emphatically that there were to be no exceptions and that, anyway, he should lead by example. That stopped him in his tracks and, after all, his shoes were about the easiest of anyone's to take off, being slip-ons!

There was all hell to pay when I caught one of the carpenters trying to sneak in with his shoes on after I had been more or less forced to leave the door unlocked when he informed me that he would need to be going in and out all afternoon and he didn't want to keep on disturbing me. After I caught him inside with his shoes on and told him exactly what I thought of him, he nearly walked off the site in high dudgeon there and then, but he did finish the job in double-quick time because he knew he wouldn't get paid for it if he did not. I had taken a calculated gamble knowing that no one, particularly the workmen, would like having to take off their shoes one little bit, and fortunately for me my gamble paid off and the room was finished not long after. Stirling was actually mightily impressed, although he didn't want to admit it at the time.

The only person in the team at that stage who was worth his salt was the electrician, Harry Whitsun. A mild, weedy man with the air of an absent-minded professor, Harry was a genius. He had a knack of never allowing Stirling to bully him and he would work day in and day out, quietly beavering away in the background, doing his own thing and with his own thoughts – and what thoughts they must have been. He was the one and only sound professional on site and was as equal a perfectionist as the boss. He never once gave Stirling a headache and would always see a problem long before it occurred and go off and discuss it with him. Harry was having to work with a new American low-voltage electrical system with touch-latch switches that Stirling had bought and had sent over from the States, and he was an absolute gem. He never took the slightest notice of anyone else in the building; he left them to their own devices and he expected the same treatment from them.

Once the central heating was working properly in the house, Stirling used to appear in the office first thing in the morning wearing a warm, grey, shaggy, knee-length robe over his underpants, and he would work quite happily in that garb until he had to go and get changed to go out. He'd had it made in Hong Kong and his name was embroidered on it in red Chinese lettering, top left above his chest. In his later years, I was amused to see that he sometimes trotted it out to wear over a top and pair of trousers to take the chill off him when we all walked down the street to go and eat in one of the local restaurants in Shepherd Market.

COME RAIN OR SHINE

With Stirling being very much more in demand, both in the UK and in all the four corners of the world, there just weren't sufficient hours in the day. The pressures of having to juggle the office with everything else became enormous and probably more so for him, although he did revel in what he was creating. Increasingly, he was being invited to attend more and more functions and the press never let up, continually asking for quotes and interviews, and his racing sponsors would wish to discuss his schedules, future advertising and other business opportunities.

One company that approached him around this time was a raincoat manufacturer known as Kagan Textiles, and because Stirling thought their raincoats were unique and practical, he agreed to endorse them. In fact, he wasn't the only person to wear this company's products – the Prime Minister of the day, Harold Wilson, also began to wear them. This company made rainwear under the brand name of Gannex. This was a type of nylon material, which was 100 per cent waterproof, although it was a little on the stiff side, and was normally backed with a black tartan type of material, which was bonded to the original waterproofed material. After a few meetings with owner Joseph Kagan (later to become Lord Kagan), a small, dark, stocky man, Stirling was happy to go along with the idea because he thought the garments would be terrifically handy in the cold and wet prevailing conditions at many of the circuits, and he thought it incredible that water would just bounce off the surface of the material whenever it teemed with rain. At one time, we even had a Gannex briefcase hanging around in the office!

It could never be said that Stirling was a hypocrite. He would only ever endorse products that he liked and thought were good enough for him personally to use. He certainly refused to put his name on anything just to make a quick buck. His main sponsorship came from BP and his face appeared on hundreds of advertising hoardings throughout the country. The BP (which probably wasn't any better than Esso, its main competitor) sponsorship not only paid him a set annual fee, but bonuses when he won races and they also paid for all the office petrol. This saved a tremendous amount of money and it wasn't any wonder that we would virtually always take the car somewhere rather than public transport. (From the age of sixty, Stirling travelled on the tube quite extensively for free with his Freedom Pass travelcard, and he always had a huge grin on his face when telling anyone about it. More than anyone he appreciated this perk.)

The cars and their upkeep were also totally free. If anything went wrong with a car on loan, I would make a quick telephone call and it would be picked up, repaired and returned to us for the duration.

• • •

By now, Stirling had become a columnist for the very trendy, new glossy magazine *NOVA* (now defunct), and he asked a young journalist on *Autosport* magazine to ghost the pieces for him. One night, this young man managed to write off rather an expensive piece of machinery that he was test driving on Stirling's behalf down the one-way Holbein Place, just off Sloane Square. Yet again, once Stirling had established that the journo was OK, he accepted the happening as being 'just one of those things' and left Ken and me to sort out the question of the insurance. His reaction to what other people might deem as 'panic stations' was always quite extraordinarily calm, cool and collected. I can't remember ever seeing him hot under the collar or bothered about anything he knew that he couldn't do anything about. And, he would hardly ever lose his temper, either. He might let off steam – and did – on many an occasion, but he hardly ever 'lost it' entirely.

All the while, the regular office procedures and tasks still had to be dealt with, such as booking hotels, confirming/changing flights, continuing researching equipment for the house and, for Stirling, personal appearances, and for me, dealing with the household chores and all the hundred and one other things which enabled his life to tick along smoothly. We were rather fortunate that members of the public very rarely telephoned the office, although they still wrote in in their hordes. Our telephone numbers were published quite openly in the public telephone directories, as it happens under both S and M for Stirling Moss Ltd and Moss, Stirling Ltd. Probably most people were under the impression that Stirling, being so well known, would be ex-directory, and never thought to look up the number in the normal way (for then).

OH, LORD!

Quite out of the blue, an envelope arrived in the post from the House of Lords, containing a letter asking Stirling to attend the inaugural meeting of an enterprise called Youth Ventures Ltd. I thought he would dismiss the invitation out of hand, but his curiosity was obviously aroused as he decided to go along to the gathering, taking me with him.

'I haven't been invited, so I can't go,' I protested.

'You are,' he said. 'I am inviting you and you can take notes for me.'

And so the two of us trolled up to a committee room in the House of Lords on the appointed date, at the appointed hour, and met the instigators of the meeting, Lords Stonham and Longford. It was explained to us by their Lordships that the purpose of Youth Ventures was to be a charitable enterprise to establish various clubs and venues around the country for young men, many of whom were becoming out of control and getting into a lot of trouble with the authorities since the demise of compulsory national service.

For some strange reason (which in all honesty could only have been because of his celebrity status), Stirling was asked to become a member of the board of Youth Ventures Ltd as indeed was Billy Butlin. Stirling was particularly hesitant to commit, especially after seeing the average age of the board and also because he knew himself well enough to know that he frankly would not have the patience to spend hours in a committee room going round and round in circles wasting his time on rhetoric. (That is not to say that the cause wasn't just; it was only a matter of his lack of time when in the country – and patience). He had been fairly and squarely put on the spot. But, his quick thinking was to save him yet again. He told the meeting that, due to his racing commitments, he would not have the time, let alone be physically in the country, to attend many meetings. He then suggested that he would lend his name to the company and I would represent him in his stead. Now their Lordships were put on the spot! Without any further discussion, the chairman of the meeting thanked Stirling and his offer was graciously accepted. In future, it was my destiny to attend all the meetings of Youth Ventures, whether Stirling was around or not. But, he did moan a lot when he was physically in the country and I had to go off to one. My reply would always be most unsympathetic and sarcastic.

'Well, if you want, you can go along instead.'

This remark was always met with a frustrated look of total exasperation.

It was one constant battle working alongside Stirling. If I hadn't stood up for myself he would have lost his respect for me, and the fact that he never did is probably one of the reasons why our friendship continued to flourish. Unfortunately, there were far too few people who did stand up to him. Most of them treated him as though they were wearing kid gloves – and that would be their downfall.

Why did I continue to swing along with all of this? Quite frankly, I never actually thought about it. Ostensibly, I was being pulled along by a strong undercurrent and it all seemed quite natural to go with the flow instead of fighting it. I wasn't really aware of the workload being so immense because one was always fighting one crisis or another. And, it was to become worse. Things eventually came to a head when Stirling was pushed to the very limits of his patience with the lack of progress on the site and he suddenly snapped, 'Right, now you are going to be foreman, Valerie.' (Uh-oh. That full name again. He means business and on no account will he be swayed.)

'Me? Foreman? I don't know anything about building,' I stated emphatically.

'Well, you'll soon learn,' he snapped back.

There was to be no argument and learn I did, in double-quick time.

SCOOTING AROUND

Somewhere during his travels after his accident at Spa, Stirling had come across a tiny motor scooter, which came in kit form (i.e. it was a self-assembly job), and he thought it would be incredibly useful for him to drive around London on it, doing his local chores, because he would be able to nip in and out of the traffic far quicker than on his normal scooter. He would also be able to use it in the paddock or chug out to some of the corners at the British circuits. The scooter, known as a Trobike, was so small that it would easily fit into a normal-size car boot or could be propped up on the back seat of a saloon car. (I think they cost about £60 back then, which was not exactly a bargain.) And, because he thought these scooters were so useful, he thought that everyone else would think so as well and that they would become extremely popular – a 'must-have' item – particularly for large conurbations. Consequently, before consulting anyone at all, he made it his business to acquire a Trobike concession/franchise for the London area. As so frequently happened, whenever he found something that he really liked, he would become tremendously enthusiastic and passionate about it and constantly talk about it to anyone and everyone who would listen to him. It would become his sole topic of his conversation other than motor racing or his house until something else attracted his attention, when he would move on and become passionate about that instead.

Such was his excitement about his mini scooter (because he instantly began driving it all around town) that he decided to apply to change the number plates to BRP777 (British Racing Partnership plus his favourite number: 7, which Ken had specifically acquired for the British Racing Partnership, I may say). By that time in his life, Stirling had already given up trying to obtain any of the SM number plates containing a 7, particularly SM7 which he was especially miffed about. The guy who owned the plate wouldn't part with it for love nor money, although Stirling did manage to acquire it many, many years later. He had also managed to obtain the number plate M7 around this time, with the help of Vic Winstone, the person who ran the NSU publicity in the UK. (I once asked the garage to put some anti-freeze into the NSU only to be looked at wide-eyed and told that it was air-cooled. Even then, I didn't cotton on!)

Once he had the BRP plates on the scooter, he personally set about calling up all the picture editors on the nationals and succeeded in persuading most of them to send their staff photographers round to Shepherd Street to take photographs of him riding his Trobike. He managed to obtain some really excellent publicity for the marque without it costing him a penny, though unfortunately all to no avail. The publicity didn't make a jot of difference. There were very few takers at all, the two main obstacles being that people didn't want the faff of putting a scooter together and the other being that many people considered them to be far too dangerous which, in a way, they were, being so small and near to the ground. Going around Hyde Park Corner on a Trobike, looking up at a big red London bus, was quite a new experience and could be compared to plankton looking up into the jaws of a whale.

The first problem could be easily resolved by paying someone else to assemble the scooters, but Stirling didn't actually want to pay anyone to do this because he felt the added cost to the basic price of the scooter would be prohibitive. Much as he would have enjoyed doing this job himself, it was not practical and this was one chore he knew that he could not put on me. I was useless at anything mechanical and I was continually asking him to mend things, such as my watch and other bits and bobs, which he did willingly, just for the challenge. However, the scooters were far too fiddly to put together and would have taken up far too much of his time pro rata to what he would have made out of them, so this was a complete no-go. He knew that I was seeing a driver, who seemed to have an awful lot of time on his hands, and Stirling, most unusually, started to positively encourage my friendship with him and made it known that he could call round at any time he liked to Shepherd Street. My friend eventually bought a Trobike from Stirling so he knew how to assemble them and afterwards he offered to build a couple more for him in the Shepherd Street garage, which again created quite a bit of interest from passers-by, but still no further sales.

There was absolutely nothing we could do about the perceived problem of the Trobikes being dangerous, even though they complied with all the rules of the road, and Stirling always worried about me when I was out on his because he knew that I was continually falling off the darned thing. I used to balance a large rectangular wicker basket on one of the handles and would forget that it was there. As a result, when I went around a corner, it would get tangled up with the wheel and I would fall sideways, into the road. In fact, Stirling banned me from riding the bike altogether in the rain, but I didn't take much notice. When the cat's away...

The Trobike phase only lasted a very short time and then another fad took precedence and making money out of Trobikes became an ignominious, forgotten pastime.

My friend who had helped him out with the Trobikes also asked me if I would like to go with him to a race in Austria, which would mean asking Stirling for some time off. I waited until I thought the time was ripe and he was in a good mood and asked if I could go off for a few days. Although he immediately agreed, he went to some length to try to discourage me from going and, in the end, I somewhat reluctantly decided to take his advice. I later found out that I wasn't the only chick on the prairie and Stirling knew this and didn't want me to get hurt. It was just as well because I was already beginning to lose my heart to this man and, in the long run, Stirling's way was for the best.

MORE CRUMPET

Once he started dating again after his separation from Katie, Stirling met a very charming model, who had classic, high cheekbones, wonderful long, dark chestnut hair and a very charming personality. She also starred in one of the Fry's Turkish Delight TV advertisements of the day, when she was pictured being swept up by some handsome man riding a dusky stallion in the desert, who galloped off with her. She had a good sense of humour and always seemed to put a smile on Stirling's face. For a person of her particular status, one would never have imagined that she would be able to produce a real workman's whistle through her fingers and she came out to the airport with me one evening to pick up Stirling. I encouraged her to produce one such whistle just as he emerged into the old waiting area, followed by a horde of cameramen. The whistle pierced the air and, as everyone looked round to see who had done it, we immediately ducked down behind one of the old sofas. Was he ever embarrassed?

The two of them never lost contact until she became hitched to someone else, but she was one of about five or six of his girlfriends with whom I kept in regular touch over the years.

Another vivacious girl, who Stirling first met in Nassau and with whom he went out for quite a long while, was a redhead with porcelain-white skin. She took us all by surprise, though, when she suddenly upped and married an American two weeks after she had met him! He was about thirty years older than her and, needless to say, the marriage didn't last very long. She stayed around in London until she went to live in New York and some years later we learnt that she and her mother had committed suicide together in Australia.

German motor races provided a good selection of crumpet for Stirling over the years and, as per usual, most of those he escorted were also models. He seemed to go for raven-haired, well-tanned beauties with the very pale pink lipstick that was the fashion of the day. The less make-up a girl wore, the better he liked it.

One afternoon, a German girlfriend of Stirling's rang up and asked if she could pop round for a cup of tea, which she did, but the look on her face later that evening was to be seen to be believed when I came face to face with her again in the Westbury Hotel! I had arranged to make up a foursome with Lucky Casner and a friend of his for dinner and, as it turned out, Lucky was to be her date for the evening! She completely froze when she saw me walk in but my face remained a complete mask. She never forgot it and she could never thank me enough.

Another fun person of whom Stirling became extraordinarily fond was the actress Judy Carne, who he met whilst she was in a musical in the West End of London. Completely outrageous, she was an absolute scream, which, normally, would have been totally out of Stirling's comfort zone, but he didn't seem to mind because she had the gift of being able to lift his spirits, whatever mood he was in. She was a laugh a minute and he even allowed her little dog to stay in the house when they went out together in the evenings. She was a hoot and she didn't have a bad thought in her head. She was extremely kind and the only fly in Stirling's ointment was that she was very ambitious and had set her mind and heart on going to Hollywood. She was quite adamant about it and no amount of persuasion on his part or anyone else's would change her mind. It was an extremely sad day when we said goodbye to her, but she promised to keep in touch, which she did. She also succeeded in making quite a name for herself in the US as the 'Sock-It-to-Me Girl' in *Rowan & Martin's Laugh-In*. She ended up marrying one of the young screen idols of the day, Burt Reynolds. The marriage only lasted a couple of years and the strain probably encouraged her to boost her confidence artificially. This habit eventually caught up with her. Some years later, she was arrested and Stirling was very supportive of her.

There was, though, one girlfriend of Stirling's who I really could not stand. She was a New Zealander and also a model, I think. He was very keen on her for a while and it was the first and last time that I actively tried to sabotage one of his liaisons. I knew that she was totally wrong for him and I would never want to see him suffer the anguish of another emotional parting of the ways although, in hindsight, it was a shame that I did not act on another, future occasion – but that particular woman was probably smarter than all of us. Personally, I could never understand why Stirling was so infatuated with Miss New Zealand, for that was what he was, but distance was to be my ally and so she gradually drifted off the scene and out of his life.

Another really lovely person who dated Stirling was Shirlee, an extremely good-looking American air hostess he had met on a flight in America, who had a particularly cute, turned-up nose. Unfortunately, the relationship was again doomed on the grounds of distance, which was a real shame but someone else took a fancy to her in the air and this someone was even better known in the world than Stirling. He was an equally nice person, one of the great Hollywood screen idols of the old school, very unassuming and natural in his personal life: Henry Fonda. He liked to keep well away from the limelight as much as he could, once away from the screen and stage at that period in his life, and the couple seemed to live a wonderfully, peaceful and retiring existence together until his death at the age of seventy-seven. Whenever they came over to London, they would ring me up and we would meet up for a chat and a cup of coffee. On one occasion, they rented Tony Curtis's London flat and were amazed to see so many photographs of the owner displayed on almost every surface there – and so was I!

On the couple of occasions that I went to New York, I would visit their house on 84th Street East and I once telephoned them at their home in California. It was 9 a.m. New York time and the phone was answered by a very sleepy-sounding Henry. He was, as usual, his charming self and he actually thanked *me* for waking him because he said that he had to be on set early. The time in California was 6 a.m. and I had been quite oblivious to the fact there were time differences across the States. I really felt dreadful.

Just like many of Stirling's other girlfriends, Shirlee kept in touch until after her husband died, the last communication being an invitation to his funeral, which I did not attend.

On another occasion, an old girlfriend of Stirling's who I knew reasonably well poked her nose into the office quite unannounced. Stirling, trying not to show that he was rather nettled at her popping in without telephoning first, suggested that we both go upstairs and make a cup of tea in the kitchen. Whilst the kettle was boiling, I asked her if she had tried taking part in any Ouija sessions, Ouija being all the rage in London at the time, mainly amongst women. She hadn't, so we wrote out the alphabet on small pieces of paper and we had just put the letters in a circle when we heard the pitter-patter of feet flying up the stairs, obviously Stirling coming to find out why we were taking so long. There wasn't time to do anything other than to try to hide the offending evidence of what we were doing, which of course was quite impossible. Obviously guilt was written all over our faces as the kitchen door flew wide open.

Intrigued at what we were up to, I couldn't believe my ears when Stirling asked if he could join in. We put an upturned wine glass in the middle of the redistributed circle of letters we had placed on the counter and each of us put the tip of a finger on the flat bottom at the end of the stem on the wine glass we were using, and waited. Almost immediately, the glass began to whizz round the letters haphazardly but when it began to spell out the Christian name of another of Stirling's girlfriends, he accused me of pushing the glass and told me to take my finger off it, which I did, protesting my innocence loudly. For some unknown reason, probably due to him, the glass still continued to spell out the other girlfriend's name and he was pretty mortified.

A WAGER

And so life continued. The more popular Stirling became in the eyes of the public, the more there was to do in the office and, yet again, there began to be a conflict of priorities. I could not be doing chores for him during the day at the same time as acting as anchorman in the office and scrambling around, trying to get through all the other bits and pieces in the time available. In addition, trying to execute my site foreman duties of constantly keeping a beady eye on what the workmen were up to could also have become all-time consuming if I had let it. One plus point was that I did begin to learn an awful lot about building-related issues.

Stirling was becoming increasingly desperate about the continuing lack of progress on the unfinished house but, ever the constant perfectionist, he refused to let his standards slip. We had more or less reached stalemate with the workers and, in sheer frustration, he decided to advertise yet again in the *Standard* for a handyman – and this time we struck gold.

Wally was an ex-merchant seaman and Stirling felt that he would be completely honest, which was always a problem when hiring ad hoc journeymen. He was an amiable character all round and thankfully he wasn't a clock watcher. He wasn't the quickest worker in the world, but he would never fail to admit that he was stuck, or when he thought he had come up against a brick wall, and would come looking to find one of us to discuss the problem and hopefully come up with an answer. And that is all that Stirling ever really asked of a person. He would far rather people asked whenever they got into a fix rather than struggle on regardless and ultimately get things wrong and then have to right them afterwards. Frankly, we could not believe our luck – or at least I couldn't, because it was me who was left to deal with Wally on a day-to-day basis. Gradually, as he became increasingly adept, we managed to get rid of most of the other workers apart from what I would call the real specialists and, with Wally keeping an ever-watchful eye on them as well when I was busy with my own work, things started to edge forward ever so slightly.

One could be forgiven for thinking that the erection of the new build in Shepherd Street was occupying rather more of both Stirling's and my time than anything else. It was. Halfway through the Shepherd Street construction, the whole of a very large block of buildings at the bottom end of Park Lane was demolished to make way for a new Hilton Hotel, which was to be built on the site. It was absolutely fascinating to watch the monstrous concrete balls, hanging like conkers at the end of a string and swaying on the end of dinosaurian cranes, smashing into buildings and toppling them. There developed quite a rivalry and our Wally had a wager with the Hilton workmen on whose building would be finished first. Unfortunately, there was no contest. The Hilton building force won hands down!

Stirling continued to research and follow through items for the house and during his travels he had ordered some specially frosted glass to be painted with cyclamen-coloured Japanese blossom for his headboard. He had already decided to have a scarlet rabbit-skin bedspread made for the especially large bed that he had ordered to be made for him, with the skins being provided by his father, and a friend in the fur trade offering to get them dyed and the spread made up for him. (At one stage, Stirling even thought of ordering a round bed but over the course of time he went off the idea.) Of course, the glass headboard arrived in one enormous oblong piece and it was so large that it was impossible to carry it up the circular staircase so it had to be returned to the depot until we managed to order a special type of suction crane to transfer it up to the third floor of the new house. One of the bedroom windows had to be removed completely and the crane operator, who was obviously a very experienced old hand, managed to expertly manoeuvre the glass lengthwise through the rather small hole that had been left. My heart was in my mouth as I watched its progress. Stirling was away, thankfully.

FILED UNDER

Once the floor in my new office had been carpeted, it became my filing cabinet and it was scattered with different piles of paper, which I would later file when I had the time. Quite often visitors en route to Stirling's office would bend down thoughtfully to pick up the sheets of paper they obviously thought had floated down from my desk. This would be met with howls of indignation from myself because, if the paperwork was touched, it would entirely upset my filing system. I suppose this method of filing could have been described as organised chaos, but it worked rather well and, surprisingly, Stirling never ever said a word about it, probably because he realised that I, too, was always under considerable strain and he didn't want to rock the boat. I found out many years later that he thought the mess was totally and utterly appalling. It was completely at variance to his naturally tidy, masculine nature and the fact that he somehow managed to maintain a dignified silence for so many years, all in a good cause, says much for his character. If it was prudent for him to remain silent and remain patient all in a good cause, he would programme himself to do so. It speaks reams about the amount of paperwork we processed and equally it speaks reams for his self-control.

Some evenings I would still be doing the filing at midnight when the doorbell would ring and I would find one of 'Les Girls' from the area, who had seen the light on, just checking to see that I was alright. One actually sent her maid round – in daylight – to ask for Stirling's autograph when she was leaving London to marry one of her clients who had a large estate somewhere in the Home Counties. Stirling more than happily obliged.

Shortly after this incident, a woman in Shepherd Street – a resident – stopped me in the road and offered to give me some uncalled-for advice; which was never to speak to any of 'that type of women'. I was pretty upset with her interference, particularly because she had never spoken to me before – although we were both residents in the same street – and I told her exactly what I thought of her suggestion. When I told Stirling about it he was equally furious as well and told me to steer clear of her in future. He was never one to stand on ceremony and couldn't be doing with any interfering old busybodies or bigots.

Rather naturally, he was never euphoric whenever he arrived back at Shepherd Street to find out, in his opinion, how little had been done on the house. I would, of course, be instantly demoted to assistant foreman and made to follow him round constantly, making notes to chase up this, that and the other for whenever he went away again. Once more, the pressure of managing the office, the house and the building along with running around all over the place and my own highly active social life began to take its toll on me. Something had to give and I felt that he would be far better off if he found someone else to run the house for him, particularly as there was now a constant stream of crumpet drifting through it whenever he was in the country. We had to find a housekeeper. Once again, choosing my time very carefully and when he seemed to be in a more receptive mood than normal, I suggested that it was about time that he should employ a housekeeper. He actually didn't need much persuasion because he could see that it really would make a lot more sense, so the next priority was to transform the basement of the new house into living accommodation and to look for the 'Chosen One'.

Advertisements were put in *The Lady* and about half a dozen women applied for the post. Once again, we did not state who the position was for and we had to be careful that anyone we employed would be exceedingly discreet, frugal and fairly open-minded. We found the perfect person in an extremely small, shy, mousey-looking person from Llandrindod Wells, who seemed to blend in with all that went on without really being noticed at all by anyone. She cut a very lonely figure and I always felt rather sorry for her because she had an aura of sadness about her. She was an excellent cook and kept house admirably whilst going around virtually unnoticed. But, even she began to tire of the merry-go-round of (rather high-handed and mostly ungrateful) women imported into the house night after night. After a while she was replaced by someone the complete opposite, although the very next appointee only stayed a week, such was her opinion of the set-up! This third housekeeper we chose was a woman of reduced circumstances and, although she was extremely efficient, she really had problems coming to terms with her newfound social status.

NO PRIZES FOR GUESSING WHO

Wally and I continued to beaver away in the house. Whilst clearing out the basement for the housekeeper, I had come across a really attractive trophy that had obviously been presented to Stirling at some stage, which someone had just left perched on some of the shelving. It was in a green leather box with two 'front-opening doors' and once I had opened it up, I saw inside that it contained a bronze of galloping horses. I stared at it for a moment, mesmerised, because it was absolutely beautiful and then I had a thought. I asked Wally to put it in the minute garden area behind Stirling's office at the back of the house, in front of the goldfish pond, and we would see how long it took Stirling to notice the addition. (Alongside all my other duties, I had to feed the goldfish once a week, which involved climbing out of a garage window into the pocket-handkerchief-sized garden.)

About a week later, Stirling noticed the trophy and thought it was such an excellent idea that he felt it would look even better if he had some little wrought-iron gates made, through which the horses could permanently leap. Once the gates had been added and the rest of the garden landscaped, it made a really good focal point. This was one of the very few trophies of his that I ever saw in my entire life. I never did know what he did with all the others – they were probably at the farm or in one of Alfred's numerous safes. At one stage, Stirling did think of having all his silver trophies melted down and made into a coffee table, which would have been extraordinarily heavy, but it was another idea which never got off the ground.

Out of sheer devilment, I was constantly testing to see what Stirling's reaction would be to certain things I would do in the house. For example, I put a small china cat that someone had sent him as a doorstop in the first-floor lounge (as it was called) next to the kitchen, which he totally ignored and it stayed there, innocuously, on the floor for decades. On another occasion, I asked Wally to erect his twisted and bent steering wheel from his accident at Spa, which I had found somewhere in the house, over the door of his office which led into the garage. I was frightfully disappointed that Stirling never gave me the satisfaction of knowing whether I had either irritated him or he thought that it was a good idea. He went one better later on, though, after his last accident at Goodwood. When I came in one morning, I found that he had put up his mangled red-rimmed Goodwood wheel next to his mangled red-rimmed Spa wheel – and I never said a word either. His sense of humour was obviously improving and he was beginning to take himself a little less seriously, which was all very good news.

SAFETY FIRST

Stirling was often looked upon by the other drivers to provide direction when it was called for and he increasingly took it upon his shoulders to be their spokesman with the various governing bodies, the main subject generally being the safety of all the drivers. He was such a sincere person that if he believed in something, it would never embarrass him to put the point across, however contentious it was at the time – a habit he developed at school. The individuals running the official body for motor racing were mostly full of their own importance (to put it politely) and had very little regard for anyone or anything.

For some time, Stirling had been concerned about the frequency and swelling numbers of deaths amongst the drivers on the circuits and, although he was certainly no trade unionist, he thought that the best thing to do would be to form an association. Its main aim would be to improve the safety and facilities at the circuits, as well as dealing with finance and the opportunity for the drivers to have a say on the rules of the sport.

He thought long and hard about what the organisation should be called and we discussed it endlessly together because he did not want the word 'Union' appearing in the title.* He eventually came up with Grand Prix Drivers' Association (GPDA). He called a meeting of all the Formula One drivers and invited them to discuss his proposals and most of them agreed in principle. (There's always at least one who doesn't.) The association was officially registered and Stirling was elected as its first president. It progressively became a beneficial force behind the drivers for many years to come.

Stirling's differences with his old friend – and subsequent god-father to his son – Jackie Stewart about the erection of Armco crash barriers on certain parts of the circuits have been well documented throughout the years and Stirling always agreed to disagree with Jackie about it. Stirling always held the view that one could have too much of a good thing and that too much Armco, to some degree, took the competitive edge out of the sport. On the other hand, it has to be said that Armco has prevented one or two deaths on the circuits and this does rather prove a point. However, Stirling being Stirling, he was always adamant that competitive drivers should be able to drive according to their own capabilities, which included slowing down or stopping altogether if they could not manage the conditions.

For example, he was simply disgusted when the organisers of a race in the Antipodes decided to stop a race, which he happened to be leading at the time, because of a torrential downpour of rain. He said that professional drivers should be able to cope with whatever challenges are thrown down in front of them whilst participating in a race, in this particular case, aquaplaning. He felt that it was 'all for

---

* There had been some such before but it was dead from the feet upwards.

one and one for all' in certain adverse conditions, be it heavy rain or tremendous heat, because the conditions are exactly the same for everyone. In his opinion, it separated the men from the boys, and that was the name of the game in his book. Also, he always said that psychologically to take a corner which should be taken flat became quite a different kettle of fish when bordered by a tight brick wall on one side and a row of trees on the other.

The fact that he won that particular race hands down once it had been restarted held very little satisfaction for him. He had already had his buzz before the race was stopped from showing everyone that he was far superior to everyone else in the competition and that he was able to cope with such atrocious conditions with hardly a bat of his eyelid.

I think his views did mellow a bit in later life because he would accept that a race should be slowed down by a safety car being sent out to hold the cars in position until an obstacle could be removed or cleared from the circuit, simply because those were the rules. Fortunately, they were not in operation during his time on the circuits because I am quite positive that, had they been, we would never have heard the end of it.

TRICKS UP HIS SLEEVE

Without stress, Stirling's life would have been empty and, if there wasn't any, he would create some. He revelled in being busy all of his waking hours. Stress was part of his life except when he was sitting behind the wheel of a racing car where, apart from the g-force, the only stress he experienced was that of warding off any other competitor until he had passed the chequered flag (preferably having won the race if he possibly could). His confidence in himself and his own abilities was second to none, and was all part of his character because he genuinely believed that he was the only person capable of doing anything perfectly, but he was far too inhibited to extol his own virtues. For example, in normal life, he would never consult instruction manuals. In fact, he would totally refuse to look at them because he knew that he would be able to work out how everything functioned himself – eventually – or at least he thought he could.

Even when he was competing in inferior cars, he would never think that the cause was lost before it even began. Quite the contrary. He would relish having to work that much harder to prove to everyone that he really was the best driver on the day and that it was possible to win a race in an inferior vehicle. He enjoyed showing off his prowess and proving that he could literally cut corners to be recognised and acknowledged as being the skilful and dedicated driver that he was. This could be considered as being terribly cocky, but he was far too modest ever to say that he was the best. As far as he was concerned, he never needed to shout about being the most talented driver around because he was content in the knowledge that he was – and that was sufficient for him. He was never smug. He just wanted to beat any obstacles that stood in his way, including cars potentially mechanically faster than his own, and improve on his capabilities. He always saw some room for development in his driving skills and a win on the day would be his bonus. He was success's biggest fan by far.

Stirling always relished the competition and, to some extent, he enjoyed being regarded as the underdog who could and – on many occasions – would, achieve the 'impossible'. When he was racing, his face would become a mask of concentration and his stubbornness and determination would become apparent for all to see.

He knew that he always had to have something up his sleeve and, if hoodwinking the other drivers came into the game, so be it. This was true in his life as well. He was an incredibly fast thinker; he could be crafty and cunning. He would drive to the limit of both his and his car's capabilities (or what he was told they were i.e. given rev limits, etc.), but he would never have been able to achieve this entirely by himself. He had to have good back-up and proficient teamwork. Sound preparation of his cars was essential. And, he also had to have the technical knowledge and be able to discuss and, on occasions, argue his point with his mechanics. He had started from the bottom rung of the ladder, using his own money, and had learnt on the job. Whether or not this was a good thing is perhaps a moot point, given his intractability. But, good or bad, this was a fact.

Being totally driven, he could, at times, be utterly ruthless and yet, on other occasions, utterly charming and humane. Because his brain never stopped working, he always found it difficult to sleep and that is probably why he liked to stay up until the early hours of the morning.

He made it his business to know all the rules of motor racing inside out and backwards, and would use them to his own advantage if need be – which he did on several occasions. Once, he tricked Masten Gregory by 'fair' means through his thorough knowledge of the rules and, although Masten called 'Foul!' Stirling was declared the winner. Masten was beyond furious but, before they came to blows after the race, Stirling suggested that they pool all their prize money to split it 50/50 and scarper, which they did. They were in Latin America at the time where things could blow up quite unexpectedly and suddenly or could often be taken the wrong way viz the kidnapping of Fangio in Cuba.

On this particular occasion, Masten had been ahead of Stirling in the race when the marshals began waving red flags. Masten slowed right down and Stirling overtook him, knowing full well that the only person who could stop the race with a red flag was the clerk of the course and, with Stirling crossing the finishing line first, he was obviously declared the winner. In fact, Stirling was once carted off in an ambulance in Argentina after having stopped out on the circuit before he could make them understand that he was not hurt. Once he eventually arrived back at the circuit, he rejoined the race!

If belief in oneself and one's ability equates to egotism, then Stirling was an egotist. His struggle for perfection in all things was his *raison d'être*. It was reflected in every single thing he did. His dedication and self-belief was second to none and he was quite capable of calling on stamina and endurance of quite unreal proportions in short spurts. He would will himself on if need be for as long as it was necessary. Stirling possessed courage as well as a sense of fear and, above all, a respect for danger. His happy-go-lucky façade, which he put on for the other drivers before a race, was strictly calculated because he was aware that such confidence would undermine and unnerve them. He had the knack of hardly ever showing what he was truly feeling inside.

A few of his tactics could sometimes have been considered as being slightly borderline, as illustrated above, yet, to all intents and purposes, they were completely legal. He could outwit many of the other drivers most of the time and his refusal ever to give up a fight was renowned. His competitiveness was such that he would, if humanly practical, do virtually anything to win – apart from cheating.

He would never give up whenever there was even the slightest chance of succeeding. If his car broke down and there was any possibility of him being placed in a race, rather than merely retiring, he would push the car – sometimes halfway round a circuit – just to cross the finishing line. He would never just give up on the spot and throw in the towel. I don't remember any other driver who would do this. It certainly was not done for show; it was done because retirement to him meant complete and utter failure, and sometimes he was rewarded with points for pushing the car across the finishing line in a point-winning place.

In fact, his character was always at odds with itself. For one who could be so vulnerable, so honest and so volatile when pushed in ordinary life about ridiculous or inconsequential matters, when racing, he was tough inside the veneer of equitability and calm. He was also the same when dealing with the larger problems in everyday life, whenever and wherever they cropped up.

PART THREE

HITTING THE HEIGHTS AND THE AFTERMATH

IN A TIGHT CORNER

The 1961 season was to be Stirling's busiest ever and, by the time the first world championship event came along on 14 May in Monaco, he had already competed in no fewer than eighteen races, including one in the infamously badly prepared Camoradi Birdcage Maserati Tipo at Sebring. This time, the car sustained a flat battery on the start line, which resulted in Stirling starting the race some six minutes down on the rest of the field after the battery had been changed. Naturally, he was working his way quite quickly through the pack when the exhaust system broke and he had to retire the car. He was exceedingly irritated by such poor preparation yet again, and let Lucky Casner know about it in no uncertain terms. He swore, once more, never to drive again for Camoradi. But, of course, when it was prepared properly, the car was very quick in his hands and Lucky's charm was equally devastating.

The Monaco Grand Prix was to prove the ultimate test of Stirling's virtuosity and doggedness. He was pitted against the strength and might of an extraordinarily strong and powerful Ferrari team and yet, during the race, he drove every lap quicker than the time that he had put up to qualify for pole position. Lap after lap, the Ferraris snapped at his exhaust and roared in his slipstream and, lap after lap, he held them at bay. For him, it was supreme. Stirling was driving at more than ten-tenths for the entire race, outwitting the opposition and driving to the car's very limits. The exhilaration and thrill of that contest and subsequent victory would stay with him eternally.

There was to be no stopping him that year but, yet again, the world championship would elude him because, despite how hard he had driven on the tight Monaco circuit in the Lotus, he would not be able to frustrate and thwart the dominance of the Ferraris, especially at some of the quicker circuits, where he would be literally powerless to do anything. Whatever work his mechanics could legally do on the engine, it was impossible to obtain improved, or even comparable, power output to those fitted in the Ferraris. At the faster circuits, where there were long straights, he had his work cut out just to keep up with them. Unfortunately, there was nothing that anyone could do about this lack of power except hope that the opposition would fail to finish. Even today, a driver can't do very much if his engine is down on power, however skilful he may be. After the Monaco Grand Prix, it was downhill all the way for Stirling driving in the Épreuves, the exception being the German Grand Prix, which that year was held on the twisting and undulating Nürburgring circuit. Stirling did manage to set up the fastest lap in many of the other championship races (although since the end of 1959 the point awarded for fastest lap was abolished; it only lasted two years) and went on to win many more non-championship events. In fact he won the most ever, but yet again, the crown would avoid his grasp.

Many people might wonder why, if he was able to put up the fastest lap in a race, he could not sustain this and win the race itself. Quite simply (and not to get too technical), it is down to sustainability, not his, but the car's – the stress and the strain on it. Long straights, particularly today, benefit the more powerful (and lower aerodynamic drag) cars. Basically, the more corners there are on a circuit, the more it benefits a skilful driver and a car that handles well. Most people can put their foot down on a straight, but it is the speed through the corners that sorts the men from the boys, even when an engine is down on power. It is the ability of the driver to make the corners work to his advantage.

If a driver can get a 'tow' in the vacuum or slipstream created by the car in front of his, the faster his car will immediately become (because it is sucked into the vacuum). In Stirling's era, the cars were not as reliant on downforce as today's F1 cars. Consequently, it was possible to use the benefits of the tow on the straights to keep up with or even overtake a more powerful car. However, if the power difference is too big and the straights too long, it makes it harder to keep up with the higher-powered cars. The same went for the corners, although Stirling also had to out-brake the competition (amongst other things) to maintain his superiority.

On the topic of modern cars, there are now some gimmicks to aid overtaking. Apparently, it is very hard to follow another car into a corner without losing downforce and aerodynamic balance. Consequently, the drivers can deploy additional electric power (from special power units) and use the drag reduction system (DRS) in one or two designated areas on the circuit, on the condition that they are within one second of the car in front. This substantially reduces the aerodynamic drag, thus increasing the speed differential to the car in front, thus potentially aiding overtaking.

During the year, Stirling also seized the opportunity to drive the new, four-wheel-drive single-seater Ferguson P99 Formula One car at Oulton Park in Cheshire, in a race that he ended up winning. The P99 had been designed as a research vehicle, the intent being to demonstrate the advantages and reliability of such a system (being four-wheel drive) and it was an extraordinary achievement for a new car to win such a prestigious event. The car had a front-mounted Coventry Climax four-cylinder engine and Dunlop Maxaret ABS (anti-lock braking system) brakes. Stirling had earlier in the season taken over driving the car from Jack Fairman in the wet British Grand Prix at Aintree after his Lotus broke down and, once again, he began to make up for lost time, weaving his way through the traffic. Eventually, he was black-flagged for not having qualified the car in practice and was disqualified. Nevertheless, he set up a new lap record with the Ferguson for 1.5-litre cars and, after this race, four-wheel drive F1 motors were banned for good. Needless to say, Stirling loved the P99.

DUTCH UNCLE

Not long after we had moved into the new offices, Stirling met an American who he came to admire greatly. But, at the same time he was also totally overawed by Ken Purdy.

Ken was a well-known American author and journalist, who was probably rather better known for the straight short stories he wrote for *Playboy* magazine every month than his articles in numerous other specialist motoring publications and books. He had a full head of white hair, neatly trimmed into a longish crew cut; a sallow, lined complexion, a cute upturned nose and a soft New England accent. He wore round spectacles and a lovely smile, and he must have been exceedingly handsome in his youth. Added to this, he was incredibly intelligent and knowledgeable. All in all, Ken was charm personified. He became quite a regular caller at Shepherd Street and was one of only a 'chosen few' who were allowed to turn up at the office without a prior appointment. I can't remember whether or not he ever telephoned to let us know that he was going to blow in, which rather suggests that he did not. Naturally, Stirling would always grumble when Ken popped his nose in through the door but, in truth, he was always delighted to see him because Ken was also a very quiet, deep-thinking and rather personal man. I believe that Stirling identified with him on many counts. He also admired Ken because he considered him to be a bit of a genius. Both were modest men, who liked to keep themselves to themselves. Ken was a person of mixed metaphors but, even so, a solid, reliable and often fun man to be around.

Imagine, one lovely afternoon when Stirling and I were working quietly together, him in his office and me in mine, when I answered the phone only to hear a hysterical female voice screaming down the line. It was a voice I did not recognise. I couldn't really make out head nor tail of what she was on about and Stirling was signalling to me to ask who was it and what was it all about? Even he could hear the somewhat muffled yet frenzied, high-pitched voice from his office. I shrugged my shoulders, asked the woman to hold on, put my hand over the mouthpiece and quickly explained that she seemed to be going on about someone who, she claimed, Stirling had suggested she should invite round to her place for lunch. Apparently, after lunch, he had tried to seduce her and he was now lying on the floor, dead drunk. Stirling looked askance and mouthed, 'What can I do about it?'

I shrugged my shoulders again and said, 'How the hell do I know?' whilst transferring the call to his office.

It transpired that the woman on the end of the phone was an old friend of Stirling's (of whom I had never heard at the time) and that, on Stirling's instigation, she had invited Ken to lunch. They had both had a few glasses of wine with their meal after which she said that

Ken had really got stuck into her brandy, with the ensuing result. Quite what she expected Stirling to do about it was anyone's guess and Stirling was clearly not going to put himself out about it one iota, but he did suggest that she should try to calm down and then bundle Ken into a taxi and pay the taxi driver to take him home. Ever the practical man.

The next time that Ken Purdy ambled into the office, not a word was said about the incident and Ken and Stirling later collaborated on a very successful book together, *All But My Life*. Ken died tragically a few years after it was published.

TIME, GENTLEMEN, PLEASE!

Often Stirling would join a little group of friends, of whom I was one, who met mainly on Sunday lunchtimes most weekends if there wasn't any racing on. The Lowndes Arms pub was situated between Eaton and Belgrave Squares (alas no more – the pub, not the Squares). The group consisted of a *mélange* of fairly normal, down-to-earth people with loose connections to motor sport, who either lived in London or in the near suburbs (such suburbs are now included as being part of Greater London).

Despite its location, it wasn't a particularly posh pub. Stirling quite enjoyed tagging along and being part of a crowd of 'normal' people for a change. No one in the pub ever considered him to be anything other than an 'ordinary chap' doing what most males did in their spare time, albeit Stirling's poison was a bitter lemon. The nicotine-fingered, beer-drinking workmen, who were there even on Sundays, with their soft caps rolled up in their hands in the public bar (through which one had to pass to enter the lounge bar), would not take the slightest bit of notice of him and Stirling was, for a change, able to enjoy just being his natural self within our group without being pestered by anyone. No one ever kow-towed to him and if he wanted to get a word in edgeways, he had to make an effort to have his say just like everyone else did. He joined in the banter and would even laugh at himself and was happy to be laughed at; no one in the group was ever spared.

Once the pub closed at 2 p.m. the group tended to stay together and drift off for a roast lunch at the home of one of the members, each of whom would take it in turns to host the meal. Everyone would muck in and lend a hand, Stirling included. His speciality was carving (no doubt learnt in the hotel trade as a commis chef) because it demanded perfection and, needless to say, he always made an excellent job of it. He would also make a big fuss about the fact that he did not eat garlic in anything because he said that he didn't like it. Most of the 'cooks', however, didn't take a blind bit of notice and would subtly include some whenever they thought it would enhance a dish and, naturally, he never once noticed, such was their expertise – or his ignorance.

The surroundings never bothered him, either. One couple lived in a fairly grotty, one-roomed garret in Earl's Court and he would happily perch on whatever was available, be it the bed or a stool or even the floor. He would also take his turn in inviting people to Shepherd Street, where I would do the honours and, although most people brought their own, he would shell out for wine, even though he didn't drink it.

● ● ●

By this stage in Stirling's career (and despite his earlier claims never to work with him again), he and Enzo Ferrari had settled some long-running scores, and the 'Old Man' had agreed to build an F1 car to Stirling's specifications for the 1963 season to be entered, run and maintained by the RRC Walker Racing Team in its Scottish racing colours of dark blue. There was nothing really around to touch the dominance and strength of the Formula One Ferraris and, although Stirling – being very patriotic and pro-British – was torn between driving a winning Italian car and a non-competitive British one, which he had been doing for the last couple of years, he was in an invidious situation because time was marching on – he would be thirty-four later on that year – and he really wanted to have a crack at the world championship in a truly competitive car. Stirling was to continue competing in Rob's Lotus until such time as the Ferrari was delivered, and around this time there was at least a faint rainbow shining on the horizon hiding that elusive pot of gold.

CAMP FOLLOWER

A couple of weeks before Easter 1962, a delightful American called George De Carvalho, arrived at Stirling's office in Shepherd Street. He was a mature man, tall and good-looking, in a craggy yet distinctive way, and his manners were second to none. He was quietly spoken and a total delight.

For his sins, George, a Pulitzer prize winner, had been assigned by *Time* magazine in New York to find out precisely what Stirling was like in real life, so to speak. He was to write the leading article for them on the first ever *professional* racing driver in the history of motor sport to be featured on their front cover. No other driver, not even a world champion, had ever appeared on the front cover of *Time*, and it was always deemed to be a great honour to be so featured. Such was *Time*'s editorial policy that this 'blurb' always had to be a fantastically in-depth piece about the featured personality and, on this occasion, George had drawn the short straw and had been specially sent over from America to find out what made Stirling tick. And so, George had arrived on the doorstep.

George was a particularly calm person; he never seemed to get ruffled or fazed by anything – although at times over the next couple of weeks his patience would be sorely tested. Stirling was rather impolite to him simply because he didn't want George hanging around him full stop, and poor George couldn't help it because it was his job to literally shadow him wherever he went.

Now, one of the things about George was that he was not particularly fleet of foot. He walked at a normal pace; he talked at a normal pace; he was just a regular kind of guy so, initially, Stirling found the whole operation to be utterly frustrating. Instead of completely ignoring George, he found his presence to be an intrusion into his privacy and a hindrance to his way of life (mainly because George couldn't keep up with him). His irritation grew until he became totally intolerant of the man and was sometimes downright rude to him. Of course, the problem had intensified because Stirling simply loathed being in the company of someone he didn't know at all for about eighteen hours a day every day, and especially someone who was so relatively slow in everything he did compared to himself. Day by day, he continued to become shorter and shorter with George until he finally blew his top in the office.

George let the fire rage and when it had abated he calmly had a quiet word with Stirling, insisting that he must, and should, do his own thing and ignore his presence entirely. George told Stirling to totally forget that he existed and that he should never consider him in any way at all. This was quite alien to Stirling because he was normally a naturally polite young man. George also said, in the nicest possible way, that he would try to merge into the background much more than before, but that he would continue to tag along because that was his job and Stirling had agreed to it. In other words, George recommended that Stirling should pretend that he didn't exist as he gently reminded him that he was being paid for George to hang around with him.

The next couple of days were hard on both of them; after this, though, they began to get on like a house on fire and really did become the very best of friends in a very short while. The transformation was quite remarkable. They acted like old chums together and what could have resulted in a total disaster was averted by a few sensible words from George.

The first time in his life that George ever attended a motoring event was at a race meeting at Snetterton in Norfolk. He instantly became an aficionado as he watched Stirling drive his Formula One car, lap after lap, until he had to retire, due to mechanical problems. Nevertheless, Stirling did manage to break the lap record in the car that day.

George was in his element when he came back to London. Attending a race meeting had given him a splendid insight into the flavour of the sport and he subsequently became very enthusiastic about it.

A few days later, he asked Stirling if he could invite his wife to come over from the States to attend the race meeting he would be attending with him, which was to be the Easter Monday meeting at Goodwood, where Stirling was down to drive the BRP/UDT Laystall Lotus in the afternoon. By this time, Stirling had become totally relaxed in George's company and had become quite fond of him because he was a genuinely charming man. Naturally, George was told that he could do as he liked providing that he made his own arrangements which, translated from Stirling-speak, meant paying for all his wife's expenses and making all the arrangements for her, which George subsequently did.

Stirling was running two main-ish girlfriends at the time – a model who nobody liked very much and a South African journalist who he had just met and who was not the average run-of-the-mill type of model that he usually went for. He opted, however, to go on his own to Goodwood and asked me to pitch up on the day, so I hitched a lift there with one of the Sunday gang.

AT THE END OF THE DAY

Monday 23 April 1962 dawned grey and grim but gradually it shed its drizzly shroud and slowly started to turn into a lovely spring morning. The sun struggled to come out as we drove along the country lanes and a few small rays of sunshine occasionally began to peep through the swirling mass of mist over the South Downs, until the haze began to roll away, leaving a patchy blue sky, streaked with forgotten strands of grey and white cloud, but there was still quite a nip in the air for that time of the year.

We arrived at the Fleece Inn quite early and well in time for breakfast. Stirling was in an unusually good mood and, when the time came for us all to depart for the circuit, Mrs De Carvalho suddenly announced that, instead of going to the race meeting, she would remain at the hotel. Try as we did, we could not persuade her to change her mind. She was quite adamant that she didn't want to come along to the circuit so we left without her, George being driven to the circuit by Stirling in his personal yellow Lotus Elite, which he had actually *bought* for his own use.

Once we arrived at the circuit, we didn't give the matter a second thought and got on with whatever we had to do. Many of the normal crowd from the Lowndes Arms were already at the circuit where most of the men used to help out, either as time-keepers or marshals, and Stirling's good mood continued. He had quite recently agreed to become a godfather to the first born of one of the couples in the gang and when he caught up with them outside a refreshment stand before the race he posed for a photograph with the baby. This was probably the last photograph ever taken of him as a professional racing driver socialising, apart from those taken on the grid at the start line.

Stirling's afternoon race, the Goodwood International 100-mile race for the Glover Trophy, was scheduled to start at 2:30 p.m. and he was still quite cheerful as he bounced into the pits before putting on his gloves and helmet and clambering into the cockpit of his car. He was on the front row of the grid, having qualified in pole position. The breeze had stiffened a little and the conditions were good.

The rumble and roar resounded around the old airfield as the start flag fell towards the ground and the cars screeched away. They were off, and the pre-race tension relaxed a little. As the cars snaked their way through at the end of the first lap, we were all craning our necks to see where Stirling would be. First to come round the chicane was Graham Hill, who led the race from start to finish, with Stirling unexpectedly lying in fourth position. By the end of the ninth lap and without warning Stirling pulled into the pits and clambered out of the car, instead of sitting there as he normally would whilst work was carried out on it. He undid the strap of his helmet and, after a brief chat with the mechanics, ambled over to where I was hunched up on the pit counter doing my own lap chart to have a quick word (the official BRP pit chart being done by the professional team of Cyril Audrey and his wife).

Stirling shouted some words in my ear but I couldn't catch what he was saying properly because of the racket of the other cars thundering by, but clearly he was annoyed about something. When I indicated that I couldn't hear what he had just said, he wagged his finger at me from left to right in his string-gloved hand and shrugged his shoulders as much as to say, 'It doesn't matter'. For the life of me now, I would love to have known what it was that he had said – those last few words…

He scrambled back into the car, pulled up his goggles and was off, joining the race in thirteenth position. Stirling was never a person to give up the chase and by the next lap, he had moved up one place, where he stayed for the next nine laps, after which he moved up further to tenth place. He stayed there for four more laps before moving into ninth, where he stayed for the next eleven laps. He went missing on the 35th lap of the 42-lap race.* By that time, he had also set up joint fastest lap: 12.2 seconds faster than his qualifying time for pole position. (This was partially because the driving conditions had changed since he qualified, the circuit being wet at the time of qualifying. In fact, in the wet, Stirling was four seconds quicker than the

---

* According to my own lap chart.

rest of the field and, afterwards, John Surtees was reported to have said, 'That Stirling Moss – he ain't 'uman!')

Everyone knew he would continue to try to better his fastest lap and also try to battle his way further up through the field, even though he was still a lap down on the leader, but no one was expecting that, seven laps from the end, he would vanish from the race entirely. We had been waiting for him to come around the chicane leading to the main straight past the pits opposite the main grandstand to start his 36th lap when he did not appear. At first, no one was unduly worried. After all, it was Easter, it was Goodwood, it was a nice day and the world was at peace. However, that peace amongst the motor racing fraternity was to be shattered for ever when the news came through the Tannoy that Stirling Moss had come off at a curve known as St Mary's at the back of the circuit. Initially, I wasn't the least bit perturbed either. I thought Stirling was invincible and I was also trying to deal with George, who began to pester me with all kinds of questions about what could have happened. Time marched on but still nothing more came over the Tannoy. The race finished and then a strange silence descended and hung in the air. There still wasn't any more news as to what was happening at the back of the circuit. By now, everyone's shock had turned into an almost disbelieving silence. A cold shiver ran down my spine and back up again when, after an agonising half an hour or so, it was announced that Stirling was being cut out of his car. The minutes ticked by. There still wasn't any more news as to what was happening at the back of the circuit and then, after what felt like an interminable length of time – but was really only an hour – the sound of a wailing ambulance siren could be heard as it made its way hurriedly out of the circuit, en route for Chichester Hospital.

A FLUKE SAVES THE DAY

Soon after that, everything seemed to happen all at once and I was, somehow, whisked away to the local hospital. I waited with a couple of other people outside a casualty operating room, in a long, bare, cold corridor on the ground floor, with its glossy cream walls and stone tiling shining brightly with the reflections of the neon light.

The tick of the second hand of a clock drummed into my head, every time it moved.

From time to time, someone passed, normally a nurse, and brightly said she was sure there was nothing to worry about. Apart from that, no one spoke. The seconds shuffled into minutes and the minutes dragged on… reminding us that time doesn't stand still, though it can pass incredibly slowly on some occasions. Suddenly, the handle on the door opposite the bench on which we were sitting rattled, and then the door flew open. Stirling, dead to the world and unconscious, was wheeled out into the corridor on a mobile stretcher, feet first, a drip held high above the end where his head was and a white hospital sheet draped over the main part of his body. The aroma of dried blood was nauseous and the sight I will never ever forget and which is for ever engrained in my mind is that of Alfred, Stirling's father, with his sleeves rolled up to well above his elbows and his forearms held upwards, as if carrying an imaginary baby up high. His arms were sticky, awash with Stirling's drying dark red blood.

The doctor on the furthest side of the bed said nothing, but Alfred, who was nearest to us, muttered, more to comfort himself than anyone else, I suppose, 'He'll be alright, he'll be alright.'

However, Stirling would certainly not have been alright had the doctors listened to Alfred when he was first brought in. Many years back, he had had his blood group engraved onto his gold identity bracelet, which he always wore on his left wrist, and when Alfred was told that Stirling required a blood transfusion, he told the hospital to go ahead immediately and use the type of blood grouping written on the bracelet. The doctors, however, decided to ensure that it was, in fact, the correct grouping, which was just as well because the blood group on Stirling's bracelet was incorrect – his blood type did not match that on his bracelet. Had it not been rechecked and he had been given a blood transfusion of the incorrect type, it might well have killed him. As it was, the medical staff at Chichester did as good a job as any of patching him up.

I cannot remember anything after Stirling being wheeled away until I was halfway home, being driven in Stirling's bright yellow Lotus Elite by a friend. The shock must have begun to kick in as we left Chichester Hospital.

A ROTATION OF DUTIES

Because of the brain damage Stirling had sustained, he was transferred overnight to the Atkinson Morley Hospital, as it was then called, in Wimbledon. As he was in such a deep coma – his brain had literally bounced across from one side of his head to the other and back again, which had bruised his brain massively – the damage had, consequently, affected the left side of his body. The doctors recommended that someone from his inner circle should stay with him round the clock, preferably talking to him, to try to bring him round from the coma. He had also broken his leg and cheekbone and his eye didn't look too healthy either. But, he was alive. Just.

We formed a roster whereby I would do the 6:30 a.m. until lunch-time stint, when someone such as Rob Walker (his patron) or Ken Gregory would come in to take over until I could get back to the hospital in the mid to late afternoon and wait for Alfred to arrive around ten o'clock in the evening. He would take over from me and stay with Stirling overnight. I would then arrive back again early in the morning to take over from Alfred, and so it went on, day after day.

Initially, the hospital found it hard to cope with the unrealistic fuss and commotion associated with dealing with such a well-known and well-liked personality. The avalanche of mail, flowers and even people who were turning up unannounced to wish Stirling well was quite remarkable. We gave most of the flowers to the other patients in the hospital and I was, naturally, in charge of the mail. In addition, I also had the responsibility of seeing that the builders and suppliers kept up to scratch with the house.

The reaction of the public to Stirling's accident was absolutely overwhelming and I went and spoke to most of those who called in person at the hospital on the off chance. He was headline news for some time. No one knew quite how badly Stirling had been injured and we wanted to keep it that way, just in case. He was to be pro-tected by a wall of silence, especially as far as the national press was concerned.

On the first Saturday after the accident, I remember a nurse call-ing me out of the room to go and meet the manager of the Grana-da cinema in Epsom, who had turned up with six or seven of the

Granadiers – the children who used to go to the Granada cinema regularly on Saturday mornings to watch specially selected films. The entire audience of kids that morning had signed a get-well card for Stirling and the manager had kindly offered to bring it and a handful of the children over in his car to deliver the card (and flowers for which a collection had been held) in person. That was a difficult one. Later, another child sent Stirling all of his pocket money 'to buy another car', which was all of a thruppence (worth about 25p today). There was a covering note from his mother, asking us not to return the money as it had taken him three weeks to save it up.

In the first couple of weeks or so, we received well over 1,500 letters and cards every day, after which the rate dropped to around 1,000 a day. (Previously, I would have answered over sixty letters a day plus a handful of requests for autographs.)

The rigid office policy of replying to every single letter received (however crackpot it may have been), was put under considerable strain, but it was also strictly adhered to so this was quite a job, and every letter was personally signed either by Ken or myself. At the height of the crisis, Ken and I decided to hire a couple of temporary, self-employed typists in the office, to whom he or I would dictate letters which required a personal input as opposed to the bog-standard letters, which I would drop off at three secretarial agencies we were using on my way back into London from the hospital in Wimbledon at lunchtime. These would be typed up by their staff. I would collect the previous day's correspondence on my way back to the hospital in the afternoon to take over from the person who had done the lunchtime shift. I could sit and sign and stamp these later whilst I spent time with Stirling in the evening before Alfred arrived. It also gave me something to talk to him about, even though, at that time, there weren't any visible signs that he was listening to me. It was not exactly easy talking non-stop to a lifeless form, but it was an essential part of the recuperation process. Something had to trigger his brain out of its stupor.

Meanwhile, George had been asking for a very long time if he could see Stirling and, on one particular evening, he turned up at the hospital because his office had called him back to the US and he wanted to see Stirling for one last time, so I broke the golden rule. I also broke the platinum rule of not getting caught. I allowed George to have a quick peep at the sleeping Stirling when... Alfred arrived early and went ballistic. I was given a good dressing down on the spot, to be honest, quite rightly so, and much to George's embarrassment. But, I guess that both Alfred and Ken felt that they could ill afford to get rid of me at that particular juncture although they did threaten to do so. I suppose they talked about it and came to the conclusion that there wasn't anyone else who could keep all the balls in the air and put in all the hours that I was doing, continually talking to Stirling, doing all the donkey work and keeping all the workmen on song.

Rather naturally at the time, I felt (wrongly) that their attitude was rather unfair, because I knew George and they did not and they were unaware of George's circumstances and that he only wanted a peek at Stirling through a viewing window on a compassionate basis before he left the country. Only I understood how close the two of them had eventually become in such a short space of time and, for George, it would be the final goodbye because, at his age, he probably would never come back to these shores.

I did not try to justify myself to them. I just kept my own counsel and thought my own deep dark thoughts about their 'ignorance' although, to be fair, I had been totally in the wrong and did, reluctantly, understand their knee-jerk reaction.

• • •

George, on the other hand, had also confided in me that the reason why his wife had not come to the circuit on that fateful day was because she had had a premonition that there would be an incident of some kind and was afraid that it might involve Stirling. She thought that by staying back at the hotel it might just have been averted.

Well, she wasn't far wrong. She was, of course, the least surprised of us all to learn of the outcome of the race – and in the end Stirling did not become the first professional motor racing driver ever to appear on the front cover of *Time* magazine.

SIGN OF HOPE

I found it rather tedious having to talk constantly non-stop to a virtually dead body. It is literally like talking to the proverbial brick wall and, consequently, I used to tell Stirling in detail what was going on at the house because I reckoned that that was his main interest.

Just prior to the accident, he had agreed to put in an internal vacuum system so all the person vacuuming had to do was pop the hose into an internal fixture in the skirting board and, bingo! However, it transpired that the system was in its infancy and things hadn't been going very well at Shepherd Street with it, and still weren't. A certain Mr Leon was the culprit; Stirling had been spitting fire and brimstone about him before the accident and I wasn't doing much better with him after it. Stirling had asked our Mr Whitsun to install internal central channelling for the whole of the electrical system and it had been decided to link the vacuum system hoses in with these internal, hidden ducts but, after arriving on site on one occasion after the accident, Mr Leon had informed me that he didn't think the system would work at all. I thought to myself that it was far more likely that he wasn't up to the job, but that was a relatively minor hitch compared to the many others that I had to deal with. Anyway, I knew that this would really irritate Stirling more than most so, after I arrived at the hospital and having been told about the prospect of the complete malfunction, I began to tell him the story, leaving no stone or detail unturned, whilst he lay there totally inert.

'And, what's more,' I trilled, at the still, prostrate body, 'that Mr Leon, he is a right little toad. He's a shit, a complete and utter bastard.'

By this time, I was pretty much yelling at the still, shrouded form when I suddenly heard a sound. I immediately stopped speaking, jumped up from the chair I was sitting on beside Stirling's bed and looked at him. He was lying on his right side and I just caught the words as he mumbled:

'Bastar… Big bastaaar…d.'

My heart jumped – this was typical of Stirling. That lifeless form had actually heard and said something. This was my first sign of hope for him.

Of course, his first words were officially attributed to his mother, Aileen, later that week when she visited him and claimed that he had said, 'Mum'. It probably made for better reading in the press than 'Bastard'!

WEATHERING THE STORM

Stirling gradually began to have lucid periods when his stubbornness would become even more pronounced. One morning, he insisted that a weird-looking mouse that he had drawn should be printed on the backs of all the office envelopes, as opposed to the plain dark green initials 'S. M.' that were embossed on their flaps, and he asked me to get the printer, Mr Wheen, down to arrange it. Of course I didn't, but I told Stirling that I had arranged it with Mr Wheen on the telephone from the office. Sometimes, Stirling would remember what he had asked me to do in his less confused periods of lucidity and at other times he would not. When he did, and I hadn't jumped to his bidding, there would be a few cross words, but then he would fall unconscious again and I hoped that by the next time he woke up he would have totally forgotten the subject, which was normally the case. But that wretched mouse was a totally different story.

One evening, I was sitting waiting for Alfred to arrive. It was dark, with the single night light casting eerie shadows over the stillness of the room, when I heard Stirling talking to himself in perfect French. He then switched to Italian and back again to French. The brain is surely an extraordinarily, wondrous thing.

One weekend, he put up a truly pitiful performance whilst he was watching the Monaco Grand Prix on television with Ken and me. First, he begged to be allowed to leave hospital that very moment to compete in the event and, when he eventually realised that he wouldn't be allowed to leave the room, let alone travel, he begged Ken to get him a car without fail for the next Grande Épreuve on the calendar. Nothing would satisfy him until Ken did agree (with fingers crossed behind his back, of course).

The accident began to take its toll on my health, what with the lack of sleep and all the added hours and responsibilities of keeping an eye on Stirling and coping with the tremendous amount of mail that continued to pour in, plus trying to keep any kind of progress going on the house. The pressure and strain were enormous and it probably affected my relationship with Ken, which was going downhill rapidly. With Ken back and virtually resident in the office, rumblings began inside the mighty volcano, which eventually erupted into a large explosion. We had an open-ended row, which made a good relationship almost impossible. Enmity hung like a shroud of death in the air.

As soon as the load of letters lightened somewhat, Ken got rid of the temporary secretaries and imported his own secretary into Shepherd Street from the BRP offices in Highgate, who sat at my desk in the front office, even when I was in there. She never offered to let me have my own chair back, let alone my own desk, so I decided to go up to the kitchen and work from there.

I made the small, two-seater fitted area in one corner of the kitchen as my small base, the kitchen by now having been transformed and more or less finished. I concentrated solely on trying to sort out the building and chasing up the furniture that Stirling had ordered, mainly through a friend of a friend in the East End of London during what little time I spent at the office because I was still doing the hospital stints as well.

The atmosphere became rather nasty and I suppose, having worked for so long on my own in the office with Stirling, with Ken hardly ever being around after we moved into 44/46, I came to resent him taking over and what I saw as his interference at Shepherd Street. I never realised that he had tremendous pressures put on him as well, probably more so, and I guess he thought that I was being pretty high-handed, full stop. I am glad to say that all the wounds on either side healed once Stirling was properly back on his feet and I went on to work for Ken on a couple of other occasions after I had officially left the auspices of Stirling Moss Ltd.

One day, after Ken's secretary had left Shepherd Street, Ken buzzed up to the kitchen from Stirling's office and asked me to pop down to see him.

Five minutes later, when I sat down at Stirling's desk, diagonally opposite Ken, who was sitting in Stirling's chair, he started a character assassination on me.

'You really are the most conceited, self-opinionated, egotistical, arrogant, selfish person I have ever had the misfortune to come across,' he said, looking directly at me.

I decided that the best thing to do was to say nothing until the storm had subsided when I then said softly, 'You are absolutely correct, Ken,' and with that I got up out of my seat and sailed out of the office and back upstairs to the kitchen to get on with my own work, somewhat shaken and upset I may add.

I was young and I was conscientious and I felt thoroughly miserable; I was not prepared to continue in this vein for much longer. This naturally troubled me deeply because I was concerned about leaving Stirling high and dry, but I suppose I was just very weary and had reached the end of my tether. I knew that I needed some good, independent advice, but the question was: who would be the best person to turn to? There wasn't anyone I thought I could trust and then I suddenly thought of Norman Solomon, Stirling's friend in the Bahamas. He had helped me out of a jam once before with Stirling regarding a personal matter so I booked a person-to-person phone call to him, but when the operator tried to put the call through, he wasn't there. I asked the operator to ask him to return my call when he could and left the details of my whereabouts for later that evening. By the time the call eventually came through, I was having a belated dinner with some friends (talk about burning the candle at both ends!) in The Colony restaurant in Berkeley Square, which was owned by the Hollywood actor George Raft, who was eventually refused entry into Britain. It was considered to be a very posh restaurant in those days and it was also a favourite haunt of Stirling's because they had a small band and a dance area where he used to dance the night away until the wee small hours of the morning.

When Norman called, I was very discreetly invited by a member of staff to use the Colony's overly ornate telephone kiosk and, whilst Norman patiently listened, I spitted out my story between little sobs. Once he had got the gist of the problem he told me, in a nutshell, that he was quite sure that Stirling would take my side and back me up 100 per cent and that I should continue on doing the work I was doing for him and that, in the meantime, if Ken would not pay me, he would guarantee my salary until such time as Stirling was capable of making up his own mind and deciding what he wanted to do. A friend in need is a friend indeed.

And so, I continued doing my two very long stints a day, sitting with Stirling in his room at the Atkinson Morley hospital in Wimbledon because he was still lapsing into complete unconsciousness in between having more lucid periods. It was awkward handing over to Alfred at night-time, because he and Ken had always been hand in glove with each other and he obviously knew of the situation, but neither of us would speak very much. A cursory nod of the head as an acknowledgement when he arrived was all that was required and I would get up and drive away from the hospital feeling dead beat and quite emotional. I didn't realise at the time quite how gruelling the strain was. I was twenty-two years of age.

UPS AND DOWNS

During the time that Stirling was in hospital, a couple of his old flames had coincidentally met and become firm friends and subsequently they decided to share a flat together. *Pro tem*, they had moved into what we called the 'Rabbit Hutch' in Shepherd Street. This property, right next door to Stirling's original maisonettes at 36/38, belonged to a Maltese 'gentleman' who let out five rather upmarket furnished rooms, one of which the girls had rented.

A Sinhalese man lived in the penthouse and Stirling and I used to have bets on whether or not his married mistress would be staying overnight whenever we knew she was seeing him for the evening. Nothing was very private in the upper end of Shepherd Street. It was a street of two parts and the upper part didn't tend to mix with the lower part and vice versa. We always knew when Rajah's girlfriend stayed over because her two-tone white and mauve Triumph Herald would always be parked at the top of the street for half of the following morning on a minute portion of private land.

Rajah was the only son of a Sri Lankan ambassador and lived royally on the 'pocket money' his father used to send him every month, rising in time to get down to the Shepherd's pub on the corner of Shepherd Street and Hertford Street at lunchtime, returning when the pub closed or after he had had a few in the private drinking club called Ruby's, which was almost next door to the pub, in Hertford Street, on the first floor. He would then amble down the street again in the early evening, as regular as clockwork, and return in the early hours of the morning not always on his own! He was exceedingly handsome and debonair, and it was unfortunate that it was still frowned upon, in some quarters, to fraternise with 'such types'. I got to know him very well over the years that he was in Shepherd Street and Stirling loved hearing all the gossip about what he got up to.

On one occasion, the police descended on our end of Shepherd Street in full force because one of Rajah's shadier Sri Lankan friends had on this occasion stolen his passport! Stirling couldn't quite believe his eyes, let alone believe his ears when he saw all the police milling around outside. Let's just say that by now, this particular friend of Rajah's had developed into a conman *par excellence* and life had become a little too hot for him. Charles, for that was his name, began by selling an imaginary fleet of ships to a rich businessman whilst travelling in first class on a train journey down from the north of England, and he even collected the money that day from a small bank on Park Lane! Rajah had warned me about him when the two of us were having a drink in a private club above Susan Handbags in Knightsbridge. On his downward path to ignominy, I believe he finally became a currency counterfeiter, after which he 'did time'. Stirling did love gossip, but rarely collected any himself, relying on me to pass on information to him. He never could understand why or how I came by it quite so easily! But he always loved it.

• • •

As for his two old flames who had moved into the Rabbit Hutch, he would have been absolutely livid had he found out that we three girls had played helter-skelter with one of his mattresses down the uncarpeted concrete spiral staircase in his new house one evening, even though it was wrapped in plastic. His two ex-girlfriends had asked me to stay the night with them in their room and their mattress wasn't large enough for the three of us. Whilst we were taking the mattress up to the first floor, we bumped into Rajah coming down, who was very keen to propose alternative arrangements! Getting the mattress back the next morning was quite a different thing altogether. Thank goodness for Wally.

Wally continued to busy himself happily around the house and, by then, he was coming to work in his Ford Anglia, which he parked off street (where Rajah's girlfriend used to park hers, Rajah having moved on by this point) in front of 44/46. One day, one of my two flatmates (I had by now moved from Shepherd Street) asked Wally if she could hire his car for the day. It was a private arrangement and one which my other flatmate and I thought was totally mad because our friend, who was going to borrow the car, happened to be a bit scatty and, to be honest, was not a terribly good driver, either. But, neither of us had been consulted on the proposition.

By pure coincidence, however, we were both standing outside the house in the street when our other flatmate came along to pick up the car. Earlier, Wally had placed a ladder against the front wall in order to carry out some work on the outside of the house at third-floor level, and we were standing near it as we watched Wally hand over the keys of the car to our flatmate. Whilst she settled herself into the car, he went back to work. He wandered over to the ladder and slowly began to climb up to Stirling's bedroom window. Just as the two of us turned to go inside the house, we heard the car start, the reverse gear crunched excruciatingly loudly and there was a loud crack and a bang. We automatically swung around and could hardly believe our eyes. The car was jerking backwards, taking the ladder with it. We looked up, dreading the worst, and thought we would see Wally hurtling down towards the ground, but he was nowhere to be seen. He had completely disappeared. Miraculously, he had been able to leap through the open bedroom window and, by a sheer and absolutely incredible fluke, someone had moved Stirling's bed out of position in the room (which was far from finished) and it had been sitting right underneath the very window that Wally had used as an escape hatch so when he sailed through it, he crash-landed onto the bed.

MILK OF HUMAN KINDNESS

The kindness of people continued unabated all through the time that Stirling was in hospital. He had always been a big fan of Frank Sinatra and once Stirling had improved sufficiently to sit in a wheelchair and talk reasonably coherently, I decided to telephone the Savoy Hotel (where I knew Sinatra was staying) to ask him, as a favour, if he would ring Stirling personally at the hospital and speak to him. I left the message, together with Stirling's hospital telephone number, with one of Sinatra's entourage and I didn't say anything to anyone.

I arrived at the hospital around lunchtime a couple of days later only to be told by one of the nursing staff that Frank Sinatra had very kindly phoned to speak to Stirling but that he had been in theatre and had been unable to talk to him. To my knowledge, Sinatra never rang back again. However, the thought had been there. I saw many years later in various publications that Stirling said that he had spoken to Sinatra whilst he had been in the Atkinson Morley hospital, but whether he really had or it was his brain still playing tricks on him after hearing that Sinatra had telephoned whilst he was in surgery is another matter. I would be surprised if he had telephoned again because Stirling certainly never mentioned this to me, which he undoubtedly would have.

Another bright ray of sunshine appeared on the scene in the form of the old girlfriend, Judy Carne, who had gone to Hollywood a couple of years before his accident. She was always a breath of fresh air and was taking a break from filming in America. She would come to spend time with him in the afternoons at the hospital and used to wheel him out in his wheelchair onto the lawn for tea, all the while trying to dodge the long lenses of the cameramen, who were still permanently hanging around, trying to take the world's first shot of Stirling after the accident. She really was the best medicine for Stirling because she made him – and all of us – laugh and, by that stage, that's what we all needed.

AFTER THE STORM

Eventually, the time came for Stirling to leave hospital, but he could still not be left on his own for very long and I was quite surprised that there was never any suggestion of him going back to Tring to be looked after by his own family. It had been decided, after a fair amount of discussion, that the best thing would be for him to go to stay at the Mayfair Hotel with a friend for a while – but that didn't last very long. There was nothing for him to do there. He did, however, manage to meet quite a few good-looking girls during this time. Once he came back to live at Shepherd Street, the problems intensified, the major one being him trying to negotiate the circular staircase. He was particularly unstable and doddery on his feet; he couldn't see properly, he wasn't particularly rational and the hardest part to deal with was the fact that he considered himself to be absolutely fine, which was a far cry from the truth.

A few weeks down the line, he determined to go to Nassau where there was an upcoming political election and he insisted on becoming involved with that and could not be swayed otherwise. At least the time that he would be away would give me some respite, even though I felt that going to Nassau would certainly not be in his best interests. Thankfully, he was to be accompanied by an American friend and, once there, Norman (Solomon) would keep an eye on him.

The family and Ken more or less ignored my thoughts on any subject to do with Stirling's health and I hadn't any rights over him; I was regarded by them as merely an ordinary worker, paid to do the job I was doing. It suited them to ignore my feelings whenever they felt like it and there was absolutely nothing that I could do about it, but I did ensure that Norman Solomon knew all the facts. I had to tread exceedingly carefully at the time because it was imperative for Stirling to fully regain his mind and his body. During all the years that I knew him, he never acknowledged my input, especially at this particular time in his life. However, as I was with him continuously, morning, noon and often in the evenings, driving him about again once he was back home, he did begin to heed my advice and support behind closed doors.

ACCIDENTS WILL HAPPEN IN THE BEST OF FAMILIES

I went to collect Stirling from the airport on his return from Nassau (he came home alone) and unsurprisingly found scores of photographers waiting to greet him. As we emerged from the terminal into the daylight, they egged him on to get into the driver's seat and take the wheel of the car so they could take their first photographs of him driving a vehicle after the crash. I took him aside and beseeched him not to drive but, ever willing to self-publicise, and thinking that he was completely well and back to normal, Stirling pleaded with me to allow him to drive. He promised me faithfully that he would only drive to the exit of the airport and thereafter we would swop seats and I would drive the car back to London. He was like a little boy begging me, determined to obtain his own way, which put me on the spot in front of such a large audience. In the end, I agreed, somewhat unwillingly, rather than cause a big scene in front of the waiting press, which would have been a somewhat larger story! Rather naturally, once we had driven away, he utterly refused to hand over the wheel of the car to me until we came to the second roundabout on the A4 back into London, which he promptly drove straight into.

'Get out, get out!' I yelled at him, and he meekly changed seats with me, looking like a little boy who had stolen the farmer's apples. Fortunately, there was very little damage to the car and miraculously no one else was involved in the incident – or saw it.

It became exceedingly difficult to ensure that Stirling did not enter into any commitments that were beyond his capabilities and, for a change, the lack of progress on the house was to prove an absolute boon because it began to consume all his waking hours, and very soon he was back on the crumpet trail again as well.

WHO WAS THE ONE-ARMED BANDIT?

In the meantime, Sir John Whitmore, who was racing saloon and sports cars, approached Stirling to see if he would like to design a special body for the Ogle car company. John was very much involved with Ogle at the time and knew that it would be a good way of obtaining publicity for the company. Stirling went along with the project and managed to persuade the *Sunday Times* to sponsor the idea as well. This kept Stirling out of my hair for a couple of months and we were all very grateful to John for collecting him and depositing him back home safely after each stint at the works in Hertfordshire.

Before Stirling's enforced stay in hospital, he had ordered a few pieces of furniture, and I had stored them in the studio at the top of the house for safekeeping, as far away from the builders' dirt and dust as possible. At one stage after he arrived home, he toiled up the stairs to inspect the goods and noticed a sofa that seemed to have something missing.

'What the hell is that, Viper?' he asked. 'Why didn't you send that back?'

'What?'

'That bloody sofa! Look at it, I wouldn't have ordered it like that.'

'Well, you did, and that was the reason I didn't send it back,' I replied.

'Oh, don't be so ridiculous,' he said confrontationally, 'I would never have ordered a sofa with only one arm.'

'Well, you did.'

'For heaven's sake, I did not,' he said vehemently.

'Oh yes, you did,' I replied, equally vehemently, 'and would you like me to tell you just why you ordered it?'

'I didn't,' he muttered truculently, 'but alright.'

Slowly, emphasising each word, I said, 'You. Ordered. The. Sofa. Like. That. Without. An. Arm. Because. You. Wanted. To. Bring. Your. Bits. Of. Crumpet. Up. Here. For. Coffee. To. Listen. To. Music.

And. Lie. Unencumbered. On. It. Until. The. Early. Hours. Of. The. Morning.'

He looked at me sheepishly and a profound and embarrassed silence ensued.

Sometimes during the day, Stirling would walk out into the street and pick an argument with a complete stranger and I had to leap out of the door to coax him back inside again. This aggression was totally alien to his 'normal' character and to how he used to behave before the accident. Fortunately it wasn't too difficult to entice him back inside because, as soon as I was aware of what was going on, I would run out and tell him that something needed to be seen to in the house and he would shoot back inside again (as fast as he was able), to find out what it was. Fortuitously, this ploy never ever failed to work. Before the accident, Stirling hardly ever swore at all. Although he would get angry, mainly caused by his inner frustrations, he would never be at all punchy but, for a while, he developed a Jekyll and Hyde personality, totally unlike the person he was before the accident. Happily, this gradually subsided with time and he reverted pretty much to type. All the time I had known Stirling up until now, he had had perfect manners and was a 'real' gentleman, even when he was in a hurry.

ROYAL TASTES

Not long after he had arrived back from Nassau, he arranged to have lunch with King Hussein of Jordan round the corner at the Curzon House Club, where we were all members.

As he still couldn't walk very well and his focus was all awry, I drove him there (it was longer to drive there than to walk) and as soon as the car drew up to the kerb, King Hussein skipped down the front steps at the entrance to greet him. After they had briefly shaken hands, Stirling took the time to introduce me. Hussein leaned into the car and we too shook hands – over the gear lever! There was very little standing on ceremony in the '60s.

By now, Stirling had become interested in karting and the King, who was also a speed merchant, wanted to import some special karts into Jordan made by a company near Tring, with which Stirling had become involved. The young King spent quite a long time in London at this stage in his life and became rather well known for frequenting the many bopping discos that were springing up all over the West End, so I suppose they also had other things to talk about apart from karts!

I think the weirdest meeting that I ever had to take Stirling to was that with the well-known film director, John Schlesinger, who was renting a flat in Hyde Park Gardens and who had requested a meeting with him. Our ring of the doorbell was answered by a butler, who informed us that Mr Schlesinger was feeling rather tired and would we mind if we held the meeting in his bedroom. Somewhat taken aback, we politely agreed and we were ushered into a darkened room. 'Mine director' lay on his back on a mattress on the floor, the lower half of his torso covered by a single white sheet. Stirling and I perched on the side of the mattress for the duration. I don't think either of us commented on the meeting when we first came out because we were too flabbergasted for words.

Back at the ranch, work on the house trickled on but life in the office was, surprisingly, just as busy as when he was racing – but with less respite, and I missed the interludes of relative calm when he was away. And, because he was around all the time and had nothing better to do, he started to try to control my free time, such as it was. For example when I could meet my friends for lunch – and an hour was precisely all that was permitted. He used to be beside himself if I was not back on the dot of the hour. This was not on in my book and we had one or two big ding-dongs about it, particularly as I was back on chauffeur duty as well as being foreman, secretary and now carer. The one thing that didn't seem to be affected by the accident, if the comings and goings at the house were anything to go by, was his libido.

A RETIRING MAN SHATTERINGLY ILL-ADVISED

Deep down in his soul, Stirling was hell-bent on going back to driving competitively. A date was eventually set for him to appraise his capabilities again at Goodwood. Coincidentally, this clashed, unbeknown to him, with a job interview I had organised with Border Television in Carlisle. By that time, I had become heartily sick and tired of being used morning, noon and night, not quite so much by him as by everyone else around him, without ever being thanked. A little bit of gratitude always goes a very long way and I was not a doormat.

Quite frankly, I personally thought it was absolutely ridiculous for him to be testing his driving skills at that particular stage in his recovery because I knew, for sure, that he wasn't the slightest bit alright and yet I had not been consulted in any way, shape or form. It was OK for me to be the dogsbody and look after him but it was not OK for me to hold an opinion about his well-being and future. Ken and his father had together taken the decision and Stirling's pitiful and fragile state had not, in my humble opinion, been considered whatsoever. I honestly thought that the pair of them were only thinking about the not inconsiderable insurance payout that would be due to Stirling if he did not compete competitively again. It was absolutely exasperating because I also knew that, if Stirling was in his right mind, he would agree with my logic and common sense would prevail.

When I arrived back in London from Carlisle and saw the evening headlines on the news-stands I wasn't at all surprised that it had been announced that Stirling Moss was officially retiring from motor racing. However, Stirling was devastated and I immediately realised that he really had believed that he was good enough to go back racing full time again. Once more, I was left with a difficult decision to make after I was offered the job with Border Television. But, loyalty won the day again and, after a full and frank heart-to-heart discussion, he started to realise just what I had had to put up with whilst he had been lying in hospital *non compos mentis*. I also told Stirling how Norman had personally backed me over the difficulties I had experienced during his spell in hospital and, as Norman quite rightly surmised, Stirling confirmed that he would also have backed me one hundred per cent in the actions that I had taken. It had really been a traumatic time for me and I had tried to cope as I knew he would have wanted me to cope. He was actually very touched at the way Norman had handled things and all three of us became much closer afterwards.

He began to set about rectifying the situation in his own way and it was around this time that I was appointed a director of Stirling Moss Ltd and, subsequently, Ken's name was removed, primarily because he had nothing further to manage. Thereafter, I remained a director through thick and thin, even when I did officially leave his employ.

The reality of this official test drive at Goodwood was, inevitably, that he would never be sufficiently competitive and capable of driving professionally in Formula One racing again. He had to face up to the hard facts that his life as a top professional driver had come to an abrupt end. This left him in shock, feeling exceedingly frustrated, angry, let down and, of course, with nothing much to do with his life. Up until then, racing had been the very essence of his being. This had formed the basis of his *raison d'être* and how he lived his life, day in, day out, from his formative years. He had never considered getting permanently 'maimed' or having to alter his lifestyle in any way, shape or form. (And neither, for that matter, had I.)

Now, he had absolutely zilch to look forward to. In one fell swoop, his chosen way of life had been shattered into a trillion pieces.

SIGNPOST LE MANS!

A year after his accident, Stirling was invited to run the *Sunday Times*-sponsored Shelby Cobra Team at the classic race, 24 Heures du Mans (24 Hours of Le Mans). He jumped at the opportunity. This was to keep him busy with meetings for quite a bit of the time but everyone inside our little team soon began to realise that he would have to be coaxed and coached into this role with me, once again, acting as nanny.

Right at the last moment and, initially unbeknown to me (because I tried to know what he said and to whom every minute of the day, but it wasn't always possible) until after the phone call, the day before we were going to leave for Le Mans, he accepted a telephone invitation from the president of the Ford Motor Company to attend a function in Paris that night. We had arranged to take our SMART Estate Cortina tow car over the Channel together with the *Sunday Times*'s motoring correspondent's wife, Pam Boyd, in the afternoon. Consequently, we had to rearrange our plans. Pam and I were still to fly the car over the Channel ourselves and pick up Stirling in France somewhere en route at a predetermined destination after the cocktail party. We were to leave before him and I had arranged for my flat-mate (the sensible one) to take him to the airport later. As soon as Pam arrived at Shepherd Street, we bundled ourselves into the estate car and set off. Ironically, as it turned out, I asked Pam if she had her passport with her. She had.

Lydd Airport is perched on the edge of a veritable windy wilderness of scrub and wetlands (known as Romney Marsh) and, once we drew up in front of the airport buildings, I looked in the back of the car for the big white leather bag, which was my hallmark and which I carried simply everywhere with me. It was nowhere to be seen. Panic ensued and Pam, thinking back to my original remark when we left Shepherd Street, began to laugh hysterically. All I could think about was Stirling being absolutely furious, arriving at our rendezvous in the dark of the night to find no one there to meet him. He would go berserk. We were literally stranded up the river without a paddle and there weren't even any public telephones around. Finally, I told Pam that she would have to take the car over to France and pick up Stirling and I would somehow make my way back to London from this utter wilderness and see what I could arrange. Pam was definitely not amused, but even she agreed that there was nothing else for it. Suddenly, over the silence of the vast expanse of emptiness, we heard the sound of a car being pushed to its absolute limit and, lo and behold, Stirling's iridescent, pale green Mini hove into view, being driven by one of our mechanics. He raced to a stop and jumped out of the car, holding one white leather bag aloft. Phew! What a relief.

It subsequently turned out that when my flatmate had gone round to Shepherd Street to drive Stirling out to the airport, she had fortunately arrived early and seen my bag on the floor. Knowing that I never went anywhere without it, she had asked where I was and once he told her that I had already left, she forced him to unzip the bag, whereupon he found my passport and our tickets.

The rendezvous with Stirling in France was accomplished at the due time, but he was none too happy about the enormous yellow and blue French signpost for LE MANS, which had fallen down by the side of the road and which Pam and I had stopped to pick up on the way. Stirling never stopped ticking on about this but was, nevertheless, quite happy to display it in his garage in Shepherd Street for many a long year afterwards. I suspect he sold it, before deciding to send my rally plates to the sale rooms, which he apparently thought were his and which had also been displayed in the garage for years ever after! I just managed to save them in the nick of time.

As usual, we were to stay at the Hotel de France at La Chartre-sur-le-Loir and I was just about to get into bed when there was a quiet knock on my door. I timidly opened it and poked my nose out only to find Carroll Shelby standing on the threshold. A whispered conversation took place. He said he wanted to spend the night with me and I told him that Stirling would be madder than hell if he did. He demanded to know whether Stirling and I 'had a thing going together', although he knew perfectly well that we did not. I was well aware of Carroll's reputation – indeed he had even asked me to marry him a couple of times previously, but I always thought that it was all a big joke – and I knew that Stirling knew Carroll far better than I did. I also knew exactly what Stirling thought of him because they had spent so much time together on tour in the past. Stirling, with his brotherly protection of me, would have been absolutely livid that Carroll had even made the suggestion because he was just as much a womaniser as Stirling, if not more so! One of Carroll's ex-wives once told me that he didn't even bother to have the make-up cleared out of the bathroom cabinet which she found when she moved into his house in America as the latest, official Mrs Carroll Shelby.

In the final analysis, we all had a very happy and fairly successful time at Le Mans with Carroll's car coming in in seventh place overall. One of the Shelby drivers at Le Mans was Peter Bolton, a motor racing and rally driver, who was in the car business in Leeds, but anyone less like a Del Boy I have never seen, holding numerous prestigious dealerships and petrol stations in the town. He was inadvertently to play a part in the most hilarious incident in which I was ever 'involved' with Stirling. But that is for later.

CRUMPET PARADISE

Early during Stirling's recovery period, an immensely colourful young individual hit town. At the time, he was considered to be a total extrovert by everyone with whom he came into contact. He could be utterly outrageous – and was most of the time – and he certainly made it his first priority and business to get to know all the 'top' people in London, whoever they were and whatever they did. He was a dark and extremely handsome New Zealander. He was personable; he was flamboyant and he drove a black, open-top sports Maserati with maroon leather seats and a thunderous exhaust, which gurgled throatily as he drove the car all over the West End of London. It would be true to say that whenever he drove down Park Lane in it, the barmen at the Dorchester would cringe and shudder at the thought of hearing his 'dulcet Strine' as he made his swash-buckling entrance into the bar. Altogether he was a larger-than-life character and was definitely not at all Stirling's speed, although many moons later, Stirling did acknowledge that he was a good sports car driver when he was in the Antipodes. But, what did attract Stirling, on some occasions, round to his house for early evening drinks were the hordes of stunning young ladies who used to pitch up in their droves every night of the week around 6:30 p.m., Monday to Friday.

Another person who also had a fine eye for the opposite sex was Kinny Lall, whose little black book was often on loan to Stirling! He certainly helped to add to Stirling's coterie of crumpet. Kinny's father was a diplomat, lawyer and a leading member of the once great Congress Party. He had been imprisoned by the British in India for his political beliefs. Amongst his many talents, he was an excellent cook and, literally on the spur of the moment one day, he decided to take over the entire kitchen of the 'society' mews house near Grosvenor Square to show us his expertise. Sending out for all the ingredients and using every single pan that he could lay his hands on, he cooked the most delicious Indian meal for everyone who was in the house that day. He was, though, equally at home eating in the Indian greasy spoons at the back of Euston Station, which were virtually the only Indian restaurants around in that era.

I had been 'collected' into the mews retinue en route as a means to ensnaring Stirling into the rarefied atmosphere of this social coterie, mainly composed of high-flying young men and starlets, models, girls with rich daddies or just good-looking chicks. Sometimes the girls were accompanied by rich entrepreneurs, but it never mattered because these early evening occasions were used as a common meeting ground for business, young love and more. Stirling never became one of the groupies and, when he did pitch up from time to time, it would only be to cast his eye over the crumpet that was hanging around. The noisy atmosphere would rather overwhelm him. Being quite reserved, he rather tended to quietly melt into the background on such occasions. He wasn't any good at small talk and I could always spot when the conversation didn't hold any interest for him whatsoever. He would adopt a rather quizzical stare and his mouth would be ever so slightly parted open, with his head tilted to one side. To everyone else, it would appear as though he was listening avidly to what the person was saying when, in fact, he was so bored with the conversation that his mind was entirely elsewhere.

The 'emporium' did, however, come in very handy for Stirling when another colourful friend (or perhaps I should say, acquaintance) of his came into town in the shape of one Mickey Thompson, the first American to drive at over 400 mph. By then, he had turned his hand to drag racing. He was rather expecting that he would be able to use Stirling's own garage at Shepherd Street to work on his dragster, but he hadn't even asked Stirling first. Not a good move. He obviously did not know Stirling that well. And, what's more, Stirling's garage was probably smaller than the length of the car itself. Mickey was smartly despatched to 'our friend' in the mews, who typically jumped at the opportunity of looking after such a well-known personality and who would probably bring even more good-looking young women round to the residence.

Naturally, 'our friend' did not own the mews house. After he arrived in London, he had somehow descended on the unsuspecting owner, who was a very rich young recluse. Rather misguidedly, the young man had offered him temporary accommodation and was now beginning to rather wish that he had not.

Mickey had some success with the car at the Brighton Speed Trials, but once he returned to America he literally became a marked man and was murdered years later.

The mews house became a meeting place for all and sundry until 'mine host' was involved in a huge motoring accident. He had got his hands on a friend's Ferrari to take a girl out one evening, and fortunately for the girl concerned it was left-hand drive, because he went roaring off from some traffic lights, across Oxford Street and went straight into some unmarked roadworks in Portman Square. As a result, the protective barrier smashed the windscreen and lunged into his face. He was carted off to the then Middlesex Hospital, where the medics literally built a scaffolding-type of contraption over his face to hold his jaw in place. It had been broken in sixteen places and his date got off more or less scot-free. As a result, he could only feed himself using a nose dropper, his diet consisting of liquids – mainly melted ice cream mixed with jam. No matter what, he decided to join a party of us, including Stirling, who were going to celebrate New Year's Eve at the Colony in Berkeley Square. With such an exhibition-ist on board, somewhat predictably things got out of hand and 'our friend' pranced around, really embarrassing Stirling. At one stage, he decided to dip his nose dropper into everyone's drinks, including those belonging to total strangers, with the inevitable consequences – not to mention the looks of horror on the other guests' faces as the second Frankenstein loomed into sight.

PART THREE

FILLING IN

Because Alfred Moss was a dentist by trade, Stirling and I both used to have our teeth looked after by him. We would generally organise to go together (although how the office would survive without both of us I really didn't know!) because by now Alfred's nearest surgery in London was south of the Thames, in Battersea. We raced over there in the Mini on one occasion during Stirling's recovery period and arrived only to find that Alfred was still in with a patient. Stirling started to fidget and became impatient and said to me, 'What are you having done, Viper?'

'I don't know,' I replied. 'An examination and probably a clean, I suppose.'

'Right,' said Stirling, 'I can do the clean for you.'

He opened the nearest cubicle door, called me to follow him inside and beckoned to me to jump up on the seat. Slowly, he raised the chair to the height where he felt he would be most comfortable working on my teeth and took a scalpel off the tray and the round mirrored instrument and began to scrape and clean the debris from in between my teeth. Suddenly, the door flew open and there stood Alfred on the threshold, absolutely seething.

'What the hell do you think you are doing, Stirling?' he said accusingly.

'Oh, just cleaning Viper's teeth, Dad,' he replied cheerfully.

'Well, you can stop right now. How dare you do such a thing?' said Alfred. 'Valerie, get out of that chair immediately and come with me.'

With that, he whisked me off into his own surgery and left Stirling rather chastened and having to spend some more time waiting.

That was probably the first and only time that I saw Stirling humbled and slightly mortified after having been castigated by his old man.

THE RELUCTANT ARTIST

People were often surprised about the odd little things that Stirling and I used to do for each other, normally far too small to mention. For example, I was changing to go out to dinner one evening from the house when I saw Stirling and Rob Walker chatting in the street outside the window. I hadn't been able to pull up the zip on the back of my dress so I clattered down the stairs and flew out of the open front door, turned my back on the two of them and said, 'Stirling, do me up, please!' He automatically did so, still carrying on talking to Rob, and I rushed back inside, having caught a glimpse of Rob's startled and somewhat disbelieving face!

During his convalescence, Rob and Betty Walker invited Stirling down to their palatial pad in Somerset where, still unwell but true to form, he had to have something to do. Books were out of the question because he had never read one from cover to cover in his entire life and he didn't intend to start then, besides which, he found it almost impossible to concentrate after the accident. Soon he became restless and bored so Betty decided that she would offer him a challenge which he couldn't refuse, if only out of politeness. She taught him to paint in oils and his first attempt, a still life, was very creditable. After he left their home, although he cherished this first attempt, he never again put a paintbrush in his hand, except to decorate his own properties! He was exceedingly hands-on about running and maintaining the various properties he gradually began to acquire. But, as far as he was concerned, he didn't have the time, or the patience, for putting oil onto canvas.

Some months later, when the workload had increased to a ridiculous point once more and I was finding it very difficult to fit everything in again, I managed to persuade Stirling that we required another 'half' person to help in the office in order to keep up with all his requirements. I never thought that he would agree to someone full time, if only because of the additional expense and more specifically because he wasn't earning any money to speak of. However, he read the situation well and decided that it would be far easier all round to find a permanent junior secretary – someone just out of secretarial college – and he naturally put me in charge of finding that someone.

Sandra Carson was a charming girl, who had been told that she hadn't a cat in hell's chance of getting a job when she left secretarial college (as indeed I had been told except that I didn't want a job in the first place) and I naturally sympathised with her plight. Although she was engaged at the time, she said she wouldn't be getting married for at least a year and I decided that she had the right mental attitude for the job. Although Stirling initially had his doubts, I managed to persuade him that everything would work out fine, which it did. She only stayed with us for a couple of years or so because the marriage didn't come to pass either.

I was quite surprised that Stirling left me to deal with that particular drama. He wasn't well but it was quite out of his comfort zone, even though he had been through a similar circumstance. He could never be described as being naturally sympathetic. Far from it.

Rather irritatingly, around that time, a member of staff from the Westminster City Council would habitually ring us up to make an appointment for the rating officer to come around to inspect the building to ensure that it was being used as a private dwelling rather than as a commercial undertaking. Sandra and I would have to down tools and transform the office into a study for the afternoon. I would run down to the market to buy some fruit whilst Sandra would hunt around for an oblong, beaten, silver bowl, yet another trophy that had at some stage mysteriously appeared in the house. We would fill the bowl with the fruit and place it on the front desk. All the other office type of equipment, such as chairs and typewriters, would be secreted in the basement and we would hang around looking like the proverbial wallflowers until the chap arrived. The council representative would then give the 'study' a cursory look and be off. It was all part of the 'great game', yet it irritated Stirling immensely because it would take up so much time that he – and we – could otherwise be putting to good use!

A SMART MOVE

Stirling's association with John Whitmore had, no doubt, given him more than just a flavour of continuing to be involved in motor sport. It had obviously provided him with some food for thought and presumably it weighed on his mind. He needed something to do; he needed to be involved and he wanted to participate even though he really was not well enough. But what could he do?

In the end, he thought the answer might be to manage his own racing team. He realised that it would help to keep his name in front of the public, as well as helping him to keep his fingers on the pulse of motor racing. All his life, Stirling recognised that his popularity was dependent on his name being kept to the fore and he had come to realise that if he did not appear regularly in the British press that it would affect his worth and livelihood.

He agreed to buy a Lotus Elan, that came with a standard soft top, from Colin Chapman, owner and designer of Lotus cars. Stirling was always a secret admirer of Colin's design skills, which was another reason why he had bought an Elite as his personal road car. (Many people were unaware that Chapman had designed the Vanwall chassis.) Because the Elan had a soft top, Stirling asked Ogle to design a hard top for it and it had been agreed that John Whitmore was to drive the vehicle in sports car and GT races. I suppose John was the natural choice to be the number one driver because Stirling had enjoyed the opportunity of getting to know him even better than he already did when they drove together between Shepherd Street and Ogle's, whilst Stirling was doing his design stint there.

The Elan was sold in kit form only, which meant that no purchase tax was payable on the vehicle. Ogle was to come up with an aeronautical design for the hard top, which would help the car to go that much faster. Stirling employed a lone mechanic, who was to be responsible for building the car at the British Racing Partnership's premises in Highgate. John had already proved his worth driving and had become a competent and capable saloon and sports car driver. He had also filched one of Stirling's girlfriends that he was seeing before he had his big shunt at Goodwood and had taken the opportunity of marrying her before Stirling was even able to move out of his bed. Quick work indeed! But thankfully, there were never any hard feelings. As Stirling was the first to acknowledge, all's fair in love and war – or it certainly used to be.

Late one afternoon, Stirling told me that his new mechanic Mike had informed him that he would be unable to finish building the car in time for its first outing unless he had some outside assistance. Apparently, Mike had suggested that he knew of a South African mechanic, Bud Rossler, who he could ask to help out and, very grudgingly, Stirling had agreed. Bud was working for Reg Parnell at the time and was willing to work overnight with Mike to get the Elan ready in time for its debut and Mike wanted permission to pay him for the night's work. Grumbling at the fact that he was having to spend yet more money on the car, Stirling instructed me to go up to Highgate that night and arrive unexpectedly to establish whether or not they were actually working on the car or just swinging the lead. Feeling awkward that I was being sent to spy on the two of them, I set out with a flask of tea and some sandwiches which they could eat whenever they felt like it during the night. When I arrived, they seemed to be getting on very well together and were both working on the car.

The Elan was finished just in time for John's first race but its handling was all to cock and more work was still to be done on it. Once again help was sought from Bud Rossler, the South African mechanic. He eventually finished up working for SMART full time – the Stirling Moss Automobile Racing Team (which first started life as the Stirling Moss Racing Team until Stirling thought up the acronym and, I may say, he was very pleased with himself for finding it).

A WEAK POINT

John drove the car to considerable success (as did I in some events, often quite unbeknown to Stirling), apart from the fact that its rear wheels were frequently flying off fairly early on in the car's existence whilst John was racing it. One day, when I was practising in it at Brands Hatch, the wheel, or rather a rear wheel hub, also cracked, and fortunately I heard it in time to pull straight into the pits. The mechanics at first didn't believe me and I could see from the expressions on their faces that they were thinking, 'Bloody woman driver'. It was not until they got back to the garage that they found that the wheel would, indeed, have come off (and what would Stirling have said then?). From that day onwards, they completely accepted that I was their joint boss.

The first time Stirling inadvertently found out that I was racing the car he became very concerned (for my welfare as it happens, and not the car's!). He telephoned the club secretary at the circuit, who put out a Tannoy announcement for me to report to race control. Guessing what the subject matter would be, I decided to ignore the announcement completely until after the race when I was, quite rightly, given a dressing-down for disregarding it, which of course 'I hadn't heard'. I was told to ring Stirling immediately. I decided, however, that it would be tactically better to see him in person after we arrived back in London because I knew by that time he would have calmed down a bit and would have moved on from that particular tack to something else on his list, which is exactly what happened. He just told me in future, whenever I was going to drive the car, to let him know in advance and he tried to make out that he wasn't really concerned about my safety.

This hub defect was, of course, a life-threatening predicament and Stirling became exceedingly angry and decided to do something about it. We had the hub metal tested by an expert and it was found to be not only made of tractor-gauge material (i.e. very thin metal), but that the design was also flawed.

Because each hub had been made with three 'holes' spaced equidistant to each other within the hub 'circle', they also were in line with the holding bolts (i.e. the nuts that hold the wheel on). The upshot of this was that the metal at these points was not always sufficiently strong to keep the whole thing in one piece when put under stress at high speeds, and the hub would consequently fracture or break completely. If the latter happened, the wheel would fly off.

Without more ado, Colin was summoned to Shepherd Street to discuss the matter with Stirling. He demanded that I should be present as well because by now I was virtually running the team by default because Stirling had very quickly become bored with it.

Colin sat in Stirling's upstairs living room opposite us and Stirling told him in no uncertain terms that the car was exceedingly dangerous and that he was thinking of suing him. Colin tried to wriggle this way and that out of this somewhat tight situation, but really there was no room for manoeuvre. Suddenly, the thought flashed across my mind that Colin was purported to have once said that if any car holds together for a whole race it is too heavy… He eventually agreed to pay a large amount of money to a charity specified by Stirling and, of course, to redesign all the Elan hubs and manufacture them using stronger metal.

We all shook hands on the deal. That was Stirling's preferred way. Calmly, sensibly, with no rancour – and secretly.

DRIVING DOWN TO SEBRING

Hugh Dibley, another sports car driver, would also be driving the Elan. At that stage in his career, Hugh was flying for BOAC (British Overseas Airways Corporation) and was consequently able to fly all over the world for virtually nothing, which was particularly advantageous to Stirling's pocket. Hugh later owned Palliser Design, and was involved with BOAC's sponsorship of what became 'the' classic sports car races at Brands, the BOAC 500 and subsequently the British Airways 1,000 km.

Stirling, Bud and I trailered the Elan down to Sebring from New York on one occasion. Stirling had bought a speed detector for radar speed traps, of which he took absolutely no notice whatsoever, and the journey took two days each way. He was not amused every time I warned him that we were travelling over the speed limit and, eventually, he got so cross with me that I kept quiet.

On the morning of the second day going south, we stopped off for breakfast at a diner in Georgia. When the time came for Stirling to pay the bill, the waitress looked at us and enquired if the car on the back of the trailer outside was ours. Once we confirmed that it was, she drawled in the broadest Georgia accent: 'Well, ain't that the dandiest li'l 'ol car that ah've ever seen.' It gave all three of us a good laugh to start the day.

Once we arrived in Sebring, we were joined by Hugh, who had flown straight across to Florida from the UK, and we all stayed together in a rented house, which Carroll Shelby had organised for us. Unfortunately, the organisers had not given us the necessary number of passes for our party and we were one short, so guess who was given the short straw? Even though I complained bitterly about it, I had to ride in the boot (or 'trunk', as the Americans would say) of the car until we stopped right inside the circuit. Rather naturally, Stirling was rubbing his hands in delight when he eventually let me out because he had got away without paying for an entry ticket.

Once again, Sebring would be unkind to Stirling and his luck would run out there, even though he was not driving. The car broke down early on in the race and there was nothing for it but for us to reload it onto the trailer and take it back to New York, where Stirling had arranged a buyer for it. Night began to fall and Stirling was naturally still driving the estate car well over the speed limit. From a brief look at the map, we saw that there wouldn't be that many more motels for quite a long stretch so we stopped at the last-chance saloon. As the car came to a halt, Stirling jumped out and ran into reception and was informed that there was only one bedroom left in the motel. Without more ado, he paid for it and bundled Bud and me into it.

The room had two double beds.

'Right,' said Stirling, 'Viper, you take that bed and Bud, you take the other.' The next thing I knew, he had jumped in beside me and Bud couldn't believe his eyes. Nor could I.

A TAXING PROBLEM

Later on, Stirling did a deal with the Porsche factory for the team to race a Porsche 904 and we both went over to Germany to see Huschke von Hanstein, the German baron who ran the competitions department. By now, we had also taken on Bud's elder brother Ed as a mechanic, who very early on had assumed leadership of the entire SMART back-up team, plus another South African, Piet van Asperen. Two of the team travelled out to the Porsche factory overland in the SMART Cortina because part of the deal was that they were going to be given a short mechanical course in order for them to maintain the infamous efficiency and supposed reliability for which Porsche was so renowned. Fortunately, they all spoke German (their ancestors having originated from south Germany), but generally spoke Afrikaans when working on the cars. Unfortunately for us, this was not to be one of Porsche's better cars and, unfortunately for them, I had picked up some Afrikaans myself and did not really appreciate it when one of them called me a bitch. We all had a good laugh.

Once the vehicle arrived in the Port of London, the fun began. I was given the task of clearing the sleek and sexy-looking vehicle out of customs, and this operation turned into a complete farce. It took weeks. First of all, HM Customs and Excise were going to tax the car at the full rate for an imported *road* car, which was approximately double the cost of the actual car itself in Germany. I had the devil's own job trying to persuade the authorities that this car was only going to be trailered on the back of our tow vehicle; that it would only be raced and run under its own steam on racing circuits and that it would never be used on the open roads in the UK, or anywhere else for that matter. After many weeks of wrangling, we were given the all-clear but, in order to move matters forward to our entire satisfaction, I'd also had to tip off the press, and they splashed the story across the nationals.

Once we were given the go-ahead, we set off down to London docks to collect the vehicle and we trailered it to Hugh Dibley's garage in Queen's Gate Mews. By now, this had been taken over by the SMART mechanics as their working garage, much to the annoyance of some of his neighbours.

Once again, Hugh would be sharing the drives with John Whitmore, but his first outing in the car was to test it at Silverstone. Unfortunately, this turned into a complete and utter disaster.

I took the call in the office from Ed who told me that Hugh had

had a shunt in the Porsche and that the car was more or less a write-off. I very quickly put him through to Stirling, who took the news as if it was the most natural thing in the world. That which was left of the car was despatched back to Germany, given a new chassis and rebuilt but, as a racing car, it was never the great success that Porsche expected this sports model to be. Indeed, it turned out to be a total disappointment all round.

The fact that the car was given a new chassis has perpetuated the myth about this car ever since because all kinds of different 'owners' have claimed, through the years, to have owned the ex-SMART Porsche. Of course, the fact that there are two cars running around with different chassis numbers obviously keeps these myths alive.

A NEW TOY

All the while, Stirling had been negotiating to buy a working garage in south-east London. America Street Garage, which also served as a petrol station because it sported a couple of battered old petrol pumps on the forecourt, was situated just off Southwark Street. Motor car repair work was carried out in the attached three or four large railway arches. Stirling decided against changing the name of the business to his because, first and foremost, its name indicated the garage in its rightful location point. It was not in a particularly salubrious part of town at that time and, *au fond*, he did not want people writing to him personally regarding any matters involving garage business, particularly any complaints, which inevitably crop up from time to time in any business. Eventually, the SMART team cars and personnel were transferred from Dibley's mews to Southwark, with

Ed Rossler ultimately taking on the overall responsibility for running the garage and the preparation of the SMART cars.

Stirling had agreed to take over the entire ASG staff in the deal so the place more or less ran itself initially, but he insisted on new systems being introduced – his own, naturally – and a number of checks were put in place. At first, this did not go down too well with the salt-of-the-earth staff who had never encountered such clerical systems before. Initially, the office in Shepherd Street ordered all the new stationery and carried out a lot of the work and back-up, apart from the actual day-to-day running of the operation. This new 'toy' did offer Sandra and me some relief in the office because Stirling would be relentlessly popping over to America Street, checking what was going on and getting in the staff's hair over there, rather than in ours.

Much later on, he lent his name to a national paint spray operation and acquired and installed a spray unit in one of the arches, which proved to be quite a money-spinning venture. Ultimately the petrol pumps were removed because they were more trouble than they were actually worth, what with insurance premiums and fire precautions taken into consideration in the cost of running the entire operation.

A WHITER SHADE OF GREEN

Stirling being such a celebrity, having the SMART team based at Southwark was quite an attraction in the local area, and one day a cool young man appeared at the door at Shepherd Street. After introducing himself as Charlie Crichton-Stuart, he asked if it would be possible for him to drive under the SMART colours. The Hon. Charles (one of the Butes) ran his own Formula Three car but wanted it to be run under the SMART colours of Renault Borneo Green (Number 173–26006 from the Valentine Varnish & Lacquer Company) with Jaguar Dark Green for the peripherals.

He also wanted it to be maintained by the SMART mechanics at Southwark, for which he would pay, naturally. After much wrangling about costs and expenses, Stirling eventually agreed to Charlie's request, having established that he was actually a more than competent driver and wouldn't let the team down.

Charlie was a real card and was actually very successful that year. In fact, he was more than a credit to the team. He lived in a ground-floor flat with Frank Williams and 'Bubbles' Horsley in Harrow, both of whom dabbled in cars. Frank went on to run his own highly successful racing team and Bubbles joined (Lord) Alexander Hesketh, who was ultimately world champion James Hunt's patron. They all got on well together and were constantly fooling around. On one occasion Bubbles got stuck in one of the downstairs windows. He was somewhat of a roly-poly and had been trying to squeeze through because the others were chasing him, feverishly firing suction arrows at him whilst he tried to escape the onslaught. By the time he became wedged in the window, screaming for help, two arrows had hit their target and were stuck firmly on each cheek. No one could help him because we were all crying with laughter. A couple of years later, Charlie went on to marry the actress Shirley Anne Field and left the motor racing scene for a few years.

The reason that Stirling had chosen the specific shade of green for the team cars was that he knew from experience that this Borneo Green photographed remarkably well and showed up best by far in black and white photographs. Therefore, if any of his cars appeared in a photograph, which was subsequently published, they would shine out like the proverbial beacon. This particular shade of green was generally regarded by the whole of the motor racing fraternity as being rather a bad joke, if not a bizarre choice of colour, but this 'old dog' did not care about what anyone else thought. He always had a reason for what he did. There were no flies on Stirling, I can assure you! He perpetually propelled me into automatically thinking of an alternative way of getting around any problem whatsoever, however large or small it may be. One had to be particularly quick-witted to live up to this particular precept, but it generally boiled down to being able to think exceedingly quickly outside the box. This was fine most of the time, but sometimes we would come up against each other and then it became a battle of willpower. Inevitably, working for him, I had to give in, but after I had officially left his employment it was a different matter. I would often stand my ground and he would back down – on occasions!

KEEPING IN THE LIMELIGHT

I was making coffee in the kitchen one afternoon in 1963 when Stirling buzzed me up on the telephone and asked if I would like to go rallying.

Of all the darn questions! Me, go rallying?

I suggested that it might be easier if we were to discuss the matter over the coffee I was making but, instead, he shot upstairs and bowled into the kitchen to mull over the proposition with me there and then.

'Viper, would you like to go rallying?' he repeated.

I frowned and answered, 'But, I don't know anything about it.'

'Oh, you'll soon learn,' he said, airily.

'Why me?' I asked. 'I haven't got a clue what rallying is about.'

'You are the only woman, apart from my sister, who I know who can drive a car properly.'

'But you haven't got a rally car,' I argued.

'Getting a car is the easy part,' he said. 'I can soon get one,' and away he bounced down the stairs back to his office.

By the time I had wiped down the bench and taken the tray downstairs with the coffee on it, he had more or less persuaded Walter (Wally) Hayes, vice president of Ford Europe, to lend us a Ford Cortina for me to drive.

'Well, you have a car, I think I will enter it for you in the Alpine Rally that is coming up soon,' was all he said.

As the comedian Tommy Cooper would have said, 'Just like that.'

The next problem was to get hold of a co-driver and qualify for an international rally licence in time for the Alpine Rally, which started a mere six weeks away in the south of France. There were only seven club rallies we could possibly enter before this event, in order to qualify for our licences, which required six signatures. John Sprinzel, another race and rally driver, who owned a specialist car repair works and a small showroom in Lancaster Mews, Paddington, quickly came to our rescue and, without him, we would never have qualified in time. As it was, we broke down on one of the club rallies because someone had put a railway sleeper on a special stage alongside a deserted railway track. Stirling was so incensed about this that he lugged me over to his solicitors to try to sue the organisers, but he was diplomatically told that there wasn't much of a case to go on as we did not have sufficient proof, apart from the shattered sump on our car. It was as if someone had personally threatened him and he wanted the culprits to be caught and given due punishment. On this particular occasion, it was not all about money; it was about the principle of deliberately putting danger in the way of other people, which could cause serious injury, or even death.

Next, he decided to design the most impractical, personalised SMART overalls for us and have them made up by one of the top 'in' fashion designers of the day, Frederick Starke. We were to wear apple green, mandarin collar-type, long-sleeved blouses underneath bib-style, black and white houndstooth overalls, with the letters SMART embroidered in pale green on the bib. This hardly showed up at all. The bib was attached by two brace-type straps in the same material, which came over the shoulders and crossed over the back, rather like those of Carroll Shelby's. They might have looked smart, but we found them exceedingly awkward – and time consuming – particularly when we wanted to go to the loo.

The car that Ford provided was a bog-standard, dark green Cortina and, after six frantic weeks of club rallying, we found ourselves driving down to Marseilles all on our own and fearing the worst. I had even been warned not to go out at night because a lot of trafficking of women went on between Marseilles and Morocco. (*Plus ça change!*)

Unfortunately, about two-thirds of the way into our almost 800-mile journey, we knew that something was not right with the car so we nursed it to Marseilles and further on up the coast to Cassis, where we knew the Ford mechanics were staying. They were not at all happy at being called out to work on our car and made their feelings very plain. The next hitch came from the organisers of the rally, who had some homologation issues. Put simply, they were implying that the car did not conform to the all-necessary official paperwork. I telephoned Stirling in utter panic but he told me calmly that he would resolve the problem, which he did, by ringing up the RAC and sorting out the whole business to his and the French rally organisers' satisfaction. As usual, after calming us down (or rather me), he was efficiency personified and told us that everything would be OK, and it was.

MOTEL MADNESS

There was a special stage on the next rally he entered me in, the RAC Rally round Britain, which included a speed test at Oulton Park. As it so happens, the Rover team had hired the circuit for a day before the event, in order for their drivers to become well acquainted with the circuit. Peter Bolton, who had driven a Shelby Cobra at Le Mans when Stirling had been team manager, was a works Rover driver, and he rang me up to invite me to come along to their test day so that I wouldn't have to do the test blind when it came to it on the RAC. When I protested that I wasn't a Rover driver he told me that he would square it with the works and that I was to come along anyway. There was one further snag: I was due to pick up Stirling from the airport the evening before I had been invited to Cheshire and I didn't know whether or not he would give me the day off. He was becoming ever more crotchety about my time. I picked him up and we were halfway back into Central London before I asked him rather tentatively if I could take the day off to go testing the following day.

He didn't utter a word. Instead, he told me to take a left turn and when I asked him where we were going he said somewhat patronisingly, 'Oulton Park, of course.'

'But,' I said, 'I haven't got any clothes or toiletries. I must pick them up before we go.'

'It doesn't matter,' he said. 'I've got mine.'

Quite! I argued my case but he wouldn't have any of it and, as soon as we hit the M1, he took over the wheel of the car. Once he decided on a course of action and his mind was made up, he rarely changed it.

Dusk turned into night as we approached the end of the motorway in Warwickshire and he was ticking on about there being a motel somewhere at the end of it. I told him that there wasn't one marked on the map and I had never heard of it but still he kept going on about it. Shortly after we came off the motorway, we literally stumbled across it. It was just after ten when we drove up to the gatehouse and I was sent to organise a room but, when I got there, the cubicle where the receptionist should have been was empty.

As I reported this fact to Stirling he hissed, 'Get back in the car,' and after I did he began to drive very slowly and quietly round the estate until we came across a cabin where the door was ajar.

'Get out and see if it is empty,' he whispered.

'I can't,' I retorted.

'Don't be so stupid, of course you can,' he answered, leaning across me to open the passenger door and push me out.

I half slid out and took my heart in my hands as I approached the darkened doorway. I touched the door and it swung eerily inwards. I held my breath.

'Go on,' he whispered loudly, 'take a look inside.'

Somewhat hesitantly, I moved a step or two inside and saw that the room was empty. I couldn't get away quickly enough and ran back to report to him.

'Good, we'll stay here,' he said.

'We can't,' I said again.

'We can,' he said, and we did.

I was instructed to use the bathroom first and I snuggled into bed in all the clothes that I had been wearing when I picked him up at the airport. It was freezing cold and there was no heating. Naturally, having been away, Stirling had all his kit with him and changed before hopping into the other bed.

My sweet dreams lasted until early in the morning when I was roughly shaken by the shoulder with Stirling whispering loudly, 'Hurry up, hurry up! I have used the bathroom so be quick. We'll get breakfast on the way.'

We drove out of the compound slowly and, once he could see that the receptionist still hadn't turned up for work and there was no one around, he floored the accelerator and, I may say, he had the largest grin of satisfaction on his face that I have ever seen.

THE CUPBOARD WAS BARE

The following year, unbeknown to dodo here, he contracted me to Standard Triumph for an undisclosed fee; he received the money and most of the publicity and I started driving for them in a works-prepared car painted in SMART colours. Initially, all went well, apart from the fact that Stirling began to make it perfectly clear – and unreasonably so – that he didn't like me being away from the office. This was probably because he felt jealous that I was able to do something that he would like to be doing himself. In fact, the whole idea about me rallying was probably that it was the nearest thing he could involve himself in without actually participating. He even accompanied me once when I went to recce for the Monte Carlo Rally. However, there was another fly in the ointment. The Triumph team manager at the time also made it perfectly obvious that it did not suit him having me in his team and when I complained to Stirling and totally refused to drive for Triumph any more, he obviously backed me up 100 per cent.*

He telephoned the directors of Standard Triumph and arranged to meet them with me at the works on the outskirts of Coventry. I simply could not believe my ears that he was prepared to shift his backside and drive all the way from London to Coventry just to support my cause – or so I thought at the time.

The problem was resolved most satisfactorily, as far as I was concerned, and the bad grace that was shown by the 'guilty' party, who had really got up my nose and obviously vice versa, has continued to cast his shadow over me ever since. This was probably because there was never any love lost between the two of us right from the start. The problem arose because, although I was supposed to be part of the official works team, he did not regard me as being a part of it (whereas the other drivers and mechanics did). On the first rally I drove the Triumph, he partnered me with a navigator who had never been to London, let alone on the Continent and, on the RAC Rally in the winter, he left me completely high and dry. I arrived at one of the service points en route only to find no one there whatsoever. I had been completely blackballed.

A couple of rallies later, the powers-that-be at Standard Triumph appointed a new team manager, which rather says it all.

A SECRET AFFAIR

The first I knew of the existence of Elaine, an American girlfriend of Stirling's, was when we were in New York and Stirling told me that

---

*   I was exceedingly surprised, but then I was unaware of the financial agreement that was in place at that time!

he had to go and see a bit of crumpet and I told him that I was off to see an ex of his who, by that time, was living just off Fifth Avenue and had some clothes to hand on to me. We arranged a rendezvous to catch our plane back to London and parted in different directions.

During the return flight to London, he began to open up to me about Elaine, the girl he had been to see. He told me that he was paying for her to fly to England in a couple of days' time and, because I thought it was so unlike him, I began to question him further. He sighed, shrugged his shoulders and told me that she had backed him into a corner during the visit and that he felt duty bound to bring her over to England for a while. Why, I do not know, but once back in London, Stirling asked me to go and buy her some underwear and nightwear. Knowing Stirling's pocket, I naturally went to Marks & Spencer to buy them. Wrong! She did not receive these at all graciously and immediately went on a spending spree, parting with rather more of Stirling's money than I had.

I tried my best to get on with her as she began to dig her heels further and further into the Shepherd Street turf, beginning to put her stamp on the rules of the property. One of these was that we (in the office) were not to use the kitchen to make coffee during the day, including Stirling. I also noticed that Stirling was beginning to backtrack in his rehab. He was becoming rude again and very snappy.

I was still rallying at this point, and imagine my surprise when, on the top of a mountain in France, Pat, Stirling's sister, called across to me and said, 'Hey, Val, did you know Stirling's married?'

Quite frankly, for a fraction of a second, I didn't believe her. But then, after it had slowly sunk in, I was aghast. It had come just as much of a surprise to her as it had to me and we both compared notes and wondered why on earth he would have got hitched without one or the other or both of us being there. It was totally out of character, even for the new Stirling.

Once back in the office, Stirling didn't mention a thing about the marriage so I eventually asked him if what Pat had told me was true and he muttered that it was. He was exceedingly non-committal and didn't want to talk about it but that was OK by me because it wasn't any of my business. I continued to try my best with Elaine, but it was pretty obvious that neither of us really liked each other.

A TEMPORARY HICCUP

A year later, Val Domleo, who was normally Pat Moss's navigator and co-driver, arrived at Shepherd Street in a works Mini she had brought down from Abingdon in Oxfordshire for us to drive in Italy. She had agreed to come along to be my navigator as part of a deal for me to take a works Mini on the Jolly Rally (Jolly being an Italian chain of hotels). The hotel group was sponsoring the Rally, which started in Palermo, Sicily. It was then to wind its way through Syracuse and up to the north of Italy, like a mini Tour de France (though with automobiles, of course). The rally consisted of driving on designated circuits, timed hill climbs and on the open roads. Stirling was exceedingly rude to her when she arrived and I was frightfully upset and embarrassed about it. I ticked on about it to her continually for the next ten days or so that we were abroad and resolved to hand in my notice when I got back to the office, which I subsequently did. Looking back, I suppose it is strange that the lighter for the fire should involve someone else rather than myself, but by then I, too, had my own principles.

For some reason, Stirling asked me to go down to the basement with him to discuss the matter of my resignation rather than doing so in the office – presumably he didn't want the possibility of Elaine overhearing what he had to say. He looked embarrassed, but there were no hard feelings and, this time, he did not really try to talk me out of leaving and I didn't rescind my notice. I was never more determined to go. We both agreed that my leaving would probably be for the best even though I did not have a job to go to.

He would not worry about that whatsoever.

MOVING ON

I do not remember anything about the day that I left Shepherd Street. I can only surmise that it must have been a perfectly normal day, just like any other. We did not go out for a meal or anything like that. After I had gone, Sandra told me that Stirling was going to give me the cheapest of the brooches that had been left lying on his desk for over a week but she had persuaded him to give me a slightly better one. These brooches had been sent round from his jewellery firm in Maddox Street on approval, and had been there for all to see on his desk. Nothing had been mentioned to me about them and I had rather naturally assumed that he was buying a present for someone else. A couple of days before the Friday I left, he tossed one of them over the desk to me – unwrapped of course – accompanied by an abrupt 'Here, this is for you.'

And, so it was, on that inauspicious Friday, that my life and Stirling's moved on in separate directions.

Eight years had gone by since we first met and, as the old saying goes, an awful lot of water had gone under the bridge.

I'M ALRIGHT, JACK!

Stirling had not been at all interested in my future welfare during those last few days. He knew I didn't have a job to go to but he wasn't at all concerned. It wasn't his problem.

He never really took much interest in what I was actually up to after I left, with one exception: he loathed my boyfriend with a vengeance and couldn't for the life of him understand what I saw in this man. He didn't like the way he treated me and was perpetually telling me to get out of the situation. I didn't ask after his personal life.

I heard that his daughter, Allison, was born on Christmas Day – I was not informed of this event – and everyone who knew Stirling had a good laugh because they joked that he would only ever have to buy her one present a year.

Then, quite out of the blue, I was invited to the party after Allison's official christening. I was in two minds whether or not to go along, but felt it would be slightly churlish of me if I did not. After all, Stirling and I had never fallen out on a personal level. As I walked into the gathering, Stirling rushed over to me and we greeted each other as if we had only seen each other yesterday, like old friends. Towards the end of the do I left, and life went on just as it had before.

PRIVATE EYE

A couple of years passed and then, a private detective, who I had introduced to a solicitor friend of mine and who Stirling subsequently used, rang and told me to keep well away from the well-loved comedian for whom I was doing some work, Tony Hancock; otherwise I could be named in his divorce case. During the course of the conversation, this chap also mentioned that he was helping with Stirling's divorce (of which, of course, I was totally unaware – and which should never have been mentioned anyway). He told me that the guilty party to be named was coincidentally living off the same street where I was living, in a small mews house. Small world!

Typically, Stirling had kept a low profile about this rather private matter but, as soon as the legalities were finished, he found himself living on his own again. By this time, his best friend David had married, and could not spend the time he would have normally spent with Stirling in such circumstances, whilst Ken was long gone and doing his own thing.

Consequently, Stirling began to ring me more regularly after the separation and divorce to have a natter. We would meet up from time to time or I would go round to Shepherd Street and he began asking me to do a few little chores for him. And, of course, our paths also began to cross because we had so many mutual friends who he began seeing again now that he was single.

And so, slowly, Stirling started to come back into my life and vice versa. The gulf that had eroded our association became the blip that never was. Our friendship rekindled and resumed as though nothing had ever happened in the in-between times, since when it has never faltered.

He also employed a wonderful new housekeeper, who was one of those very grounded, comfortable people, who was very good for him and, gradually, he began to come out of his shell and started to do the rounds again, crumpet-wise. I was also being asked to pop round to have a snack and a catch-up and once I even used his place as a haven to stay when I was having boyfriend problems.

THE FLAME REKINDLES

Stirling subsequently began a couple of long-term affairs, naturally run in tandem. The two bits of crumpet involved were completely different. One was an air hostess, kind and loving and who was comfortable in her own shoes, and the other was a go-getter, elegant in the extreme, who dated scores of men and, although she tried to pin Stirling down, he, thankfully, was not really up for it, though she definitely seemed to hold a certain fascination for him. He could never really get rid of her because she would have made a scene and, *au fond*, Stirling was all for the quiet life.

After going out with both women for many months, the air hostess began to feel that she wanted to know if there was any long-term future in her relationship with him. She firmly but kindly put her foot down and gave him an ultimatum – either they would become a properly 'recognised' couple or she would leave him completely.

Up until then, they had been quietly going out for meals together, but he hardly ever took her along to official functions, preferring to parade the more glamorous alternative on his arm. He was in a total quandary because he really did not want that to happen, but neither did he feel that he could give her the commitment that she was looking for. Being true to his better feelings and self-imposed standards, they decided to part amicably but, to my knowledge, they never saw each other again. The split was final. That left the way clear for the 'nearest competition' (or so the other person thought) and who, quite frankly, Stirling was even less likely to commit to. When she was finally edged out, she took the final snub with such bad grace that she caused him a multitude of problems.

THE BRAZILIAN CONNECTION

Quite out of the blue, a couple of years later, Stirling rang me up to ask me if I could come and meet some Brazilian drivers to whom he wanted to introduce me. Unusually, I could not pin him down as to precisely why he wanted me to meet them. In the end, it was just easier to agree. We arranged a date and a time when it suited us all to meet up at Stirling's house, when he introduced the two boys to me. Stirling explained that they wanted to join the Stirling Moss Automobile Racing Team, which had been dormant pretty much during the years since I had officially stopped working for Stirling Moss Ltd.

Stirling might have been self-centred – and I dared to tell him so very many years later – but he always knew how to work certain people and because he had moulded me more or less as he wanted me; he knew which buttons to press to access what he required. On this particular occasion, without ever coming to the point and actually asking outright, he wanted me to manage SMART again, part time. He considered these boys to have potential, but, more to the point, they owned their own cars and had come over to the UK with their own sponsorship. All they wanted was to be seen to have the backing of Stirling Moss. They also required the necessary 'behind-the-scenes' back-up, such as management and mechanics to maintain their cars, preferably in Central London. What could be more ideal than America Street Garage? And, of course, me, to supervise the whole operation. I was put in such a position that I could hardly say no to becoming involved on the management side (naturally without any payment), and SMART was resurrected. This meant that our old South African mechanics, who were, by now, working at America Street Garage, would have something to do that they really enjoyed, and their wages would be covered by the Brazilian sponsorship monies. By this time, I was running my own PR business so I had to juggle my life accordingly, but this commitment certainly took up most of my spare time at night and at the weekends during the season.

We began on a winning streak; the sole problem to arise was another Brazilian who had become our main competition by the name of Emerson Fittipaldi. He had arrived in the UK earlier in the year before our two Brazilians and was driving under the beady eye of Colin Chapman, who he had impressed originally, I believe, as a test driver. As soon as our boys began racing, we began beating the Fittipaldi car, which really upset the Lotus apple cart in Formula Ford. (We were running Merlyns as opposed to Lotus.) Stirling did not interfere very much with the day-to-day running of the team, but he was always on hand to give support and advice, when asked. Emerson would go on to become a two-time F1 world champion in 1972 and 1974.

It wasn't long before Stirling began to complain about the cost of running the team. Because of the number of races the two cars had been entered in so far, they had used more engines and tyres than anticipated, quite apart from anything else. Life on a shoestring was proving difficult yet fun. Even so, Stirling didn't really understand what was happening, but enjoyed ticking on just for the sake of it! I would always give him short shrift if I could because, quite frankly, life was so much easier when he did not interfere.

I had tried to keep the team outgoings down to a bare minimum and, in fact, we had spent less than we normally would have done because the two cars were so successful. Even so, motor racing is not cheap and any prize money that was received just ended up covering hotels and travelling expenses. We were approaching a crossroads when a lifesaver loomed onto the horizon.

Once SMART started to become a winning force and the boys began scooping up some trophies, we were approached by one of the engine suppliers, Chris Steele, who asked if he could look after our engines and strip them down after every meeting, free of charge. In return, all he asked was for permission to use the team name in connection with any publicity for his engines. This was a no-brainer because, quite apart from anything else, the cost of looking after the engines was going to cripple us. And, if you don't look after the engines properly, there isn't much point in competing, no matter who is driving.

However much Stirling may have grumbled, he definitely still had his uses. Yet again, it was his name that was in demand.

FATHERLY ADVICE

On one particular occasion, I had to get in touch with Stirling because one of 'our' drivers did not like competing in the wet and wanted to pull out of the race before it even started. He wanted to know what Stirling would think of this, which was an easy question to answer. In a phrase: 'not very much'. However, to keep faith, I did speak to Stirling on the telephone and he told me what I already knew and to tell him to drive to his capabilities and to feel as happy as he could be with the conditions. This advice worked like a charm and, after a couple of laps, our 'timorous wee beastie' was well up with the leaders and went on to win the race.

At the end of the season, it was announced that the chief of Brands

Hatch, John Webb, was organising a Torneo in Brazil and was inviting over certain teams to compete in five races there; two were to be in Rio de Janeiro, one in Curitiba, in the south-east of Brazil, another in Fortaleza, right on the north coast, four degrees south of the equator and the last in Sao Paulo. The SMART team was invited to participate and we decided to send the cars over because it would be a good opportunity to try to sell them there, which is, indeed, what happened. It was an absolutely crazy trip from start to finish and I was even asked to run the official Lola works car as well but, when I returned from Brazil and told Stirling that the motor racing had not cost him a penny, apart from a set of tyres, he simply could not believe how I had managed it. Even he, for once, was overawed and totally flummoxed.

• • •

Stirling was an orderly person in absolutely everything he did but, rather surprisingly, he never berated me even if I left any of his cars looking like a dog's dinner. Curiously, he never said a word and, as time went on, he actually found it rather amusing that I treated my own cars in exactly the same way – or even worse than I did his. I hardly ever cleaned the interior of a car and I would probably only wash mine about once a year, if that. I always felt that it was such a waste of my time. It rained pretty often and that was enough for me. Often, people in Shepherd Street used to look at me rather strangely when I would sweep into Stirling's pristine garage to park one very scruffy, dirty old Fiat Uno. It certainly never embarrassed him and, in actual fact, he became very fond of the old vehicle. We always referred to it as 'the skip' and he never quite got over the fact that eventually a young man in a white van crashed into the side of it whilst stationary in Central London and it had to be towed to the great big parking lot in the sky. He missed the Uno more than I did and he would continually ask me time and again, 'Viper, have you still got the skip?' He had a memory like a sieve – out of sight, virtually out of mind. The Fiat was almost a quarter of a century old by that time – a third of Stirling's life – and it had never once let me down.

CAPITAL ADVICE!

From time to time, Stirling would ask me to do personal jobs for him, such as going through his diaries for certain pieces of information or to check copy for accuracy, which I always found particularly tedious and time consuming. Rather naturally, he liked to try to keep up with modern technology, such as the internet, and I was always giving him bits of advice once he began using an Apple Mac. Coincidentally, we both had the same laptop. If I couldn't help, we would nip off on his scooter to seek some professional help at Apple in Regent Street. How he got away with what he did on his scooter was quite beyond belief, because he never considered anyone – he knew he didn't need to. He typed some of his own letters and most of his emails, the latter always being in capital letters. Many of them were classics: short, sharp and to the point and, sometimes, they were very funny. I particularly liked one very clipped email I received in reply to a question that I asked him about someone he didn't particularly like.

It read: 'BECAUSE HE IS A PRICK. Ciao, Stirling.'

In his later years, Stirling standardised his personal emails, finishing them with: 'Ciao, Stirling', plus his address and telephone numbers, but when he wasn't in a hurry, he would personalise them more – or at least he did when writing to me.

We also had many other common interests, not the least of which was property, and he would often call me up to discuss what was on the market and the valuations. Sometimes, we would go and view the properties together and, on one occasion, he asked me to go along to an auction and bid for him.

•   •   •

Stirling's eyesight – and consequently his judgement (in terms of measuring distances) – was phenomenal, and this was probably why he had such fine intuition when it came to driving. But, when his arms gradually appeared longer and longer, he eventually gave in to age and began to wear glasses. I continually baited and teased him about this and he would always defend himself and say, 'Viper, you just don't understand – I can't see.' He eventually had his eyes surgically corrected.

Before the operation, accompanying him on a scooter was sheer murder as he weaved his way through the traffic with just a couple of millimetres to spare, and many a time I would tap him vigorously on the shoulder and tell him that even if he was happy cheekily squeezing past, I was not. It was little wonder that he landed in hospital so many times as a result of scooter accidents. He always got short shrift from me on such occasions, when I would call him a bloody fool. Eventually, Susie banned him from riding his scooter. With the amount of time he spent there, it is little wonder that, to this day, we still confuse the word hospital with hotel.

Stirling often used to help me out when he was running around London on his scooter doing little chores, such as delivering my film for processing or collecting the contacts for me. People were frequently amazed when they recognised the 'messenger' under the helmet!

As time went on and I moved house, we would discuss builders and decorators, plumbers and electricians. Now and then he would ask me what I was doing, which I learnt meant the prelude to: would I like to go back and work for him, but I don't believe it ever does to go back – I am positive that it would have been a sure way to ruin our friendship.

MORE FATHERLY ADVICE

At the end of the '70s I had a strange, whirlwind romance. I was married under unusual circumstances, eventually tying the knot at Caxton Hall, Westminster, after Stirling had warned me against it. I had popped into Shepherd Street just prior to the date of the ceremony and he begged me to reconsider getting married to this particular person. I immediately responded by pointing out that he had already had two goes at it so now it was my turn. He didn't try to argue. He just looked at me, sighed and said, 'You are making a big mistake, Viper.'

And, as usual, he turned out to be correct.

But, of course, it was he who came to my rescue when troubles arose during the breakdown of my marriage, but he never rubbed salt into the wound. Far from it. When I considered it prudent to move away from home for a while, it was Stirling, ever practical, who suggested that I should move into Shepherd Street to let things cool down whilst he was away. I had fallen headlong into this whirlwind romance and, as often happens, true love stories can have particularly sad endings. Life happens.

FUN WITH THE FAMILY

A couple of years after that, I was invited to attend the blessing at the church in Chester Square of Stirling's marriage to Susie Paine, his third and final wife, who had been the little girl he had first met in Hong Kong at the age of five. It was she who subsequently took on all the responsibilities surrounding his well-being and business activities. His bride was twenty-five years younger than he was and she had sat tight during all the goings-on and melodramas that had taken place since the disintegration of his second marriage. Her reappearance into his life completed the circle.

I have to admit, I did wonder how she would view me and whether I would be accepted or whether, perhaps, I would be considered as being the enemy. Fortunately, we gelled together excellently and, because Stirling and Susie's son, Elliot, was born three or four years after my daughter, Mia, we started to get together to do family-type things over the years. At Christmas, Susie would put on the most magnificent feast for us all. And as the children grew older, we would play games after Christmas lunch, but, when the kids became too bright, Stirling would throw all his toys out of the pram and refuse to play with us! At first, we would go round to Shepherd Street, but later Stirling would pay for me and my daughter to fly to Florida to join them at their house in Fort Lauderdale and, later still, Miami.

When the children were really quite small, Elliot and Mia decided to put on a special Christmas play for us but, unfortunately, after lengthy rehearsals, whatever action there was, it was far too slow for Stirling and after many cries of 'Get on with it!' the play was abandoned.

On another occasion, he decided, quite on the spur of the moment, that we should take the children to Disney World and the Epcot Centre for a couple of days. Stirling obviously felt that he was being somewhat hampered by the children always being around and was bored. He thought a trip to Orlando would bring some light relief and give him – and secondarily the children – something more positive to do, as opposed to what he really enjoyed doing most. Generally, he liked to potter at a Hells Angel pace around the house, doing practical chores, or he would drive to the shopping malls to see what was available. But, because he was a sun-worshipper, most of all he liked to relax by the pool, trying to make himself look busy with a laptop and taking the occasional dip. Of course, with the children hovering all the time, he found it rather difficult.

As per usual, when we left for Orlando he sped off as though he had been stung by a bee and fortunately we had a pretty uneventful three-hour or so drive. After finding some accommodation, we drove into the enormous Disney World complex. The children had made up their minds that the one thing they really did want to have a go on was the Magic Mountain but, as luck would have it, it was closed. After coping with that disappointment, 'Note Man' Stirling decided to make a list of what was open, what we would do and the order in which we would visit the attractions. We methodically went through it like a dose of salts – apart from the inevitable queuing.

The queues in America zigzagged to and fro, which has become the norm in the UK today. Impatient as always, Stirling was hopping from one foot to the other with the monotony of it all when suddenly, out of the blue, a woman opposite to him in the queue asked, accusingly, 'Aren't you Stirling Moss?' This was probably the first time that I had ever seen him pleased to chat to a complete stranger! The kids could not understand why the woman had accosted him and they began asking all the normal questions that children do at that age to try to find out the facts, such as 'Do you know that lady?' and then, when he said no, 'Well, why did you speak to her then?' Where ignorance is bliss...

Ever since we'd left Fort Lauderdale, I had ticked on about Epcot being an acronym for 'something' and Stirling was adamant that it wasn't. He was, therefore, surprisingly embarrassed when I stopped to ask a giant Mickey Mouse in Disney World what the initials stood for.

'Experimental Prototype Community of Tomorrow'.

So then we knew.

By the end of the first full day, we had visited the majority of sites on the list and that evening, in a diner, Stirling saw an advertisement where we could get free tickets to a Water World event if we attended a presentation for a timeshare. He was absolutely over the moon about this, but Susie certainly was not and refused to go with him.

'Viper will come with me, won't you?' he asked, expectantly.

'She's welcome,' said Susie, but there really wasn't going to be any argument with free tickets on offer for the five of us. (I must admit that the tickets were frightfully expensive.)

Next morning, Stirling and I pitched up to listen to the spiel, politely refused their kind offer, collected our free tickets and off we went to pick up Susie and the kids to see the afternoon performance. This was more or less the last item on our agenda and immediately after the show finished, Stirling decided that there wasn't any point in hanging around in Orlando any more, wasting another evening in the motel. So, off we sped into the night, homeward bound.

Things tended to move so fast with Stirling that the children were quite used to being just swept along on the tide, and this was advantageous as well because they didn't come to expect anything unless it was absolutely promised. There was one slight hiccup on the return journey, though, when Stirling was pulled up by a speed cop and had to pay a rather large fine (which rather defeated all the economies of the day), but the children saw it all as part of the entertainment. Susie and I, of course, bit our tongues.

Naturally, this was not the first time that Stirling had been apprehended by a speed cop in America, the previous occasion being a year or so before I joined him on holiday. He landed up in jail for the night and one could say that he did not enjoy the experience at all – but it hadn't seemed to deter him from speeding much either.

Apparently, our reactions to situations had become totally predictable by anyone who knew us well enough, and who knew us better than the children? Whenever Elliot and Mia were together, they could often be seen doing a number of high fives and, initially, no one thought anything more to it, even though it was always followed by muffled laughter. Then, after yet another outburst, someone asked them what it was they were exactly laughing at.

'Nothing,' came the typical response of children being asked a question they do not want to answer.

'It can't be nothing because you are still giggling.'

It transpired that they were laughing because, by that time, they had realised that they could set up Stirling or me, or both of us, and predict exactly what our reactions would be to given circumstances, which would, of course, be pretty well identical. They thought this to be a great joke I may say, and it became a never-ending game to them, even as adults.

AS TIME WENT BY

Our get-togethers at Christmas continued until Stirling had his prostate problems so that year, 2000, Elliot came skiing with Mia and me whilst his father underwent an operation in America. Even after that, Stirling would often pay for me to join him and Susie during their summer break in Florida and we had a lot of fun together. Susie made my sixtieth birthday extraordinarily memorable because she put on a special dinner and the pair of them had hunted around and found a fluorescent plastic viper, which glows in the dark, and which still lives on in my house today, hanging from one of the main lights! It always gives me a laugh when people try not to notice it.

● ● ●

It rather surprised me that Stirling did not take more of a firm hand in bringing up his son. Once, when Elliot was being particularly naughty, I asked Stirling why he did not tell him off. Being the wise old owl that he was by then, he told me that in order to prevent disagreements with Susie he thought it was better if only one parent took on the primary responsibility of bringing up a child, and that included discipline. This was a valid point, but I don't think Stirling really would have had the patience for it either, particularly when Elliot went to school.

The three of them attended my daughter's christening when she was about five, and at one point Elliot began toddling around on his own, socialising and apparently asking many of the adults for sips of their champagne, with inevitable results. And who was the one who received all the blame for this? No surprises there! I was always blamed for everything. Stirling could not, however, hold me responsible for the couple of floods that occurred after he had revamped his house. I was a key holder and would be woken at all hours by security, and would have to climb out of bed and drive round to Shepherd Street to try to sort out the problem if there was one. One never knew.

I was often asked to make up dinner parties at Shepherd Street, first and foremost because I found it easy to chat about inconsequential things and, secondly, Susie thought that she might be able to find someone who I might be interested in, but even she couldn't find anyone to take my fancy.

As the years went by and the children left home and went their separate ways, Stirling, Susie and I continued to meet regularly and we often watched the Grands Prix on television together. The children were never particularly interested in motor racing, especially as they grew older. Woe betide us if Susie and I had a bit of a natter during a race, which of course was inevitable, and poor old Susie would always get it in the neck. It was as if Stirling knew that if he chided me for speaking at the same time as the TV commentary I would give him as good as he gave, even in his own house. Eventually, Susie and I would gang up and shout him down and he realised that it was far more prudent for him not to argue with us because he could get back to watching the race on the box that little bit quicker.

MUTUAL RESPECT

I met an extraordinary number of people from all different walks of life during the time I worked for Stirling, from royalty and top celebrities to criminals. We were running the racing team at the time of the Great Train Robbery and, as it turned out, we knew one of the members quite well because he drove a Formula Junior car. Subsequently, once he had been captured Stirling was asked if he would give a character reference for him. This, however, was never followed through by the barrister. The chap had, in fact, gone on the run the day before the Tourist Trophy race in which our team was due to take part at Goodwood and had chatted to me in the pit. Whatever status a person might have and whoever a person may be, Stirling would unfailingly treat everyone with precisely the same respect and courtesy as the next person. It came as second nature to him to be extremely civil and charming to everyone he met, with the exception, on occasions, of those in his immediate family and his small circle of friends! He did not suffer fools gladly, yet he would never belie what he was really thinking about them at the time.

I have always been my own person and, as such, once I left his employ and was on my own, doing my own thing, I would never let Stirling get away with anything. That was probably one of the reasons why we have had such a long and close friendship: because he respected me as I respected him. I would sometimes argue and tell him to his face exactly what I thought and, although he would argue back, he would always respect that I had a different point of view to him (if I did – we generally agreed on most things, though). Of course, he was always the first to concede that, to a large extent, he made me who I was as an adult and I think he was rather proud of this fact. Although we lived very separate lives all through the years we have known each other, we have always been there for each other. I don't think Stirling ever liked any of my boyfriends very much and, probably like a parent, he didn't think any of them were good enough for me. On some occasions, he would even ring them up to find out what their intentions were. He would always spring to my defence and would generally take my side in any dispute; on a couple of occasions, he even became involved in disputes within my own family.

When he inadvertently fell down the lift shaft in his house from the second floor (because he was talking to his daughter-in-law as he automatically opened the door to go inside and the lift wasn't where it should have been), it was truly amazing that he survived. Naturally, he was very, very sick and shaken afterwards. But, as per usual, he put a brave face on everything. He was in a lot of pain though. Once he had substantially improved and was feeling a little better, I went round to sit and chat with him to give Susie some slight relief, as I did many times when he was hospitalised after falling off his scooter. He didn't receive much sympathy from me, though! But, just like any other adversity he had ever faced, whenever he had to stay put, he always tried to beat the problem far quicker than anyone else, and his determination for self-preservation was unfailing. Being in bed for such a long time, he was so bored that he had become totally mesmerised by many of the rather mundane programmes on the box. I guess there wasn't any alternative for him, lying prostrate in bed for hours on end, because he didn't read. He became totally hooked for a while on an American TV programme about the extreme mess in some people's houses, and he really could not believe that people could live in such disgraceful conditions. No doubt the producers felt the same way! For someone who was always so neat and tidy, this was an entirely different experience for him, seeing how some of 'the other half' live.

SHARED UPS AND DOWNS

For well over half a century, we shared the ups and downs of each other's lives – the triumphs and the disasters, the misery and the jubilation, the sorrows and the laughter, the gossip and the secrets.

It is quite impossible to work with someone for decades without caring for them and forming a close attachment to them. Yes, Stirling had a great influence on my life and we have always worked as a team. Of course, we have had our differences, but we have never actually had a row when the other has stormed off, even if we did come close at times! But if someone tried to cause trouble, or there was the slightest doubt about the other's actions or character, we would defend each other to the hilt. Of such attitudes are unbreakable friendships made.

Stirling never wavered in his support for me (and this has been true throughout the entirety of his life). He would voice his opinion quite vociferously at times, but he would always support me when the chips were down, and vice versa. He was just like a good father or brother should be, and never once failed to give me moral support whenever it was called for (with the exception, perhaps, of the five years or so after I left his employ – but then there was no call for it). He was always there for me and never let me down once during the time that I have known him.

It was inevitable that Stirling would become a very different but still lovable person after that fateful St George's Day in 1962, because it was the end of everything he had always known. He was cut short in his prime by the cruellest of fate. Sometimes, I think he would have preferred to have died rather than live the future he was to inherit but, once Susie came along, she helped him put all that behind him.

However, the accident unquestionably ended life as he knew it and he would be the first to acknowledge that it was a dream of a life. Somehow, he did find the strength to struggle on because he has always been a fighter, but, whether or not he was ever truly happy again, no one will ever know.

He was probably lucky to be born at the right place at the right time and to be able to earn his living out of his great gift and natural instinct to master the unpredictability of cars driven at high speeds, whatever the circumstances threw at him. And, even better still, to get paid for doing something he enjoyed so much. He was the first of the all-professional drivers to be in this position and he forged the way for all those who came after him.

In only fourteen short years, the name 'Stirling Moss' became a household name and has remained so ever since. His was a name that was known all over the UK and in virtually every corner of the world. He gave much pleasure to millions of people, including himself, but spent the rest of his days behind an iron mask.

No one is perfect, but I personally couldn't have asked for a better friend.

He has been that friend.

Thank you and ciao, Stirling,

Viper

ACKNOWLEDGEMENTS

My sincerest thanks go to my agent, Peter Buckman, from the Ampersand Agency, for his help and encouragement. Also, to my editor, Stephanie Carey. Additionally, I would like to thank those who have written such warm endorsements.

My grateful thanks also go to Graham Cruickshank, Hugh Dibley, Ross Ferguson, James Healey, Roz Hubley, Marcos Lameirão, Inge Ostermayer Wulff, Terri Parish, Andrea Parrino, Alan Zafer, Nonie Zaremba and to professional photographers Andrew Boyd and Maurizio Rigato, and my daughter, Mia, for giving me and the publishers the copyright of their photographs free of charge.

INDEX